Thinking-Driven Testing

Adam Roman

Thinking-Driven Testing

The Most Reasonable Approach
to Quality Control

 Springer

Adam Roman
Jagiellonian University
Kraków, Poland

ISBN 978-3-319-73194-0   ISBN 978-3-319-73195-7   (eBook)
https://doi.org/10.1007/978-3-319-73195-7

Library of Congress Control Number: 2017964013

Printed on acid-free paper

This Springer imprint is published by Springer Nature
The registered company is Springer International Publishing AG
The registered company address is: Gewerbestrasse 11, 6330 Cham, Switzerland

To Marcin, Denis, Daria and Danuta

Trademarks

The following registered trademarks and service marks are used in this book: CMMI®, PRISMA®, TMap® and TMMi®.

CMMI is a registered trademark of the Software Engineering Institute.
PRISMA is a registered trademark of Improve Quality Services, The Netherlands.
TMap is a registered trademark of Sogeti, The Netherlands.
TMMi is a registered trademark of the TMMi Foundation Ireland.

Figure 1.16 is a public domain picture from commons.wikimedia.com

Preface

Why This Book?

If you read this book, you probably want to become a tester or to improve your testing skills. There are many books on software testing, but this one is quite unique among them. It is not just another, regular lecture on software testing, test management, tools, test automation, etc. Much has been said on that and this knowledge is easily accessible in many books or on the web. I would like to invite you for a completely different journey—a journey to the roots of the testing craft. If you want to become a good tester, learning some theory and mastering your technical skills is definitely not enough. These are of course very important and necessary skills, but there is one more indispensable ingredient of your success as a tester: **thinking**.

It may sound trivial, but think about it: all books on software testing present to you the theory, techniques and tools. Most of them teach you when and how to use this stuff. Some of them give you detailed examples and exercises. But none of them really tells you how to master your tester's skill set. Notice that the books on software testing usually do not tell you:

- *why* are these techniques and tools important and useful?
- how *exactly* to perform testing for a given testing problem?
- how to behold a *holistic* 'big picture' of the software development process in the context of quality assurance?
- how to use *analytical and critical thinking* in testing and why use them in the first place?

By 'mastery in testing' I understand the ability to test *consciously* and *rationally*. The IT industry loves new technologies, tools, programming languages, etc. We naively think that new tools will automate all our work, including its most creative parts, and protect us from the poor quality—just because. This is very dangerous, as it distracts testers from their most important activity: thinking.

Whether we like it or not, we're living in the times of incredible progress in technology. The changes in the IT world are vertiginous: a solution that is brand new today, few months later becomes completely useless. The famous so-called 'Moore's law' states that the number of transistors in a dense integrated circuit doubles approximately every 2 years. Thirty years ago Apple produced a 5 MB disc that cost $3500, which gives ca. $700,000 for one gigabyte. Today one gigabyte costs less than 7 cents. There are thousands of programming languages and every year the world welcomes several new ones. For example, only in 2014 we got Hack (Facebook), Swift (Apple) and C++14—a new version of C++. For each language developers create tens, hundreds or thousands of libraries, packages and frameworks that make programming more and more faster and easier. A modern smartphone has more computational power than the whole NASA had in 1969.

All of this is really amazing and one would expect that the same should be observed in software testing. Unfortunately, the analogous progress does not seem to hold. Despite the spectacular successes in technology, somehow we are still unable to provide a good quality software. Each computer user encounters software failures every day. Some of them are just funny or irritating, but some may have really serious consequences. As in the famous case of Therac-25 radiation therapy machine, where the concurrent programming errors resulted in radiation doses hundreds of times greater than the admissible dose, causing the death of six patients in 1985–1987.

Why is it so? What is the reason for our notorious handicap in software testing? If we constantly encounter software quality problems, despite the progress in technology, then two things should be more than obvious:

- quality increase is not correlated with technology progress,
- it is not the technology—the problem must be somewhere else.

Software development is a very complex and subtle process. It is impossible to control all the processes, changes, relations, constraints, dependencies and logic connected with development activities. But the software quality depends directly on all these things. A sole testing theory, knowledge of test design techniques or the ability to use many different tools will not help you to gain more of this control. To do this you need to involve rational and critical thinking, that is—a *conscious human factor*.

In this book I will try to show you how to develop these crucial skills and how to achieve a real mastery in (software) testing. In the following part of the book I will often use the phrase 'professional tester', by which I mean a tester who has indeed achieved the above-mentioned mastery.

What Is This Book *Not* About?

This Book Is Not About Test Management Test management is an important activity in the software development process, but it is an organizational area. Managing means dealing with complexity. A manager needs to plan, estimate effort, delegate tasks, talk with stakeholders, negotiate, hire and fire, report to higher management, coordinate different activities. But no matter how good the manager is, she will never be able to perform well the work done by the team members she manages. If you are interested in test management, you can get familiar with some books about it, for example [1], [2] or [3].

This Book Is Not About the Test Process Itself Although testing *is* a process, we will not be interested primarily in this aspect of testing. Of course, if you want to be a good tester, you need to know what a test process is. But if you want to be a real professional in testing, you also need to be aware of all relations, dependencies and constraints that the test process implies. These things are usually not discussed in the literature on test processes, such as norms and standards like [4]. The test process, like any other process, can be improved. But this kind of activity is usually a managerial task, and—as we stated above—this book is not about management. If you are interested in test process improvement, you may want to read books [5] or [6].

This Book Is Not About Tools There is a plethora of books, articles, documents, websites, blogs and conferences on testing tools. Tools are extremely important in testing, especially in test automation. But learning a tool is a pure technical competence. It does not include the creativity factor: just being able to use a given tool will not help you to test software effectively. Think about it this way: knowing how to ride a bicycle is definitely not enough to win Tour de France. Tools are important, but testers' skills are far more crucial.

This Book Is Not About Test Automation Knowing how to automate test execution is, as in case of the tools, a technical competence. It may save you a lot of time needed for test execution, but will not help you to learn how to test wisely and effectively. And, as in case of the tools, there are thousands of books on automation. An example may be [7], but there are also many books on using specific tools (like Selenium, Robot Framework, etc.) in the context of test execution automation. It does not make any sense to write another book on this topic.

What Is This Book About?

This Book Is Primarily on Thinking Thinking is the fuel of creative, wise, smart and clever acting. It allows us not only to test effectively, but also to continuously improve our testing skills. If we achieve this conscious and rational way of acting, the whole theory on test management, risk-based testing, test design and so on will be utilized by us in a very natural way. How can you know that you achieved this level of mastery? It may sound a little bit mystical, but if you achieve it, you will know it—you will intuitively *feel* that you act the way you should act.

The progress in developing your skills is not an easy thing. It requires time, gathering a lot of experience and making a lot of mistakes which you can learn from. People who already have some experience know that very well. It is much harder to explain it to the ones who are just at the beginning of their professional career. To illustrate this progress, imagine that you face some testing problem and use some technique to solve it. The following ways of approaching this problem may show you the levels of a tester's awareness and professionalism, from the lowest to the highest:

1. I use this technique because someone else told me to do so.
2. I use this technique because I know it and I know that it may be applied in this case.
3. I use this technique because I understand it and I know the profits it gives.
4. I use this technique because *it is natural for me to act this way* in this particular situation.

In this book we will try to answer the following question: what does it mean that something is *natural* for a tester and how to master this skill? It is far from being trivial! If something is natural for us, we must be deeply convinced that this is the right thing to do. We must have a very solid basis for such acting. This basis needs to be built of:

- advanced knowledge on testing and software engineering (theoretical foundations, test design techniques, solid math background, software development life cycle, etc.),
- systems thinking (understanding the context and the relations between different areas of the software development process, going far beyond processes, tools and techniques),
- critical thinking (making clear, reasoned judgements [8]),
- analytical skills (analyzing the risks, test basis, designing a test strategy, etc.),
- design skills (using cognitive abilities to improve the process of designing [9]),
- deep understanding of the nature of testing, our role as a tester, business context (why we test, what we test, what is a bug, who influences us, who is influenced by us, etc.),
- wide range of soft skills, like: communication, creativity, curiosity, meticulousness, etc.

The book is organized in the following way:

Chapter 1 introduces the fundamental ideas underlying software testing. Some of them are of philosophical nature, some are related to more practical issues. But they have one thing in common: they are *universal*, that is—independent of technological progress and other factors. They are like mathematical theorems—they will always be true and will never change. If you want to achieve mastery in testing, you need to be aware of them. Remember, however, that this is just the tip of the iceberg. A real craftsman in testing should have a solid background in areas like software engineering (including requirements engineering), discrete mathematics, theoretical computer science and so on. Some good references to start may be [10], [11] and [12].

Chapter 2 is about meta-strategies in software testing. By '*meta*'-strategies I mean general approaches that can be adapted to many different situations in your real work as a software tester. They include psychological aspects of testing as well as methodological laws and tools. I describe the role of planning, documenting, estimating and simulating. This may sound a little boring (besides, many books discuss these concepts as well), but I focus here on how these activities can bring a real added value. When you really understand *why* should you plan, document, estimate and simulate, you have a very powerful tool in your toolbox. I also discuss the very important concept of *error model*, which is one of the central notions in software testing.

Chapter 3, together with the following Chap. 4, is the central part of this book. In this section I describe the concept of Thinking-Driven Testing (TDT). This approach utilizes the concepts discussed in the two previous chapters and introduces two main ideas that underlie the reasonable and optimal approach to software testing. The first one is a set of universal rules that any tester should follow if she wants to be a successful professional in testing. The second one is the concept of systems thinking [13]. It is a powerful tool that allows us to look at the software development process as an ecosystem in which many different elements such as testers, developers, processes, structures, behaviors, procedures, test artifacts, etc. work together and influence each other. By using systems thinking we can reason on how each of these elements affects other elements. We may deduce then that, for example, reinforcing or reducing one of them will have a concrete impact on reinforcement or reduction of another one. This way we are able to improve the whole process of software development. Systems thinking forces us, so to say, to look far beyond our comfort zone, restricted to particular testing activities. It allows us to understand how different actions undertaken by us impact other processes and how then these processes affect us.

Chapter 4 proposes a specific approach to testing, called TQED. It uses an analogy between software and a real, physical world. The analogy constitutes the basis for the test design approach. You might already figure out that in this book I want to focus on general ideas and very fundamental things related to software testing. The same is with the TQED model: it is not a detailed set of rules saying exactly how to construct the test cases. It is a general approach that allows you to increase your creativity in delivering effective, optimal test ideas. The TQED model is universal in the sense that *every* testing problem can be reduced to the elements and relations described by the model.

Chapter 5 describes different types of testing techniques. Again—I do not go deeply into technical details of particular techniques, although I present here some concrete approaches. There are many books on particular test design techniques, like [10], [14], [15], [16], [17] or [18] to mention the most important ones. I rather focus on the *ideas* that underlie the concrete test techniques. This bird's-eye view will allow us to understand the fundamental concepts of test design. When you understand them, you will be able to design not only your own tests, but even your own test design techniques, tailored to a given problem. I also show how to utilize the TQED model in different techniques.

Chapter 6 is closely related to the skill of critical thinking. It presents many different kinds of pitfalls you may encounter in your job as a tester. These traps come from a wide range of testing process areas: from test planning, through test design, reporting, estimating, to the dangers of improper use of many popular models, like test pyramid. I also discuss here how to use critical thinking in order to avoid such pitfalls. This is very important, because when we a make decision upon wrong or low quality data, this decision will probably be harmful or at least far from optimal. Wrong decisions may put the whole project at risk and our role as the testers is to *reduce* the risk as much as possible.

Chapter 7 contains several exercises for testers. Apart from the 'typical' exercises the chapter also contains so-called 'kata'. These are the exercises named after the detailed choreographed patterns of movements practiced in the Japanese martial arts, like karate, aikido, judo or kendo. Kata will help you to develop several skills crucial for a professional tester: logical thinking and reasoning, out-of-the-box thinking, creativity, counting and estimating, analytical thinking. Despite the fact that kata can be practiced on the normal, everyday situations, they allow you to master the skills that are extremely important in software testing.

I assume that a typical reader of this book has some fundamental knowledge on testing theory and—in particular—is familiar with the most important terms, vocabulary and processes used in testing. However, if you are completely new to testing, Appendix A may be helpful in understanding some technical parts of the book. It contains a glossary of technical terms that show up throughout the book. Appendix B, "Testing in a nutshell", in turn, describes in a concise form the software testing process and the most fundamental ideas about what software testing is.

Figure 1 shows schematically the structure and content of this book regarding the test activities. Fundamentals of software testing (Chap. 1) are necessary for a proper use of testing techniques (Chap. 5), avoiding pitfalls (Chap. 6) and developing necessary skills (Chap. 7). The general approach to testing should result from one or many testing strategies which may also involve ideas from different fields of science and humanities (Chap. 2). The whole process should be rational and in the first place should involve thinking—critical, system and analytical (Chap. 3). Good testing is driven by reasonable test ideas, which can be generated using the TQED model (Chap. 4).

In this book I would like to show subtle and sometimes counterintuitive issues related to software testing. I also would like to convince you that many different ideas in testing can be inspired by seemingly distant areas, like economy or philosophy, making the testing more efficient. A deep, holistic broad view on the discipline of testing may show us that some 'obvious' dogmas of testing are in fact not so dogmatic. That some 'good practices' really make things harder, not easier. That testing is not only a technical IT activity, but is a fascinating, beautiful and difficult craft, whose practice can be a lot of fun.

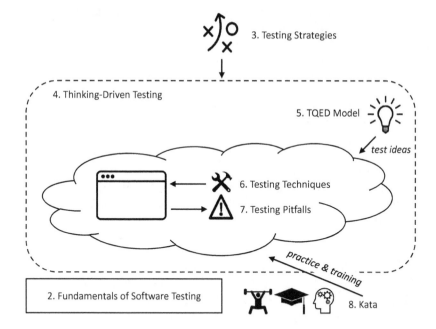

Fig. 1 Structure of the book

This book doesn't give any direct answers. There are no such answers—anyone who claims that, lies. Therefore, do not expect any straightforward recipes for particular problems. I rather show the possible ways of self-development and rational acting, which—if applied well—may simply result in better testing. Reading this book will not make you a better tester, but may inspire you to the unceasing self improvement in this demanding, but beautiful craft.

References

[1] Spillner, A., Rossner, T., Winter, M., Linz, T.: Software Testing Practice: Test Management, Rocky Nook (2007)
[2] Pinkster, I., van de Burgt, B., Janssen, D., van Veenendaal, E.: Successful Test Management. An Integral Approach. Springer, Berlin (2006)
[3] Farrell-Vinay, P.: Manage Software Testing. Auerbach Publications, Boca Raton (2008)
[4] ISO/IEC/IEEE 29119 – Software Testing Standard. International Organization for Standardization, 2013-2016
[5] Koomen, T., Pol, M.: Test Process Improvement: A Practical Step-by-Step Guide to Structured Testing. Addison-Wesley, Reading (1999)
[6] Bath, G., van Veenendaal, E.: Improving the Test Process: Implementing Improvement and Change, Rocky Nook (2014)
[7] Graham, D., Fewster, M.: Experiences of Test Automation. Addison-Wesley, Upper Saddle River (2012)

[8] Beyer, B.: Critical Thinking. Phi Delta Kappa Educational Foundation, Bloomington, Indiana (1995)

[9] Cross, N.: Design Thinking: Understanding How Designers Think and Work. Bloomsbury Academic, London (2011)

[10] Jorgensen, P.: Software Testing. A Craftsman's Approach. CRC Press, London (2014)

[11] Pressman, R., Maxim, B.: Software Engineering. A Practitioner's Approach. Mc Graw Hill, Boston (2015)

[12] Biggs, N.: Discrete Mathematics. Oxford University Press, Oxford (2002)

[13] Senge, P.: The Fifth Discipline: The Art and Practice of the Learning Organization. Random House, New York (2010)

[14] Whittaker, A.: Exploratory Software Testing. Tips, Tricks, Tours and Techniques to Guide Test Design. Addison-Wesley, Upper Saddle River, NJ (2010)

[15] Thomas, T., Badgett, T., Sandler, C., Myers, G.: The Art of Software Testing. Wiley (2011)

[16] Patton, R.: Software Testing. Sams Publishing, Indianapolis, IN (2006)

[17] Beizer, B.: Software Testing Techniques, Dreamtech Press (2002)

[18] Koomen, T., van der Aalst, L., Broekman, B., Vroon, M.: TMap Next for Result-Driven Testing. UTN Publishers (2006)

Acknowledgements

This book is based on my knowledge and experience with software testing, gathered during the last 10 years of my work at Jagiellonian University, Rivet Group and Society for Quality of Information Systems. But knowledge always comes from other people, and the experience—always thanks to them. In my professional career, I had the great luck of meeting a lot of such great personalities. The discussions with them—even in the form of a quick exchange of views—were a true intellectual adventure. These experiences allowed me to learn a lot and have shaped many of my views not only on the software quality but also on how to think about it.

Therefore, I would like to express my gratitude to the following people (in alphabetical order): Bogdan Bereza, Tomasz Bonior, Monika Braun, Alexandra Casapu, Maciej Chmielarz, Krzysztof Chytła, Daniel Dec, Olivier Denoo, Dariusz Drezno, Marta Firlej, Remigiusz Gadecki, Joanna Gajewska, Paul Gerrard, Arnika Hryszko, Jarek Hryszko, Wojciech Jaszcz, Agnieszka Kaczor, Krystian Kaczor, Piotr Krzosa, Monika Lichota-Cywińska, Sebastian Małyska, Paweł Noga, Ingvar Nordström, Tomasz Osojca, Jędrzej Osiński, Łukasz Pietrucha, Jakub Rosiński, Jan Sabak, Ina Schieferdecker, Radek Smilgin, Lucjan Stapp, Jarek Szewczuk, Piotr Ślęzak, Tomek Watras, Piotr Wicherski, Karolina Zmitrowicz and Wiktor Żołnowski. I realize I may have forgotten someone. If so, please accept my apologies for my fallibility.

I would like to thank my editor, Ralf Gerstner, for enabling me to publish this book with Springer and for the professionalism he has shown in every aspect of the publication process. A special thanks goes to Bhisham Bherwani, who copy-edited and polished the final version of the manuscript. I would also like to express my gratitude to the anonymous reviewers—their thorough reviews and insightful remarks allowed me to significantly improve the quality of the text.

Contents

List of Abbreviations

API	Application Programming Interface
CLI	Command Line Interface
CMMI	Capability Maturity Model Integration
COTS	Commercial off-the-shelf
GUI	Graphical User Interface
IT	Information Technology
MTBF	Mean Time Between Failures
MTTF	Mean Time To Failure
MTTR	Mean Time To Repair
PRISMA	Product RISk MAnagement
QA	Quality Assurance
QC	Quality Control
REST	Representational State Transfer
SaaS	Software as a Service
SDLC	Software Development Life Cycle
SUT	System Under Test
TDT	Thinking-Driven Testing
TMap	Test Management Approach
TMMi	Test Maturity Model integration
TQED	A model of testing; an acronym for the 'Time, Quantity, Events, Data' or 'Tested. Quod Erat Demonstrandum'
UI	User Interface
UX	User Experience

Fundamentals of Software Testing

1

1.1 Introduction

In this chapter we review some of the most fundamental and important issues related to the software testing craft. We show the difficulties and ambiguities related to them. We also discuss some topics that receive a lot of controversy in the professional testers community. After reading this section you will get familiar with the reasons that make software testing a difficult and demanding profession.

1.2 The Beginning: What Is Testing Really About and Why Is It So Difficult?

Testing is a jungle. A jungle of notions, ideas, methods, tools, models, frameworks, techniques, and approaches. The reason is that software testing, like software engineering itself, is a relatively young discipline. It's still in statu nascendi,[1] and therefore it develops very rapidly, in directions being very hard to predict. Figure 1.1 presents the number of scientific books and articles published in years 1972–2015 by just one publisher, Springer, that contain the phrase 'software testing'. You may notice the exponential growth in the number of such publications. It is both impressive and frightening!

The development of software testing is a little bit chaotic. In the testers community there are still many ideas that are unclear, insufficiently explored or even contradictory: is exploratory testing better than scripted testing? Is agile approach better than other life cycle models for achieving software quality? Are test design techniques effective? Should we follow norms and standards like ISO/IEC 29119 or are they just unnecessary or even harmful? What is the role of documentation? What does the notion of 'test case' really mean? Can we predict the quality? And what

---

[1] A Latin sentence which means 'in the course of being formed or developed'.

© Springer International Publishing AG 2018
A. Roman, *Thinking-Driven Testing*, https://doi.org/10.1007/978-3-319-73195-7_1

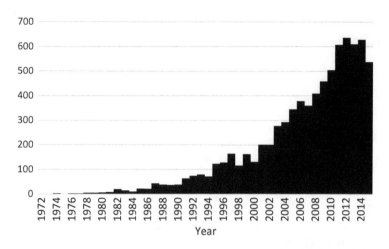

Fig. 1.1   Number of articles on software testing in the Springer database from 1972 to 2015

exactly do we understand by 'quality'? How can we effectively improve testing process in our organization? Which tests should be automated? And so on, and so on...

Many years must pass before testing, understood as a well-defined software engineering area, will stabilize. The whole problem is that on the one hand we just cannot wait that long, and on the other hand we do not have an established, trustworthy theory on software testing. What is even worse, even if we finally create the Unified Theory of Testing, it probably won't be able to give us simple answers to the problems like the ones mentioned above. It seems that software design is a much more complicated process than any other engineering activity. In 1969 (!) we were able to build a spaceship that successfully landed humans on the Moon, but almost half a century later we are not able to produce a simple piece of software that is free from defects...

The conclusion is clear: software engineering is difficult, and so is software testing. Take this, add the 'jungle' factor, and we have a really big problem. Imagine someone who wishes to become a tester. Of course, not an ordinary one, but a real *professional* in testing. It may even be you yourself! Such a poor guy has absolutely no idea where he should start. What should he learn first and from which sources?

In this chapter we try to remedy this problem. We introduce the fundamental aspects of software testing. They are fundamental in the sense that you really need to understand them well if you want to go any further in your career as a tester. They also form a basis for the rest of the ideas presented in this book. Moreover, reading this chapter will let you see the 'big-picture' of testing: its main ideas, the challenges and its opportunities it gives. It will also give you a sense of direction in this difficult and complicated domain. You will be able to better assimilate from other sources both theoretical and practical knowledge on testing.

Even if you have some experience in software testing, you may want to get familiar with these ideas. Returning from time to time to the basics of our craft is always good and refreshing. It allows us to get out from the routine, so common among experienced professionals. Routine kills creativity. That is why it is highly recommended, for example, to include in an inspection team someone inexperienced. Such a person has a clear mind and looks at many things in a completely different way than people that spent most of their life on those issues. Her comments may be very inspirational for other team members. This is a classic example of synergy[2]: by delivering the added value to the process we create something that is greater than the simple sum of its parts.

It is surprising that such reflection—almost philosophical—on software testing fundamentals is very rare among testers. Most of them consider themselves as *engineers*—even their job positions usually have titles like 'QA engineer', 'engineer in test', etc. But being an engineer does not mean being a geeky tech guy. You will never achieve mastery as a tester if you just learn some tools and blindly follow technical procedures. Being an engineer means being able to think. As Terry Pratchett wrote in 'I Shall Wear Midnight':

> If you do not know where you come from, then you don't know where you are, and if you don't know where you are, then you don't know where you're going. And if you don't know where you're going, you're probably going wrong.

You need to know where you come from. That is, you need to know and understand the fundamental ideas behind software testing. IT people usually do not care about such things. Many tech guys tend to avoid things like philosophy, thinking about ideas, deep reflections. Maybe this is the reason why their testing is often so poor. They are indeed 'going wrong'.

To better understand the peculiar notion of 'idea', look at Table 1.1. It presents two different approaches, two different ways to grasp some exemplary concepts from software testing.

As you can see, we will not just scratch the surface—we will go much, much deeper. In this book we try to answer the fundamental questions about testing. We are definitely not satisfied with formal, abstract definitions, techniques and procedures which give us simple (often *too* simple) answers about what to do and when to do it. This is delusive—testing is much more complicated. When you think more about this, you immediately realize that such coarse rules are just ineffective and ludicrous. We want to discover the nature of testing, we want to know why different ideas about testing are useful and what is their meaning, their gist. But to do this well, you need to be open-minded and you need to *think*. If you are familiar with some books on testing, you have to be prepared for changing your perspective. We will consider testing in a very different way than it is usually done.

---

[2]The term *synergy* comes from the Attic Greek word συνεργία (Eng. 'working together').

Table 1.1 Two different approaches to the ideas on software testing

Issue/concept	How most books approach it	How this book approaches it
Test case	What is the definition of a test case? What does IEEE 829 standard say about the structure of a test case document? What fields should you fill in? Which fields are mandatory and which are optional? Let us give you an example of a nice, formal test case document that you should use on a daily basis.	What *is* a test case really? What is its *nature* and its function in the whole testing process? How should we use this concept to bring added value to the process, that is—to increase the quality? How does the information contained in the test case allow us to improve the process?
Test design techniques	What is the definition of a given test design technique? Let us introduce it in a very informal way and let us give you some trivial examples of its application! Remember: if you have problem X, then you must use technique Y. It is important to distinguish between exploratory and scripted testing—just because. You don't really need any explanation about this. Just accept this.	How does a test design technique work? How can we *design* a test design technique? What sources can we use for that and in what way? When should we use these techniques? What benefits do they give us? What kinds of errors are they (not) able to detect? How can we use these techniques in a real, non-trivial software? How can we combine them to be more effective?
Test process	What is the definition of a test process? What types of test processes are there? What are the names of their consecutive phases? Let us list the tester's tasks for the given phases. Here you have an abstract picture of the process from the ISO 29119 standard, which you should follow to achieve success.	Why, in the first place, should we consider the idea of a 'test process'? Who works on the software? What do these people do? How are their roles related to each other? How does their work impact others? Let us grasp the process as a big system with many subtle relations and let us discover these relations. Let us *understand* this system.
Coverage measure	Let us give you all possible definitions of the coverage, both for the source code and for all other software models. The higher the coverage, the better!	What does the coverage measure really say? Is there a relation between coverage level and software quality level? When it is beneficial to use these measures? Can we use them only for measuring the risk level or can they tell us something more about the software, tests, process. . .?

1.2.1   Testing as a Unique Activity. Why Testing Is So Hard?

In a sense, tester is a very unique and very specific role. It combines many different skills, but—in contrast to other roles—their overabundance is not detrimental. In other words, you cannot overdose on any skill as a tester.

This is schematically depicted in Fig. 1.2. It presents a desired (optimal) level of four types of skills for four different IT roles: manager, developer, analyst and tester. It is 'optimal' in the following sense. When the skill level is too low, its growth will result in better job performance. But when the skill level is too high, it will either have no impact on the quality of work, or will result in decline in quality. When the

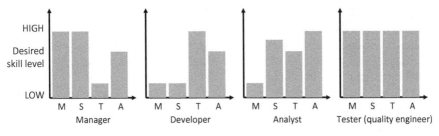

M = managerial skills   S = soft skills   T = technical skills   A = analytical skills

Fig. 1.2 Comparison of desired skill level for different IT roles

skill level is HIGH it means that there is no limit for this skill: the higher, the better. Otherwise, it represents the optimal level.

For example:

- For a manager it is quite obvious that both managerial and soft skills should be developed as much as it is possible. But if the manger has too many technical skills, he might be biased and have, for example, a tendency for micromanagement, which is usually very harmful to the project, team morale, etc. A manager needs to be a good analyst, but again—if he possesses too much of the analytical skills, he may be missing the big picture of the project and may tend to focus on some technical details.
- A developer usually possesses almost no managerial skills. He does not need them, because developer is a technical, engineering role. It does not involve much management. Developers spend most of their time on writing code and do not interact with other team members, not mentioning the clients, users, top management, etc. as much as managers or testers. The increase in the level of social and managerial skills will probably not result in increasing a developer's efficiency.
- An analyst, like a developer, does not need to have many managerial skills, although his social skills need to be much more developed than in case of a developer, because he is 'closer' to the client than a developer. However, as analyst is also mainly a technical role, skill increase in these areas will usually not be beneficial.

The ideal tester, in contrast, should have all skills developed as much as possible—it is impossible to overdose on any of them:

- **managerial skills**—to be able to plan, estimate and coordinate test effort and activities, to manage requirements and tests, to be able to own and maintain the test process, to understand the development process as one big ecosystem with its all connections, constraints and dependencies, etc.;
- **soft skills**—to negotiate with managers, to be able to convince them of his opinions, to communicate with clients, analysts, developers and managers, to be able to understand all stakeholders and their expectations, etc.;

- **technical skills**—to be able to use tools for optimizing, automating and improving the test activities, to understand technical documentation, etc.;
- **analytical skills**—to be able to define the testing problem, decompose it, analyze, estimate, and perform its abstraction, build a proper model, provide efficient solutions and translate them back to the original domain; to be able to predict the future quality level based on the present activities, etc. The tester should also possess domain and business knowledge, to understand what she is testing and why.

Of course, Fig. 1.2 is a little bit exaggerated and one may argue that for each and every role the higher level of *any* skill, the better. But still, the role of a tester is distinctive—we will discuss this in detail in Sect. 1.8. If we agree that testers play an extremely important role in improving the final product quality and proving it has reached a given level, we will immediately understand how important it is for each tester (even the one working in a junior position) to be able to convince team leaders and managers that solutions they propose may be very bad for the project.

Example
If you had any experience with performance tests, you might have been faced with a situation in which you had to create several hundreds of user accounts for performance testing, but the organization policy had a 'one account—one real user' rule. You needed to be able to convince security officers that you just have to create these accounts. If you don't have soft skills, like communication and negotiation, you will fail. If you can't write scripts, you won't be able to optimize and automate part of your work, which means that you won't have time for other important testing activities. This will obviously cause a decline in quality.

Good developers and analysts usually have a technical background and this is perfectly enough. Great managers frequently graduate from humanities, like philosophy, philology, psychology, and this is perfectly OK. But if you are a tester who is a 100% geek or a 100% humanist, you will never be as effective as the one who possesses both of these skills and, therefore, be able to utilize a natural synergy between the two.

You might have heard about a position in development called 'full stack developer'. A full stack developer is a software engineer who understands all development layers: network communication, data modeling, business logic, API, GUI, user experience, user requirements and business needs. The rationale for hiring such a person is that a full stack developer has the ability to optimize the code on all layers.

Hence, the software is much more effective than if it would be optimized only on, let's say, GUI level.

A professional tester has a similar position—it's like 'full stack quality analyst' who is able to control the quality in all possible aspects. It is definitely not restricted to clicking in the app and finding bugs. Here are some concrete examples:

- if you deal with user requirements, you need to understand the user's business needs and you need to have the excellent communication skills,
- if you inspect architectural design, you need to be familiar with formal software models,
- if you test a business process, you need to understand the business logic behind it,
- if you inspect a source code, you need to have at least passive knowledge of a programming language the code was written in,
- if you design a test strategy, you need to have knowledge on test techniques, maybe some programming skills, and you need to know how to extract test conditions from the available documentation and from other people,
- if you test a web application, you have to understand the OSI/ISO model, be familiar with things like the TCP/IP protocol, HTTP, REST and so on,
- if you test any software quality characteristic, you should know and understand it (for example: usability, security, performance, maintainability and so on).

This is the reason why good testing is so hard: you have to be a one-man band. Let me put it in other words: imagine a symphonic orchestra performing a great masterpiece, like Beethoven's 9th symphony for choir and orchestra. It consists of many different people with many different roles. A conductor rules the whole band, but he does not need to be a perfect instrumentalist to conduct a concert. A violinist must understand the conductor's gestures during the performance, but he does not need to know how to play trumpet to be a perfect soloist. A singer does not need to know how to analyze the masterpiece in order to sing it well. But a composer, in order to write this masterpiece, needs to know the technical details of all instruments, the abilities of human voice, the harmony, the instrumentation, the history of music and many, many other things.

Software development is like performing a masterpiece by an orchestra. And a tester is like a composer of its quality.

It is tempting to think about the role of a tester as the one responsible only for testing the software. But it is far beyond that. A tester does not only test software. She should be everywhere and she should test everything: requirements, documents, processes, clients, developers and even her own manager. Improving *all* aspects of the organization, especially the people's *thinking* on quality, is the best way to achieve this quality.

Example

This example is a little bit theoretical, but its intention is to show a very important thing. Namely, it illustrates that the proper allocation of the tester's resources to different process areas may result in much better results than his focusing all his efforts on only one aspect of the process. Suppose there is a very simple development life cycle consisting of two phases: requirements specification (REQ) and coding (CODE). Both REQ and CODE are characterized by a 'quality effort' (expressed as a natural number between 0 and 100, denoted by Q_{REQ} and Q_{CODE} resp.) that represents the amount of quality activities in this phase. These activities allow us to detect bugs, but they also generate costs.

Assume that in REQ 90 defects are introduced and $m = 0.9 \cdot Q_{REQ}$ of them are found and corrected. The rest of them escape to the CODE phase. In CODE $180 - m$ new defects are introduced.[3] Together with the escaped ones we have $270 - 2m$ defects in CODE and $n = (27 - 0.2m) \cdot Q_{TEST}$ of them are found and corrected. Therefore, after release (in operation) there are $270 - 2m - n$ field defects, which are assumed to be detected and raised by the users. We have two types of quality cost: the cost of bug detection and the cost of bug correction. These costs are different for different phases, according to the following table:

Phase	Cost of detection	Cost of correction
REQ	$1 per defect	$(Q_{REQ})^{1.2}$
CODE	$5 per defect	$(Q_{CODE})^{1.7}$
In operation	None (raised by users)	$53 per defect

We want to minimize the total cost, that is, the sum of detection and correction costs for all phases. Suppose that the initial quality effort for both REQ and CODE phases is 70, which gives the total cost of $4381 (see Table 1.2 for the exact calculations). Now, assume that we are able to improve the testing process with 10 additional quality effort units. How should we partition these 10 units across REQ and CODE in order to minimize the total cost? If we allocate all 10 units in REQ, we increase the REQ quality effort to 80 and the total cost is $4088. If we allocate all of them in CODE, the total cost

(continued)

---

[3]The number of defects in the CODE phase depends on the number of defects found in the previous phase (REQ), because the defects propagate: a defect in design may cause one or more defects in the cde. Hence, we assume that the more the defects removed in the first phase, the fewer the defects introduced later.

will be $4058. But if we allocate five of them in REQ and another five in CODE, the total cost will be $4040.

Table 1.2 Quality cost simulation for a simple two-phase life cycle

Phase	Defects from previous phase	Defects introduced in phase	Total defects in phase	Quality effort	Defects detected	Cost of quality actions ($)	Defects escaped to next phase
REQ	–	90	90	70	63	227	27
CODE	27	117	144	70	101	1875	43
Operation	43				43	2279	
Total cost						4381	

This example shows that the quality effort distributed over all process areas and activities may be more beneficial than focusing all our efforts on improving just one single phase or task. In a real life this is almost always the case.

1.2.2 Testing Finds Bugs, But This Is Just the Tip of the Iceberg

There is a Big Question (and a big discussion) about the primary objective of testing. You might already have found many blog posts, articles or books that say—what a surprise—completely different things. However, most of the authors agree that the primary objective of testing is, generally speaking, quality control. Some of them add that another important goal is to provide information. These authors usually definitely emphasize that 'the purpose of testing is not to find bugs' [19], 'testing != bug finding' [20], 'if you think it is to find defects then you are wrong' [21], etc.

However, there is a big misunderstanding here. We have to understand that there are two completely different issues when trying to answer the Big Question about the software testing goals:

Question 1. What is the *essence*, the *true nature*, what are the *direct attributes*, of software testing?
Question 2. What do we *use it* for?

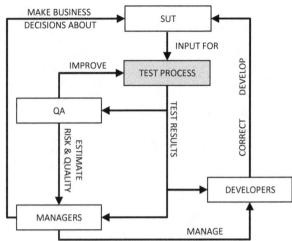

Fig. 1.3 The role of testing in the development process

The answer to Question 1 is this: testing is *only about finding bugs* and nothing more. Imagine this: if we remove the ability of finding bugs from the testing activity, what will remain? Well. . . nothing! Testing becomes a useless and pointless activity. But, of course, this is not what we are *using* testing for. The answer for Question 2 is the one given by the above-mentioned authors. We may use testing for:

- assessing the software quality level,
- providing information about the software to all stakeholders,
- verifying that the software works as expected, and so on.

Notice that all these goals can be obtained by testing. For example:

- the number, type, severity and location of bugs found is a valuable measure of the software quality level,
- the defect density or defect frequency can be translated into information for stakeholders about software maturity/reliability,
- the lack of bugs found when software is used under normal conditions by a user is a simple verification that the software works as expected.

You may ask: why do we even discuss such things? This is weird, peculiar and artificial: it seems like an abstract, senseless, academic discussion: why should we split the Big Question about the software testing goal into Question 1 and Question 2 as above? Well, there is a very important reason for that. We need to understand the difference between the *business goal* and the *means* for reaching this goal. The business goal is related to Question 2. The means to reach it are hidden in Question 1. If you are aware that the direct goal of testing is to find bugs, you need to focus on a very important concept in software testing—an error model—and use it to be more effective as a tester (because you should be aware what are you looking for). An error model impacts the tester's actions and activities, and hence his effectiveness in bug finding. We will talk about error models in detail in Sect. 2.6.

What about the business goal? Look at Fig. 1.3. It presents a simplified model of testing within the development process. We have a test process, which takes the System Under Test (SUT) as an input and returns the test results. Notice that the SUT has not been changed by the test process—testers cannot change anything in the SUT! The only output they provide is the information about what they exactly did with this SUT and what kinds of defects or failures were found.[4] This information goes to the developers, quality assurance (QA) engineers and managers. Developers use the feedback from testers to fix the bugs in the code. This increases the software quality level. QA engineers can measure it and—using the feedback from the testers—propose some actions to improve the testing process itself. They may also report to managers the information about risk and quality of the software. Although not shown in the model, information from the QA engineers may be also used by developers to increase the quality of the development process. Managers, using the information provided by QA engineers and testers, make 'technical' decisions about the development process and also make business decisions about the software product.

As you can see, testing provides only the information about bugs found (or not), but this is just the tip of the iceberg. This information is used by all stakeholders to make the reasonable, thought decisions about the coding, business issues, testing process and many other things. Testing directly finds bugs, but indirectly influences the software quality. Only when you perceive this big picture of the development process, you will understand the answer to Question 2.

The information provided by testers should be as accurate as possible. That is why a tester needs all those skills we were talking about in the previous subsection. The ability of using the error model is one of them. When you master this skill, you will understand not only the answer to Question 1 and all its consequences, but also a reason why we split the Big Question into two separate questions.

There is one important thing to remember when we talk about 'finding bugs'. By 'bugs' we understand not only the observable failures, but any suspicious program behavior or characteristic, such as: run-time longer than usual, wrong screen appearance, lack of software ease of use and so on. Remember also that the absence of such issues is also information.

1.2.3   Quality Control vs. Quality Assurance

For some unknown reasons people often confuse quality assurance (QA) with testing, a part of a quality control (QC) process. For example, in Poland it is very common to put in a job offer statements like 'we are looking for a QA engineer', while from the job description it is clear that the company is looking for a tester. The reason may be that 'quality assurance engineer', 'software quality engineer' and other similar titles sound more serious and more official than just an ordinary 'tester'.

---

[4]This is the reason why removing the bug finding ability from testing makes it useless: in such a case there would be no output of the testing process!

Many people say that these two terms: QA and QC are interchangeable or that they do not distinguish between these two roles. Some others claim that a tester needs to be a quality engineer as well. However, again—as in case of the primary objective of testing discussed in Sect. 1.2.3—there is a very important reason for distinguishing between these two activities.

Quality control is a process of checking the quality level. It is usually done by testing. The quality level can be expressed in terms of the number of defects found. It is commonly said that QC is about defect detection. Notice that in some sense this is a passive process: we are given a SUT and we have to test it. As testers, we don't make any decisions about the SUT itself. Quality assurance, on the other hand, is a completely different process. Its aim is to *prevent* the introduction of defects into software. This process is much more proactive and much broader than QC.

QA is simply a set of all actions that improve something in the development process. Here are some concrete examples:

- checking the quality of the test basis (for example: is the code testable enough? is it properly commented? are the code metrics, like Lines of Code, cyclomatic complexity, etc. in a normal range?),
- checking the quality of the tests (for example: are they correct, understandable, easy to maintain?),
- proposing the corrective actions (for example, suggesting code refactoring, organizing the training for developers or testers, etc.),
- performing the inspections of the requirements, documentation, design, code, tests and other SDLC artifacts,
- checking whether the process performs well (by auditing and measuring),
- checking whether the corrective actions have a positive impact on both process and product,
- checking how the process can be improved,
- ensuring the adequate stakeholders commitment,
- analyzing and selecting the purchase of the suitable and necessary tools,
- setting up the standards for test management, defect management, tool usage, reporting, etc.
- taking care of the constant improvement of testers and developers,
- facilitating the communication between all stakeholders,
- increasing the satisfaction of employees (for example, by organizing events, keeping a good wage policy, offering social benefits, etc.).

Notice that all these activities are done in order to *prevent* the defects, not *detect* them. For example, if we organize a training on good practices of code writing for the developers, their skills will be improved, so they will make less mistakes when writing code. Moreover, their code will be easier to read, so the code reviews will detect more defects in a shorter time. These actions will also impact the QC process: the code will be more testable, so testers will be able to write better tests and detect more defects. If, as part of the QA activities, we also train the testers to write good, professional defect reports, the communication between them and the developers will improve. This will make the defect removing process more efficient. All in all, at the end, the final product will have a better quality.

Tester and QA engineer are two different roles, but they may be performed by one person. In fact, the professional tester is a great candidate for the QA role. This is because he knows how to test, and QA—from a certain perspective—can be viewed as *testing the process*. Just instead of designing the software tests, a QA engineer can perform a process audit and point out things that may be improved. For a professional tester it is not important what is tested—it can literally be everything, not only the software. That is why good testers should definitely participate in the QA activities: because of their creativeness, inquisitiveness and a pursuit of perfection.

QA is usually more subtle than QC. For example, any action that increases the employee satisfaction may result in the quality increase in the final product. This dependence may be very indirect and may be even not seen at first glance. Also, QC activities are much more 'controllable' from the financial perspective: we know what exactly we pay for, we know exactly what the results are (number of defects detected), we may even calculate the cost-per-defect metric, although we should be very careful with that.[5] In case of QA it is often very difficult to perform such cost-benefits analysis. This can be facilitated by performing the accurate process and product measurement and analyzing the influence of different short- and long-term QA activities on the final quality. But doing this right requires an advanced statistical and modelling knowledge. This topic is far beyond the scope of this book. However, simulations together with systems thinking can be used to assess the impact of different QA activities on the product quality. We write more about simulations in Sect. 2.10 and about systems thinking in Sect. 3.7.

1.2.4 It's Not About the Working Code, But a Solution to the Business Problem

There is an analogy between the Big Question about testing and the Big Question about development. The direct goal of the development is to create the code, but the code *itself* is not so important. It is created for a client, who doesn't care about the software itself. The client buys it because he needs to solve his business problem by using the software. The analogy is presented in Fig. 1.4.

If you tell a developer that a working code is not the main task of the development process he will probably go crazy. Every programmer knows that the final product of the development process is code, so the most important thing here is his own work! This is very typical, because people tend to perceive and value their work through the filter of their 'own ecosystem'. A single team worker usually doesn't see the

---

[5]As Jones and Bonsignour rightly point out in their book [28], the widely-cited 'cost-per-defect' metric actually penalizes quality and achieves its lowest values for the buggiest applications, due to ignoring fixed costs. Also, the cost-per-defect metric focuses too much attention on defect repairs and ignores the greater economic advantages of high quality in shortening schedules and lowering costs.

Fig. 1.4 The analogy
between the goals of testing
and development

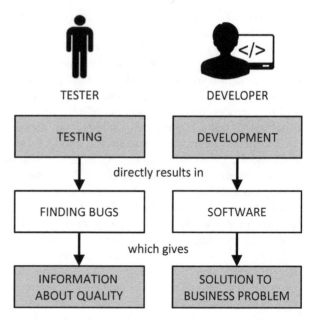

whole, subtle network of connections between the different parts of a team (this can be changed; we will talk more about this issue in Sect. 3.7). A developer's world consists of the requirements he gets and the code he writes. Nothing more.

But there is much, much more than just his code. All this work of the developers, testers, managers, architects, business analysts and God knows who else has just one goal: to solve the client's problem. Software is just a tool, just a means for reaching this goal. Therefore, during their work all the team members should have—in the first place—the business solution in their minds. Otherwise they will tend to focus on the technical aspects of the system being created. Of course, this kind of verification is also important, but it becomes harmful if done as art for art's sake.

What is the moral from this story, in particular for a tester? It is mainly about the quality. A tester must understand how different aspects of both product and process quality impact the quality perceived by the client (let us call it the Final Quality). Informally speaking, the Final Quality is the quality of the business solution delivered to him in a form of the software. We said that the software itself is not so important, but of course the source code *quality* is an important part of the whole puzzle.

Garvin [22] introduced five distinct views on quality: product-based, user-based, manufacturing-based, value-based and transcendent-based. Each of them is related to some part of the Final Quality, for example:

Product-Based Quality Relates mainly to non-functional characteristics, such as reliability, portability, usability and so on. The non-functional requirements are often not given explicitly, so it may be easy to skip testing in these areas. This is very dangerous, because the lack of non-functional quality may make software completely useless, even if it has implemented all functionalities desired by a client. The testing process that evaluates a product-based quality is called a non-functional testing.

User-Based Quality Relates mainly to the needs, wants and desires of the user. It is a degree, to which software provides desired functionalities. The testing process that evaluates a user-based quality is called a functional testing, and is also a part of the validation process. The user plays here a very important role. The decisions need to be made on which part of the software should be tested by the testers and which by the users and to what extent.

Manufacturing-Based Quality Measured by the degree to which a product or service conforms to its intended design and requirements. This kind of quality arises from the processes used. The testing process that evaluates a manufacturing-based quality is called verification. The impact of the manufacturing-based quality on the Final Quality is very often intangible, therefore hard to provide and to measure. This is because people learn best when they see an effect occurring directly after a cause. Here, the effect (client's satisfaction) is far away in time from its cause (for example, some good practice implemented in the development process). A professional tester should be focused on this type of quality and should very well understand its importance.

Value-Based Quality Related to the price/cost of the product. A quality product or service is one that provides desired performance at an acceptable cost. The testing process that deals with this kind of quality is often referred to as a risk-based approach. To achieve an acceptable level of a value-based quality, some economic decisions need to be made. These decisions should be made upon analyses and simulations that take into account trade-offs between time, effort and cost aspects, involving quality costs. For example: will it be worth it to perform an inspection of the design project X? The inspection may discover some design defects, so this may be a cheap way to detect and solve a serious defect. On the other hand, the inspection itself is expensive. What is the optimal trade-off here? Another example: we cannot test everything—what should be tested first and to what extent?

Transcendent-Based Quality According to Garvin, it cannot be precisely defined—we know it when we see it or are aware of its absence when it is missing. It depends on the individual perception. However, if we assume that this individual is feeling results from the other four quality types, we may identify a transcendent-based quality with the Final Quality defined above.

To make the long story short: the most important thing is a business problem the client wants to solve. A software is the solution to his problem. The solution's quality depends on many different factors. Therefore, the tester's activities should not be limited to functional testing, but should also include all other quality factors. However, when undertaking any action (be it requirements inspection, code review, performance testing, etc.), the tester should *never* lose sight of the main goal.

Therefore, the right question for a tester to ask is not 'does the software work correctly without any bugs?', but: 'is the client able to solve his problem with the software?' The latter implies the former and corresponds to the ultimate goal of quality.

1.2.5   Your Real Boss Is Your Client

As we said earlier, the most important thing is the solution to the client's business problem. So, when you think about it, your real boss is your client. You have your job because he needs your help. Unfortunately, this boss is very often whimsical. You might have heard the saying 'The client does not know what he wants'.

This is some kind of a paradox: everything we do, we do for our client. But very often he really does not know what exactly he wants. Why is it so? It seems that business problems are much more difficult to grasp than the 'traditional' engineering problems. For example, in general, building a bridge is much easier than building an application in the sense that all bridges usually share *the same kind of functionality*. Therefore, one methodology can be easily applied to most bridge building projects. Also, for the bridge's primary role it is not really important what the color of its spans will be or what kind of material the walking surface will be made of.

Building an application, on the other hand, is completely different. Each application has its own set of functionalities. This results in the fact that at the beginning of the project it is very hard to describe all requirements and functionalities in a complete and detailed way. Also, from the *technical* point of view, introducing a change is much easier in the case of a software than in the case of a bridge.[6] This is one of the sources of the persistent 'I don't know what I really want' problem.

The client usually *understands* his business problem intuitively. But very often it is problematic for him to express it in a transparent manner to the development team, especially if he speaks business language, and the team speaks a technical dialect. Another problem is that we cannot really help him, because we usually do not understand the business. When it comes to envisioning the solution, the client may also make mistakes.

---

[6]This is, by the way, why engineering and architecture projects can be easily conducted within a waterfall model; also, their costs can be estimated more precisely than in the case of a software project.

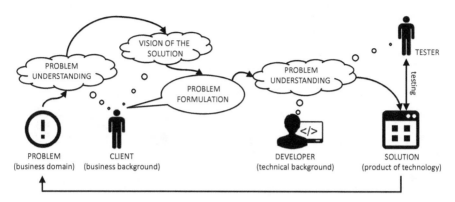

Fig. 1.5 Typical and problematic communication between client and team

Example
A client's concern is a low sale. He wants to improve the business processes using some application. This should facilitate the communication with the clients, make the choice of product more accurate, allow for better CRM and so on. The client orders such an application, it is well designed, has all required functionalities, is stable with no bugs. But it turns out, that the problem was lying somewhere else—in the sales market. People just want to buy a different kind of product. Besides, the customers hate the loyalty system that is offered by the company.

It is very hard (if possible) for a tester to diagnose such problems. But these are extremal situations. Usually we deal with the kinds of problems that we are able to solve. The crucial thing here is the proper management of the communication process. The typical (and problematic) communication process is depicted in Fig. 1.5. Let us investigate it in detail.

The whole process starts with the client's problem understanding and envisioning the solution. These two steps usually take place in the client's mind, which, unfortunately, we cannot access. The problem formulation is the first visible and tangible thing from a tester's perspective. For a developer we have a reverse process: given the problem formulation, he creates a problem understanding in his mind, so that he is able to implement the solution. Remember, that the development process is an intellectual activity driven by our minds, not formal documents. These documents need to be processed by our brains.

The same process takes place in a tester's mind. He also needs to form a problem understanding in his mind. The problem is that tester's and developer's

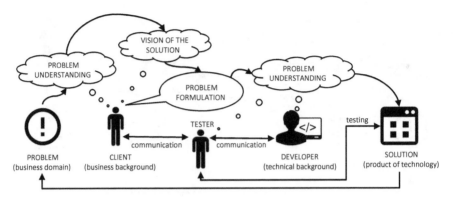

Fig. 1.6 A better model for communication

understandings may differ. Even worse, their understandings may be completely different than the client's one. The result? A classical Chinese whispers. In the case of most development projects the situation is getting even worse, because there is little or no contact with the client.[7] A tester can communicate with a developer and they may even get to the common problem understanding, but this can still differ from the client's vision.

To avoid such situations, we should modify the communication model. There should be a feedback loop between the client, developer and tester understanding (see Fig. 1.6). The conclusion? The most important things happen when people talk to each other. It is even more important than producing a massive amount of the documentation that will never be read by anyone. If, in any agile methodology, we remove all its parts except the frequent contact with the client, the model would still work well!

A tester needs to be a good interlocutor. From the managerial point of view, the communication and—in general—a human factor are the most important parts of the development and QA process. If this were treated seriously by all managers, clients and the development teams, many problems could be avoided and projects would succeed more frequently.

A conversation with a client has one more positive side effect. When we organize a meeting with two or more client's representatives, and the conversation starts, the clients frequently... start talking to each other, because it turns out that they have a completely different understanding of the problem being discussed. Such meetings help us to make sure that we all are on the same page. Never underestimate the role of the meetings and conversations.

It might seem that tester activities related to understanding the client's needs are a classical part of a QA process. But this can be thought as a *client testing*. We check

---

[7]The irony is that in most cases it is the client who avoids communication. Many clients assume that they will be completely understood and will not need any feedback loops when they say what they want once, at the beginning of the development process.

whether a client is precise in what he says and if we understand the problem in the exactly same way as the client does. A great help here for the tester is the knowledge of communication theory and a practical experience in this field. We will analyze this problem in more detail in Sect. 1.7.

1.2.6   Continuous Scale of Tests: From Confirmation to 'Dirty' Testing

There are two extreme types of testing, between which there is a whole continuous scale of testing. At one end of the scale we have so-called 'confirmation testing'.[8] This type of testing checks whether the software realizes the client needs. It is usually related to the typical use case scenarios that describe the system use. At the other end we have so-called 'dirty' testing. This type of testing tries to 'destroy' the software. Sometimes it is called the 'negative' testing. Between these two extremes there is a variety of other testing types.

Example
Assume we have to test the functionality of a simple login screen for some web application, shown in Fig. 1.7.

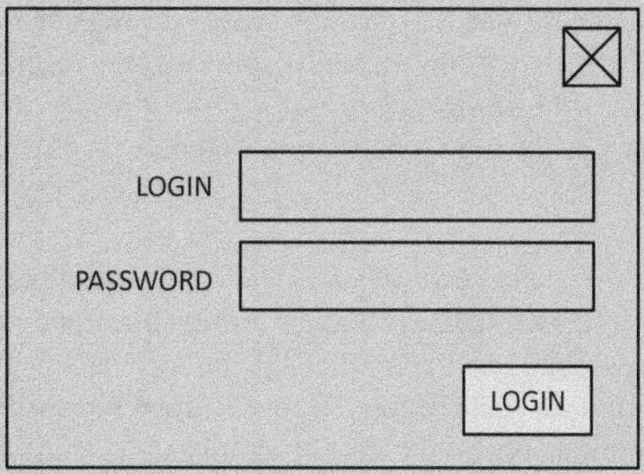

Fig. 1.7 Login screen

Let us give a few examples of possible tests, starting from the most 'confirming' and ending in the most 'dirty' ones:

(continued)

---

[8]Do not confuse it with re-testing, which is also commonly referred to as 'confirmation testing'.

- Enter a valid (existing) username, a correct password, and then click 'Login'. The expected behavior of the system is to switch to the initial screen for a logged user. This scenario is a typical, 'happy path' scenario: all steps in our test case were correct and everything worked as expected. We conclude that for the proper data the software works as intended: the logging process works.[9]
- Enter a valid username and password, but don't click a 'Login' button. Instead, after entering a password, hit the Enter key. What should the system do? This may be considered as a valid action, and hitting Enter may be equal to pushing the 'Login' button.
- Enter a valid username, but an invalid password, then push the 'Login' button. Such user behavior may be unintentional, but the resulting action is invalid and should be rejected by the system (for example, by communicating a 'Wrong password' textbox).
- Enter the non-typical characters (blanks, non-ASCII characters, etc.) for login and/or password. Check how the system reacts (it should reject this request).
- Enter a valid username and password, click the 'Login' button, intercept a POST message that is sent from the client browser to the server. Check if you can use this data again, for the new logging session. If the system is secure, it should not allow this (for example, by using a session id mechanism).
- SQL Injection attack, which dynamically changes SQL statements executed at the server side; if an application is vulnerable, we may return all the records in the table, retrieve the user's passwords or even damage the database. This kind of testing is trying to intentionally attack the software.

As we can see, the valid test case and the SQL Injection examples are two extremes: one test assumes that everything works fine (and mimics the normal user's behavior), the second one tries to damage the software on purpose. In between there is a large, continuous scale of tests. Some of them represent the situations that may happen in a normal operation (like user mistake), some of them are rather impossible to occur in the case of the normal users, but may be for example performed by hackers and should also be verified.

Some people understand testing as the solely negative process, that is, they consider the 'dirty' testing, which tries to destroy the software, as the only true and valuable testing. However, you should never underestimate the 'confirmation' testing. Testing the normal, typical scenarios is very important for at least several reasons:

---

[9]Another thing that should be checked here is the proper masking of the password—it shouldn't be visible on the screen. The password letters should be represented as dots, bullets or other symbol of this kind.

- if no failures are found, it increases our belief that all the intended functionalities work as expected and that the user can perform all the actions that are offered by the software; in other words—it increases our confidence that the software is able to solve the user's business problem,
- it represents the typical use of an application and allows us to perform the testing based on the operational profile, that is—testing that is performed under conditions very similar to the real ones,
- the 'simple', confirmation tests like 'create a user account', 'perform a valid login process', etc. can be used later to create more complicated scenarios on the business process level; this may save much time,
- when a failure is found, it is usually a very serious one; this may indicate that the software is not stable, not secure enough, not usable, etc.

Here is an instructive example supporting the last one. In 2013, in Gdańsk, a city in northen Poland, one of the ATMs was disbursing in one case twice as much cash as it should (100 PLN instead of 50 PLN). It is obvious, that such behavior is a really critical failure that needs to be fixed as soon as possible. It could be discovered with a simple, 'confirming' test suite containing four simple tests: try to withdraw an admissible value in one banknote (20 PLN, 50 PLN, 100 PLN, and 200 PLN). The reason of this failure was a human mistake: it turned out that the ATM operator incidentally switched two cassettes with 50 and 100 PLN banknotes when putting them in the ATM. Notice that a simple, confirming test has two advantages here:

- first, it is able to detect this error by performing a test 'withdraw 50 PLN' (expected result: 50 PLN withdrawn; observed result: 100 PLN withdrawn); if we have only 'negative' tests, like: try to withdraw maximal possible amount (2000 PLN), try to not withdraw any money at all, etc., it would probably be perfectly OK—in the first case the ATM would withdraw 20 times 200 PLN banknotes, in the second it would do nothing, and both tests would pass,

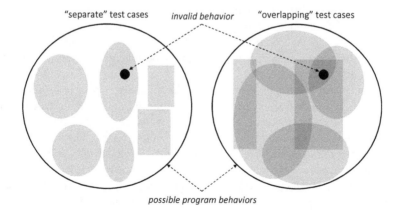

Fig. 1.8 Overlapping of test cases helps to identify defects

Table 1.3 Comparison of 'separated' and 'overlapping' approach to test cases

Aspect	Separate test cases	Overlapping test cases
Test development **cost**	**Lower** (less number of tests is required to achieve a given coverage level)	**Higher** (the same coverage level is achieved, but we have more tests)
Defect detection **time**	**More difficult** (the feedback about the failure comes only from 1 test)	**Easier** (more tests detect the failure, so more information about the defect is provided)

- second, the test suite helps us to identify the root cause of this failure more easily: observing two tests: for 50 and for 100 PLN we see that their results are switched, which immediately suggests the cassettes have been exchanged.

1.2.7 Test Redundancy Is Not Always Bad

It is obvious that the test suite should consist of 'different' tests, that is, the tests that are able to detect different types of failures in different areas of the SUT. Most literature says that 'a good test should not be redundant' (for example [23, 24]). However, a little 'overlapping' or 'redundancy' may sometimes be helpful in terms of test process efficiency. Look at Fig. 1.8. It symbolically represents test cases (gray ovals and rectangles) that are able to detect different incorrect program behaviors. The black dot represents the actual defect. If tests are more 'separate' (left part of the figure), there may be only one test that results in a failure caused by this defect. On the right side the tests overlap, which means that a single failure can be detected by more than one test. In our example, a failure was detected by three test cases.

However, as usual, there is a subtle trade-off between the extent to which the test cases are 'separate' and the ease of potential defect detection. This trade-off regards the cost and time issues. The pros and cons of both methods are summarized in Table 1.3. It may be difficult to define the optimal level of the redundancy. In fact, the sole notion of 'redundancy' may be intangible. Also, there may be other factors impacting the whole analysis (for example, the cost of further detection and correction). Nevertheless, it is important to bear in mind the concept of 'overlapping' when designing a test strategy.

The concept of overlapping is more understandable, when you think about software testing as a detective work at the crime scene (failure). You search for the traces (testing process) and then, collecting all the clues (tests that failed), you try to figure out who was the murder (which defect caused the failure). The more clues you have, the easier it is to identify the murderer (defect). If you have several failed tests, each of them can give you some other data. Collecting them together may help you in localizing the defect locus in the code, its type or even the root cause. Of course, to be more effective you can also use other standard tools, like debugging activities, running some additional exploratory tests, etc.

Let us recall the ATM example from Sect. 1.2.6. If our test suite had only two tests, for 20 and 50 PLN, the failure would occur due to the second test. The only information we would have is that instead of 50 PLN it returned 100 PLN. If our test suite would also have a test for 100 PLN, this test would also reveal a failure: 50 PLN instead of 100 withdrawn. Analyzing the two failed tests together might lead us easier to the root cause, despite the fact that the extended test suite might be considered as more redundant (if we check the ATM for 20 and 50 PLN, do we really need to check it also for 100 PLN?).

1.2.8   Disregarding Risk Is Risky

Testers are often called quality *engineers* and engineers work with concrete, *quantitative* data. Qualitative data is of course also important, but quantitative data can be processed, analyzed and interpreted in much more ways. The measurement theory defines four main types of measurement scales:

- **Nominal**—it just labels the variables, they cannot be compared in any way. An example of a nominal scale is OS type: Linux, Windows, Unix. It does not make any sense to claim that 'Linux is greater than Windows', although there may be a significant group of people who exactly claim this...
- **Ordinal**—it introduces the order of the values, e.g.: satisfaction level: very unsatisfied, unsatisfied, neutral, satisfied, very satisfied. You can compare the values, but you cannot say that the *difference* between 'very unsatisfied' and 'unsatisfied' is the same as between 'neutral' and 'satisfied' or half as much as the difference between 'neutral' and 'very satisfied'.
- **Interval**—it introduces not only the order, but also the exact differences between the scale values. The interval scale allows us to use the operations like adding/subtracting and to use metrics like median, mode, standard deviation and so on. Unfortunately, the interval scale has no 'absolute zero'. An example may be the Celsius scale. You can say that the difference between 20 and 30 °C is the same as between –2 and 8, but you cannot say that the object with 20 °C is twice as warm as the one with 10 degrees.
- **Ratio**—the 'richest' scale. It gives us the order, the intervals *and* the absolute zero (which, for example, allows us to claim that something is twice as big as something else). The ratio scale allows us to use all descriptive and inferential statistics procedures.

If we want to measure something, we need to define a measurement scale for it. The broader the scale is, the better. When it comes to the software quality evaluation, the management always asks you: how *good* is our software? The main problem is: how to express the 'goodness' of the software? How to express its quality?

One of the possible solutions is the concept of *risk*. In fact, the risk-based strategy is the most popular test approach. It allows us to express the software quality level, at any stage of its development, in terms of the so-called residual risk, that is—the risk that is expected to still exist in the software. But how should we define the risk? And—what is more important—how should we define the *operational metric* for this notion, that is—the way it should be measured, assuring the consistency of the measurements?

In fact, there are many ways to do this. A tester should choose the method that is reasonable, easily measurable, and understandable for all the stakeholders. Unfortunately, it may be hard to fulfill all these conditions. For example, if we define the risk in terms of the defects remaining in the code (ratio scale), it may be difficult to measure them (actually, we *do not know* how many residual defects there are!). We could only rely on some predictive models, which are not 100% accurate. We can define risk in terms of the coverage (like requirements, code, functions coverage, etc.; also on ratio scale), but this is very dangerous and may not be properly understood by our clients and the management. Risk may be also described in terms of the money (again, ratio scale), for example using the 'value-at-risk' concept, that is, the amount of money that we may lose if the field defects are found by the client, not during the testing process. This notion may be comprehensible for finance guys, but is definitively not intuitive and does not seem to reflect the *direct* quality level.

Regardless of the pros and cons of each of the above-mentioned methods, it is wise to use *some* form of the risk metric. Disregarding risk is risky. If you don't use this concept, you don't measure your software. And, as Lord Kelvin wisely said: 'if you can't measure, you can't improve it'. He also said, that 'to measure is to *know*'. Your ultimate goal is to solve the business problem, but how can you measure a progress toward this goal, if you have no idea about the current quality level of your software? You *don't know* whether it increases, decreases or is stable; you don't know whether it is economically viable to release the software now, or whether it is better to wait a few more weeks (because, for example, within this time a certain number of additional defects could be detected and thus eliminate the potential costs of fixing them after release).

It is also important to understand that there is a strict relationship between risk and the economics of software quality. To be honest, it is not fully understood yet by the contemporary software engineering, but there is one, simple fact that every tester should remember. This fact is the so-called *law of the diminishing returns*, which, in economic terms, means that the marginal output of a production process decreases, as the amount of a single factor of production is incrementally increased, while the amounts of all other factors of production stay constant.

This somehow complicated statement means just one important thing for a tester: at some point, our quality-related efforts stop paying us. So, at some point it does not make any sense to improve the quality at all costs. We shall discuss this issue in more detail in Sect. 2.2.3.

In some projects, especially the ones from the agile world, it is common to operate with a qualitative risk level scale. In such a case, the risk level is expressed with the ordinal scale (like: very low, low, medium, high, very high). Such an approach is quite convenient, because the 'more qualitative' a metric is, the more uncertainty it

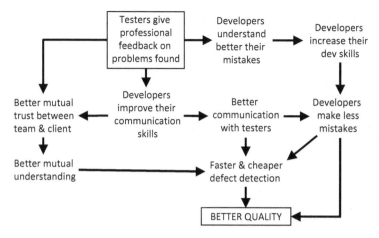

Fig. 1.9 Indirect soft skills impact on the final quality

has.[10] Unfortunately, the measurement process is usually based on the risk level individually perceived by all the team members, so it is not objective.

1.2.9   Feedback for the Team

Testing does not change the software itself. The only added value of testing is *feedback*. Usually, because of the nature and the role of testing, this feedback is bad and negative and may be viewed as pessimistic. That is why it is so important to 'communicate it in a professional way'. It is a standard catchword present in all textbooks on testing and IT project management. But the benefits of a professional communication reach far beyond the simple making sure that there won't be a war in the team. To understand it, we need to utilize a systems thinking and see the testing process in a broader context.

Let us look at Fig. 1.9. It shows some relations between the project stakeholders and their skills. Suppose that testers start to communicate their findings in a very professional, neutral way. This results in a few things. First, developers may understand better their mistakes. Second, the communication between testers and developers improves. Third, it introduces more trust between the team and the client. These phenomena result in subsequent occurrences, like increasing the developers' skills or better understanding. At the end, developers work better (make less mistakes), and all problems are found more efficiently, which results in... better quality!

---

[10]For example, the 'number of defects found' metric is very precise, but the number of predicted, future defects is not so clear. The risk expressed in money is even less precise (it would be insane to claim that the present risk level is, let's say, *exactly* $1,832,334.65).

As simple as that? Unfortunately, there are at least three big problems here:

- this whole delicate network of relations and dependencies will work only if *all* team members will have a willingness to change,
- introducing the change in the process requires management support (which usually means: costs!), so the management really needs to be convinced and to understand the possible benefits of a change...
- ...which may be difficult, as the process usually needs to take some time and the change resulting in better quality is slowly increasing, almost invisible, very subtle and hardly measurable in a short period of time.

The communication issues are discussed in Sect. 1.7. In order to convince the management to support the change process, some proof of concept may be helpful. The testers can use the simulations and systems thinking that might visualize the potential benefits in a convincing way. We will talk about simulations in Sect. 2.10 and about systems thinking in Sect. 3.7. The willingness to change is stronger if one understands better how and why it may make his life easier (analytical and critical thinking) and if one sees clearly the possible ways of self-development. Both these issues will be discussed in the following parts of this book.

1.2.10 It Is Not About Test Execution

Testing is a very wide and complicated engineering process requiring many technical skills, composed of dozens of relations, constraints and dependencies. It is therefore very tempting to perceive it through the technical aspect, as some kind of an 'engineering abstraction'. Hence, it is very easy to forget about the most important thing: a human factor.

Testing indeed is full of technicalities and abstract processes: defining the test environment, assigning the tasks, planning, scheduling, writing the scripts, using the tools, executing the tests, reporting, measuring, and so on. All of this is important and you can see it from the topics of all testing conferences all around the world. Tools, automation, processes. Scripts, reports, certifications. Standards, DevOps, agile... This makes it even more urgent to ask the testers community, as Pio XIII in the brilliant Sorrentino's TV serial 'The Young Pope' asks the crowds gathered on the St. Peter's Square: what have we forgot? What have we forgot?!

We have forgot the tester himself. We have forgot the ultimate goal of testing. What is the most important part of the testing process and where it happens? It is definitely not the proper use of tools, possessing the technical skills or following ISO 29119 standard. It is not even the 'agile'. The most important thing, the most valuable part of the testing process is thinking and it takes place in the tester's head: tests can be executed by a tool, but first they need to be *thought*. All other things are technical: writing a script, generating the data, running a test. If you are not able to design a *good* test, even the best tools, processes and standards won't help you. A good tester is not only an engineer, but primarily a *thinker*. Being an engineer is just a side effect. The tools are of course important, but the most valuable tool in the tester's toolbox is his own brain. The excessive affection for a certain type of tool may bias the tester's way of thinking and decrease his ability to provide good, effective tests. We discuss this problem in Sect. 6.9.

All this may sound trivial and obvious. But did you notice that it is very common for technical people to instantly start working on a problem's solution before *thinking* about it? Yes, we all live in a hurry. We all have to deliver our work in increasingly shorter iterations, resulting in more frequent releases, needed for speeding up time-to-market. But haste causes carelessness and carelessness causes big problems. This issue is discussed in detail in Sect. 6.8. A professional tester knows that his primary task is an intellectual process: thinking before solving, and planning before acting. This is the only possible approach to avoid the problems.

1.3   The Mythical Test Case

The Internet is full of information on what a test case is, 'how to write a good test case', what are the mandatory and optional fields in a test case specification and so on. Unfortunately, it is much harder to find there an explanation *why*, in the first place, we should use test cases. A thinking-driven approach forces us not only to think before acting, but also to think broadly. So, let us look at the test case issue from the broader perspective. It should be obvious that test cases—regardless of their definition, form and other factors—are used by testers in their everyday work. Hence, the following questions immediately arise:

- what is the primary function of a test case?
- should we always use test cases in testing?
- how can we, other team members, client and process benefit from the information gathered in a test case specification and from the data on the results of its execution?

1.3.1   A Primary Function of Test Cases

There are many definitions of a test case. For example, ISO/IEC 29119 Standard defines it as a 'set of test case preconditions, inputs (including actions, where applicable), and expected results, developed to drive the execution of a test item to meet test objectives, including correct implementation, error identification, checking quality, and other valued information'. Ignoring the fact that this definition is incorrectly constructed,[11] let us look at this problem bearing in mind the fundamental ideas about software testing. In the following discussion, we assume that test

---

[11]The defined term is used in the definition itself: a *test case* is a set of *test case* preconditions (...). Fortunately, in this case the methodological error (called *idem per idem*) can be easily corrected by removing the words 'test case' from the definition and just saying that a test case is a set of preconditions (...).

cases are related to a so-called *dynamic testing*, that is, a form of testing being conducted on a running software.

The primary role of a tester is to test. Test cases are the ideas on how to do it. From this point of view, a test case—to have any sense—needs to *rationally define* the eligible testing activity. By saying 'rationally' I mean that it needs to bring an added value, be it finding defects, improving the test process, performing an educational function, providing a means for collecting quality data and so on. Testing uses the software, and test cases are the ideas about this usage. These ideas may take different forms: they can be written, mental, concrete, abstract, detailed, general and so on. The only thing that distinguishes test cases from the ideas of a 'normal' software usage is that the test cases are directed at finding specific information about the software, while the latter is directed at achieving the business goal, without any reflection on the software itself. We should not confuse test cases with tests. A test is a physical realization of a test case.

1.3.2 When Should We Use Test Cases?

In fact, we always use them. The above-mentioned considerations imply that any testing activity related to software execution is a form of some test case realization. Having said that, we identify two important test case characterizations:

- the meaning—related to what a test case really does,
- the form—describing what kind of information a test case provides us.

A form relates to the technical realization of a test case. The form can vary, from a very informal test case, whose execution leaves absolutely no trace, to one very detailed, richly documented and tracked. The choice of both meaning and form of a test case depends on many factors, which can be brought to one general question: what is the expected benefit to the quality?

1.3.3 Benefits from Test Cases

It is not possible to present a closed-form list of all potential benefits that we may achieve by using the test cases with different meanings and forms. In Table 1.4 we give a few examples. Some of them are quite obvious, while others are more sophisticated.

As you can see from the table, test cases play different roles in different contexts. They may be a formal documentation, an informally written test idea, a model, an abstract thought. Some of them must explicitly define the input and/or expected output, some of them may, and some of them can't. We shouldn't really follow any standard that imposes the predetermined form of a test case. There are at least few good reasons for that:

- generalization can never catch special cases—each test idea is different,
- test case form standardization kills tester's creativity,

Table 1.4 Sample benefits from different types of test cases

Sample test case meaning	Sample test case form	Expected benefit of using the test case
Checking whether software realizes its intended function	A simple user story or a detailed written scenario derived from a specification	Better confidence in software; also a form of software documentation
Checking different combinations of parameters	Orthogonal table for parameter combinations providing pair-wise coverage	Test suite size reduction (optimizing run-time while maintaining the test suite ability to detect defects)
Deviation from a defined functional test	Loose idea in tester's mind during manual testing	Higher chance for defect detection by following the 'weird' software behavior
Collecting quality data for further analysis	Written document with obligatory field 'test type' (e.g., functional, usability, performance, etc.)	Distribution of defect types that will allow us to identify 'weak', 'undertested' quality areas
General idea of what to test	A general description of what to test	Better creativity when test case is realized by more testers; better communication with client
(Arbitrary)	Richly commented, written set of steps	Educational purpose for other testers; also a form of documentation

- we will not be able to optimize the test process,
- it will be hard to communicate with the client with use of test cases.

Example

Suppose you test a borrowing system installed in the university library. There are different types of borrowers and different business rules about the maximal number of books a user can borrow, borrowing terms, and fees. These requirements are shown in Table 1.5.

Table 1.5 Business rules for a borrowing system in the university library

Borrower	Items	Borrowing terms
Undergraduates	10 books, 3 DVD/videos	Standard loan: 4 weeks Fee: $1 per one book per one day of delay
Postgraduates	15 books, 3 DVD/videos	Standard loan: 8 weeks Fee: $1 per one book per one day of delay
Research staff	40 books, 4 DVD/videos	Standard loan: 16 weeks Fee: $0.5 per one book per one day of delay

Below are given the examples of three different types of test cases designed to verify different aspects of the system.

(continued)

Test case 1: checking, whether software realizes its intended function, by providing a scenario to be tested.

Actors: Undergraduate, System.

Initial condition: clear account

Steps:

Undergraduate logs into the System.

Verify that Undergraduate is logged in, authorized to borrow the books, and has no borrowed books.

Undergraduate selects 6 books and 1 DVD to borrow.

Verify that Undergraduate was able to select 6 books and 1 DVD.

System verifies that the books and DVD are available and assigns them to the Undergraduate account.

Verify that Undergraduate has 6 books and 1 DVD borrowed and that it is shown in his account.

System shows the information where the books and DVD can be picked up.

System shows the information about the return date.

Verify that System shows this information in a proper way.

This is an example of a "high-level" test case: it does not provide any concrete input values (for example, user id, current date, return date, book titles, etc.). The idea here is to provide a general scenario describing a valid, eligible, normal borrowing process. When executed, this test case must be "filled" with the concrete values. This may be not highly reproducable, as each tester may use different test data for performing the test case. On the other hand, this may increase the coverage, as each test case execution will be slightly different than the others.

Test case 2: checking different combinations of parameters. Suppose we want to check whether the system works correctly with different combinations of: user type, actual number of borrowed books, number of books to be borrowed. We identify the following possible values of these variables (MAX denotes the maximal possible number of books that can be borrowed by a given user type):

- user type: Undergraduate, Postgraduate, Researcher
- actual number B of the borrowed books: 0, typical (between 1 and MAX– 1), MAX
- number $B2$ of books to be borrowed: typical (such that $B + B2 < MAX$), boundary value (such that $B + B2 = MAX$), incorrect (such that $B + B2 > MAX$)

(continued)

We want to cover every pair of values for every pair of variables. Table 1.6 shows all these combinations.

Table 1.6 Test cases covering the combinations of values

Test case	User type	B	B2	Result
1	Und	0	typical	OK, total = typical
2	Und	typical	boundary	OK, total = boundary
3	Und	MAX	incorrect	NOT OK, total = incorrect; borrowing is impossible
4	Postgr	0	incorrect	?
5	Postgr	typical	typical	OK, total = typical
6	Postgr	MAX	boundary	?
7	Research	0	boundary	OK, total = boundary
8	Research	typical	incorrect	NOT OK, total = incorrect; borrowing is impossible
9	Research	MAX	typical	?

This set of nine test cases is written in a completely different form than the Test Case 1. Each test case is defined here by three values: user type, B and B2. For each two of them and each possible pair of their values, we can find a row with these values. The possible pairs of variables are (User type, B), (User type, B2), (B, B2). For example, for a pair (User type = Postgraduate, B2 = typical) we have this combination in Test Case 5. For a pair (B = 0, B2 = incorrect) we have this combination in Test Case 4; and so on. It would be very hard to express such a set of combinations using the test case form from the previous example.

Notice one interesting fact: after designing the test cases we see that we cannot really define the expected result for Test Cases 4, 6 and 9. In Test Case 4, if the actual number of the borrowed books is 0, we cannot borrow more than MAX books. This situation is infeasible. In Test Case 6, the actual number of the borrowed books is MAX. So, we cannot borrow the books in a way that the total number of B and B2 will be the boundary value, as B is already this value. The same problem is with Test Case 9. Hence, due to the 'negative' test case input values, we see that some combinations of the values may be infeasible. Notice, that it may be impossible to detect this by designing a 'positive' test case as in the previous example.

Test case 3: general idea of what to test. Delays in the return are penalized. The business rules give the information about the fee. As the books can be borrowed in different days, it may be worthwhile to check whether the fee calculation system works correctly. This general idea may be then transformed into a test scenario, for example:

(continued)

Undergraduate borrows book A in day 0, books B and C in day 17, book D in day 28 and book E in day 29. What should be the fee value after day 28? How will these values change in different scenarios of book returning? A tester may even write a script that would simulate random borrowings and returnings, calculate the fee in consecutive days and compare it with the behavior of the system under test. Such an automation project may optimize the test process in terms of the test execution effort, as it allows us to quickly execute thousands of randomly generated scenarios.

Another example of a test idea may be this: is there a maximal fee value? If not, the client may never return the books. So, let us check what happens if we borrow a book in day 0 and never return it. Will the account be finally blocked?

1.4   The Nature of Defects and the Myths About Them

A good detective needs to have a knowledge about the ways the criminals act and think. This helps him to solve his cases more easily. A good tester should have the same knowledge about the nature of defects. Of course, the number of defects, their types, and place of occurrence depend heavily on specific, process-related factors. But there exist some patterns which seem to be common for most projects. These phenomena are a kind of 'laws of defect nature'. There are also some myths about defects or, at least, the popular claims that do not have enough support in data. We will now discuss both the 'laws' and the 'myths' about the defects.

1.4.1   Defect Distribution in Time

Regardless of the SDLC, if there are no serious obstructions and impediments during both software development and testing processes, the distribution of the number of defects found in time looks more or less like the one depicted in Fig. 1.10. It is usually similar to the Rayleigh distribution [25]. At the beginning, the rate of the defects found grows rapidly, then it stabilizes, and in the late phases it slowly decreases.

Fig. 1.10 Distribution of number of defects found in time

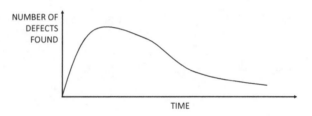

The shape of this function can be easily explained by the nature of the development process itself and by the team dynamics. In the early phases the team needs to understand well the project assumptions and requirements, set up all necessary environments and do many other 'technical' things. At this stage, there are not many occasions to insert a defect. Then, the team starts the implementation, much of the code is produced, so this stage is naturally the heavily error-prone one. Many defects are introduced, so many of them are also discovered. Then, the development phase starts to phase out. Less defects are introduced. Testers successively discover both the defects from the last phases, but also the ones from the earlier phases that were not detected earlier. This makes the distribution fat-tailed.

The knowledge about the defect distribution in time may help to allocate the resources and organize the testing process more effectively. But the wise tester should be aware not only of the crude number of defects found, but also of their *criticality*. The large number of defects found in the middle SDLC phase may be related to trivial or not very critical problems. Usually, the most important errors are the design errors and usually they are introduced at the beginning.[12] Therefore, the quality introduced in the beginning phases is the crucial success factor.

Another important thing, when using predictive analysis like this, is of statistical nature. You should never use such models uncritically. Each model has its assumptions, so you should always check if they are fulfilled, and if not—it would be a big problem for your modeling. Also, you need to understand the notion of variance, which represents uncertainty. We will talk more about this in Chap. 6, especially in Sect. 6.6. There is also another danger—when people know that the defect distribution should look like the one in Fig. 1.10, they will subconsciously endeavor to make it real. For example, in the early phases they may tend to design many, but poor, test cases, to find most of the defects, and in the late phases they may unintentionally perform poor testing to find a lower number of bugs, which will be 'confirmed' by the model [26, 27].

1.4.2 Cost of Defect Removal

It is said that the defects should be removed as soon as possible because the cost of defect removal grows rapidly in time. Some sources even claim that it is exponential. However, as Jones and Bonsignour point out, it is not so obvious:

---

[12]In [28] C. Jones gives the following data on defect origins (Tables 4.1 and 4.4): for small software projects (<1000 function points or <50,000 source code statements) the number of defects that originate from Requirements and Design phase is equal to the number of defects that originate from the Code phase. For large projects (>10,000 function points) he claims that "front-end defects in requirements, architecture, and design are much more numerous for large systems than for small applications". There are 2.7 defects per function point that originate from Requirements, Architecture and Design, and only 1.77 defects per function point that origin from the Code phase.

the 'cost-per-defect' metric actually penalizes quality and achieves its lowest values for the buggiest applications. This problem is due to ignoring fixed costs. The oft-repeated aphorism that 'it costs 100 times as much to fix a bug after release as during design' is based on a flawed analysis that ignores fixed costs. Due to fixed costs, the following rule applies: 'Cost per defect is always cheapest where the number of defects found is highest'. This is why front-end defects are always cheaper than tail-end defects. Worse, the cost-per-defect metric focuses too much attention on defect repairs and ignores the greater economic advantages of high quality in shortening schedules and lowering costs. [28]

So, the cost-per-defect metric is valid mathematically, but not economically. Jones and Bonsignour notice, that this metric tends to escalate as quality improves and does not capture the real economic advantages of higher quality. They propose that instead of 'cost-per-defect', a 'defect repair costs per function point' should be used, as 'it gives much better picture of the real value of quality and how fixed and variable costs interact'.

1.4.3   LOC Metric as a Defect Predictor

It is a well-known fact that the simple 'Lines of Code' (LOC) metric is a good predictor of the number of defects. This seems to be obvious, as the bigger the program is, the more chances to make a mistake, and therefore, more defects introduced into the code. However, there are two important things that tester should keep in mind:

- it is not the only defect predictor—the number of defects depends on many factors; the LOC metric can be used as a rough measure of the potential future problems with a given module, but other factors should also be considered, like: the complexity of the module's logic, the degree of interaction with other modules, the developer experience, the language used and so on,
- the LOC metric should be used coherently across all the project in the organization; it should have the operational definition that gives the unequivocal way of measuring it (for example: do we count comments or function signatures as separate lines? Do we count only executable lines? And so on).

1.4.4   Defect Grouping

Defects are not uniformly distributed not only in time (see Sect. 1.4.1), but also in space. It is therefore reasonable to find the most error-prone areas and focus more on them. How to identify such areas? From the tester's perspective, it is much better to classify bugs by their root cause and not by their outcome. The root cause is able to not only identify the 'areas' themselves, but also identify what the 'areas' really are. For example, the analysis may find that 80% of bugs come from 20% of certain modules, but it may also find that most of the bugs come, for example, from calling the same library or querying the database with the same type of SQL query. In such a case, the defects seem to occur in different places (modules), but their common root cause is the library or database, not the individual modules.

The root cause identification allows us to improve the process by removing the underlying cause. Therefore, it is important to gather as much data as possible when reporting defects. Having such data we can analyze them and find some patterns. For example, we may find that most of the bugs come from module X, or that most of the bugs have something to do with performance issues and so on. This allows us to prioritize test activities, hence, solving most important problems at the beginning and removing most of the issues with low costs.

1.4.5 Defects Resulting from Interaction of Parameters

From the empirical data it is well-known that the majority of defects is caused by a single factor or by an interaction of two of them [29]. Kuhn and Reilly [30] analyzed 171 defects in the software for Apache server and discovered that 70% of them were due to the interaction of two modules. The maximum degree of interaction in actual real-world faults so far observed is six [31].

This observation is very useful when designing the tests. A tester should always try to identify the combinations of factors that may lead to a failure. Here are some examples:

- different actions that the user can perform in the system may be combined with the user's role (administrator, unlogged user, logged user, etc.),
- trying to force the combination of factors that should not happen due to the business logic, e.g., trying to obtain a reduced ticket for a person with an age that does not allow that,
- 'interaction with time', for example closing the application during some operation and checking if it can restore its state after re-opening it.

In Chap. 4 we introduce a TQED model that helps a tester in designing good tests by stimulating her creativity. One way of doing that is using the concept of factor interactions, which is directly implemented in the model.

1.4.6 Module Structure vs. Defect-Proneness

There are many metrics that try to predict the defect proneness by catching the relation between the defects and some structural properties of the modules. However, a tester cannot be uncritical about them. It is a big problem in software engineering: there is plethora of defect prediction models, but most of them were not tested in real environments. Also, the experiments that study the metrics are often inconclusive.

For example, a number of authors suggested that there is an optimal size of a software module, which results in the optimal defect density, that is, the number of defects divided by the module's LOC [32], [33]. This phenomenon was called a

Goldilocks Principle.[13] Both smaller and larger modules were supposed to have a greater defect density. However, in [34] Fenton and Neil critiqued this model as well as studies intended to validate the conjecture. They noticed that if it were true, the whole idea of decomposition—fundamental for software engineering—would just be wrong (the smaller the modules are, the greater is the defect density). After investigating several studies that were supporting the Goldilocks Principle, Fenton and Neil found the following problems:

- no study defined 'module' in such a way as to make comparison across data sets possible,
- no study explicitly compared different approaches to structuring and decomposing designs,
- the data analysis or quality of the data used could not support the results claimed,
- a number of factors exist that could partly explain the results which these studies have neglected to examine.

They also performed an analysis on the large data sets taken from big industrial systems. No relationship between module size and defect density was observed. The reason that some authors believed in the Goldilocks principle was that they were trying to explain the complicated concept of 'defect density' with only one, simple metric: module size. But the defect density depends on a huge number of factors, some of which are even impossible to be accurately measured.

There are some better measures than LOC, for example a cyclomatic complexity (CC), which measures the degree of a structural complexity of a module. Technically, CC is the number of decision points in the module plus one. There is an engineering rule saying that CC should not exceed 10. However, this is still a single metric and it will not predict well the defect density. The example below shows in a simple way why this is so.

Example
In Fig. 1.11 three control flow graphs are shown. All graphs have the same cyclomatic complexity, CC = 4. However, the third program seems to be much more complicated, because there are two nested loops and a decision one that is not structuralized (it jumps inside a loop). Clearly such a program will be much more error-prone than the two shown on the left. So even in the case of one, single, structure-related metric like CC, we can construct two programs with identical metric value but with completely different susceptibility to defects.

(continued)

---

[13]The name was given after the protagonist in the children's story 'Goldilocks and the Three Bears', which introduces the idea 'not too big, not too small, and just right'.

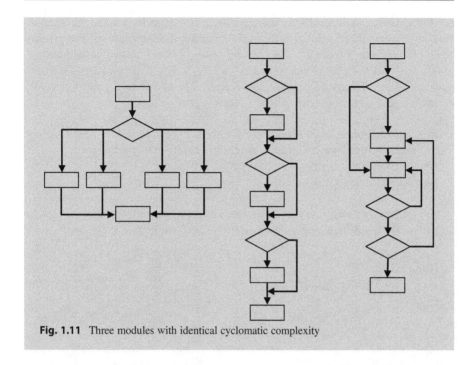

Fig. 1.11 Three modules with identical cyclomatic complexity

Apart from the structural complexity, there are many other types of complexity that influence the defect-proneness, like: algorithmic, code-related, combinatorial, computational, data-related, diagnostic, entropic, essential, fan-in based, flow based, function point based, logical, mnemonic, organizational, perceptional, problem based, process based, semantic, syntactic, topologic and many others.

1.5   Exploratory vs. Scripted: An Apparent Problem

In the software testing community there are present two test approaches, which are acknowledged as the opposite ones. These are so-called *exploratory* and *scripted* testing. Exploratory testing is usually defined as 'simultaneous learning, test design and test execution'. This means that the tester uses her knowledge, intuition and analysis of the current software behavior in order to decide what should be the next test execution step. Exploratory testing should therefore be performed without any prior detailed planning and designing the predefined test cases, which later on should be just simply followed. Scripted testing, on the other hand, is presented as the opposition to exploratory approach. In scripted testing test cases are first designed, and then executed.

In recent years there was a wide discussion about which of the two is better. There are advocates of both methods and the arguments often contain more ideology than merit. However, as we pointed out earlier, a professional tester is not an ideologist, but a pragmatic and rationally thinking engineer. So, let us look at the 'exploratory vs. scripted' problem from a broader and more reasonable perspective. The primary goal of testing is to find defects. The method we use to reach this goal is secondary—in fact every method that works well is acceptable. It would be unwise to claim that only one of the two extreme approaches is right. The choice of the method should depend on several factors, including the following:

- what is the required level of documenting the testing process?
- how much time do we have for the preparation and for the testing?
- what level of 'thoroughness' is required?
- what level of test repetitiveness is required?

For example, we may find the test design process very useful, because we may be able to find many design defects just because of performing the design activities.

Example

Suppose we have to test the requirement that describes a piece of a business logic for an e-shop. This logic defines some rules for offering (or not) the customer a discount and for sending (or not) the special offers via e-mail, depending on three factors: is the client registered, what is his average basket value, and is he a regular customer. The requirement is as follows: if a client is not a registered one, don't offer any discount and don't send special offers. If the average basket value is greater than $100, offer a 10% discount. If the average basket value does not exceed $100, and a client is regular and registered, offer a 5% discount and send him the special offers. For the regular customers send the special offers.

It is difficult to test such a requirement just following an exploratory session without any model of this logic. We need a model that allows us to systematically check all possible combinations of conditions (is he registered, is the average basket value > $100, is he a regular customer) and for each of them identify the expected actions (give a discount, send a special offer). A decision table can serve as such a model. We design the test cases by constructing the decision table that describes the relationship between the conditions and actions. A decision table for our problem is shown in Table 1.7.

Table 1.7 A decision table showing defects in the business logic

CONDITION: registered?	Y	Y	Y	Y	N	N	N	N
CONDITION: mean basket value > $100?	Y	Y	N	N	Y	Y	N	N
CONDITION: regular customer?	Y	N	Y	N	Y	N	Y	N
ACTION: what discount?	10	10	5	**?**	**0/10?**	**0/10?**	0	0
ACTION: send special offer?	Y	**?**	Y	**?**	**Y/N?**	N	**Y/N?**	N

When we fill it according to the rules given above, immediately several problems occur (the corresponding fields in the table are bolded). First, we

(continued)

have several different (contradicting) actions for 'discount' (registered customer with basket value > $100) and 'special offer' (unregistered, regular customer). We also have missing requirements: for example, the requirement does not say whether we should give a discount or send a special offer in case of a registered, non-regular customer with basket value not exceeding $100.

This simple example shows that the sole process of *test case design* is able to discover many defects, especially in the requirements and in the architectural design. Having no such model it might be difficult for us to systematically test all the combinations.

On the other hand, exploratory testing also uses some form of a scripted approach. A so-called session based exploratory testing uses a testing chart as a guideline for a tester during the exploratory testing session. This chart may be considered as a form of a high-level test script. As you can see, the whole 'exploratory vs. scripted' problem is fluid. Every test activity has some form of 'exploration' and some form of 'scripting approach'. When manually executing a test script, a tester may decide to 'explore' some untested paths or scenarios. On the other hand, when performing an exploratory session, a tester may use formal models to design some test cases and therefore discover potentially interesting test paths or scenarios. The extent to which we utilize these two aspects depends solely on us. And the choice should be dictated by the only reasonable goal: to create an effective test.

The above-mentioned rationality in acting should also be reflected in the process activities. Management should never impose one particular way of testing (like: 'you may only use exploratory testing and you can't design any test cases'). This would be the ideology, not rational thinking. The decision belongs to a tester, who is an expert in the field. Of course, this decision may be based on some managerial decisions, like: general testing approach, general test strategy and so on. But when it comes to *testing*, it is a tester who takes over the command.

There is also one subtle benefit from a scripted testing, which seems to be neglected by some advocates of a 'pure' exploratory approach. Such scripts may be viewed as a software 'live' documentation. It is 'living' because when software changes and a test does not pass, we are forced to change the test. So, tests reflect always the current, desired software behavior. Scripts also have some educational value: other testers can learn and improve their creativity using the well-designed tests.

Some advocates of the exploratory approach, gathered around a so-called 'Context-Driven School', redefined lately the 'exploratory testing' term. They noticed that actually every testing is exploratory: '*testing is the process of evaluating a product by learning about it through exploration and experimentation, which includes: questioning, study, modeling, observation and inference, output checking, etc.*' [35]. This is consistent with our above-mentioned remark, that each testing includes some form of a 'pure' exploration (experimentation, observation) and some 'pre-design' process (study, modeling).

Hence, the 'exploratory vs. scripted' is an apparent problem. Some scientific experiments seem to confirm this thesis. For example, in a recent study of Itkonen and Mäntylä [36], 'pure exploratory' and 'pure scripted testing' were compared in a real experiment performed on a group of computer science students. Both methods turned out to have the same effectiveness (number and type of the defects found). Pure exploration was slightly more efficient, but it is more efficient by definition, since it requires less design effort. However, as we pointed out before, we may benefit from the design effort in other ways than just simply finding bugs. The interesting observation from the experiment was that scripted testing produced significantly more false positive test results compared to exploratory testing. The final conclusion was that both approaches have problems, but of different nature: in exploratory testing it is managing the testing activities and reporting; in scripted testing it is the quality of the test cases.[14]

1.6   The Ideal Tester's Skill Set

In Sect. 1.2.1 we mentioned that a good tester needs to have a really broad skill set. This is because of a very specific role a tester plays in the organization. The tester's toolbox includes both technical and soft skills. They are related to knowledge, abilities and competencies. To be effective as a tester you need to be constantly improving all of them. You can develop at least some of them by:

- drawing inspiration by learning from different areas of science and humanities (see Chap. 2),
- mastering the analytical skills, improving critical thinking and practicing continuous learning (see Chaps. 3, 5 and 6),
- using models that stimulate your creativity (see Chap. 4),
- practicing kata for strengthening of what you have learned (see Chap. 7).

In Fig. 1.12 we present an ideal tester's skill set. As you can see, we depicted there really a lot of skills and probably much more could be added. You will never master all of them—none of us is perfect and omniscient. But this is not the point. The important thing is that you should not focus only on some specific skills, but try to self-develop in many dimensions.

Some of the skills may seem to be not so obvious when we think about testers. For example, the ability to observe carefully is important, because no detail can escape the tester's notice. Even the most innocent symptom, if ignored, may lead to very

---

[14]The authors of a cited study also show its several threats to validity, so the results are not 100% conclusive. But, unfortunately, this is very characteristic of all studies in the experimental software engineering.

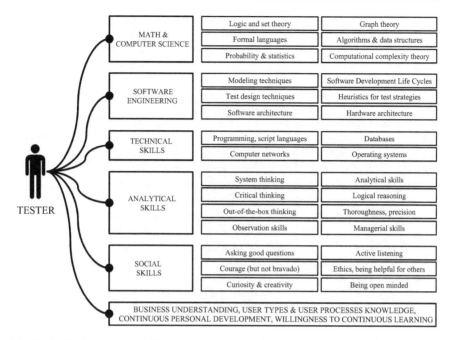

MATH & COMPUTER SCIENCE	Logic and set theory	Graph theory
	Formal languages	Algorithms & data structures
	Probability & statistics	Computational complexity theory

SOFTWARE ENGINEERING	Modeling techniques	Software Development Life Cycles
	Test design techniques	Heuristics for test strategies
	Software architecture	Hardware architecture

TECHNICAL SKILLS	Programming, script languages	Databases
	Computer networks	Operating systems

ANALYTICAL SKILLS	System thinking	Analytical skills
	Critical thinking	Logical reasoning
	Out-of-the-box thinking	Thoroughness, precision
	Observation skills	Managerial skills

SOCIAL SKILLS	Asking good questions	Active listening
	Courage (but not bravado)	Ethics, being helpful for others
	Curiosity & creativity	Being open minded

BUSINESS UNDERSTANDING, USER TYPES & USER PROCESSES KNOWLEDGE, CONTINUOUS PERSONAL DEVELOPMENT, WILLINGNESS TO CONTINUOUS LEARNING

Fig. 1.12   The ideal tester's skill set

serious consequences (a very edifying example here is the case of Ariane 5 rocket, see [3]).

Example

Here's another, very interesting example of how the combination of different skills might prevent the American Army barracks from being hit by a Scud rocket during the Gulf War in 1991. The Scud should be intercepted by a Patriot missile, but it failed. The problem was related to the arithmetic errors (rounding) in the tracking and intercepting system. As it was stated in the GAO report:

The range gate's prediction of where the Scud will next appear is a function of the Scud's known velocity and the time of the last radar detection. Velocity is a real number that can be expressed as a whole number and a decimal (e.g., 3750.2563... miles per hour). Time is kept continuously by the system's internal clock in tenths of seconds but is expressed as an integer or whole number (e.g., 32, 33, 34...). The longer the system has been running, the larger the number representing time. To predict where the Scud will next appear, both time and velocity must be expressed as real numbers. Because of the way the Patriot computer performs its calculations and the fact that its registers are only 24 bits long, the conversion of time from an integer to a real number cannot be any more precise than 24 bits. This conversion results in a loss of precision causing a less accurate time calculation. The effect of this inaccuracy

(continued)

on the range gate's calculation is directly proportional to the target's velocity and the system's runtime. Consequently, performing the conversion after the Patriot has been running continuously for extended periods causes the range gate to shift away from the center of the target, making it less likely that the target, in this case a Scud, will be successfully intercepted. [37]

The time in tenths of second as measured by the system's internal clock was multiplied by 1/10 to produce the time in seconds. But 1/10 has an infinite binary expansion: $1/10 = 0.000110011001100...$ This value had to be rounded, as it was stored in 24-bit register. The very small rounding error, when multiplied by the large number giving the time in tenths of a second, led to a significant error.

The knowledge of a low-level hardware architecture (representation of numbers in the binary code), combined with analytical thinking (careful documentation reading), logical thinking (reasoning) and out-of-the-box thinking might have prevented Americans from this terrible disaster, in which 28 soldiers died. You never know which exotic skills (in this case, hardware architecture) may be helpful!

You shouldn't try to master all the skills at once. Some of them require more experience and prior knowledge than others. Also, some skills form the foundations for developing others. Figure 1.13 presents a simple model that shows how different dependencies of skills create an opportunity for professional development as a tester.

We can symbolically distinguish between three basic levels in a tester's development. The first one is reached, when a tester possesses the foundation of the testing craft. This means that she is familiar with technical vocabulary, foundations of testing theory, and software engineering. She need also to possess elementary soft skills (especially communication skills) and—to have the opportunity to reach higher levels—the ability to learn.

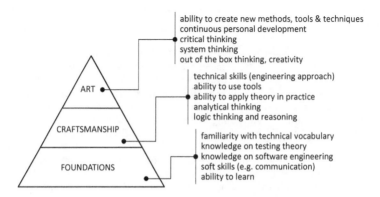

Fig. 1.13 A tester's way to success: the model of professional development

When she achieves that, she starts to gain experience. She becomes familiar with test tools, applies the theory learned in practice, uses an engineering approach. She is able to perform the independent analyses using logical thinking and reasoning. She becomes a craftsman—an independent, technical expert in the field.

But there is something more—she may reach yet another level. By mastering the critical or systems thinking, creativity and out-of-the-box thinking she becomes 'an artist' in testing. To remain on this level she needs to continuously develop her personal skills. On this level she is able to not only effectively use all techniques, tools and approaches, but also to improve *herself*. It's something like the fifth level that an organization reaches in the TMMi[15] model, which means that the organization is able to improve not only its processes, but also its own improvement process.

The model looks quite reasonable, but in practice we may observe a certain problem that does not allow many testers to reach the final level. Suppose that our tester possesses the ability to learn, so she is on a good way to develop and reach the next levels. She decides to participate in many testing conferences to get familiar with things other testers do, to discuss with them, to learn some good practices. But when you look at the programs of most testing conferences, you will immediately notice, that they heavily focus on tools and automation. Most talks have titles like 'how to use a tool X in a project Y'. So, most of the testing activities in the community are related to the second level of development—a 'craftsmanship' level.

At the same time, there is far less talk on the foundations of the testing craft. This is because people usually think that a theory is boring and not applicable to the real testing problems. But you can really act *meaningfully* and *rationally* only when you have the theoretical foundations. Because only then you understand 'why', not only 'how'. And if you know *why* things look as they look, you can consciously develop your testing skills and be able to create your own context-dependent testing strategies. Only then you take a real part in the advancement of testing. Otherwise, you just flounder in the dark and become only a professional who can operate smoothly one or two tools.

There is also lack of talks about 'art' level skills, like system or critical thinking. So, on the one hand, there is lack of foundations, on the other, lack of more advanced topics. This is the worst combination. The result is that testers without a solid background in testing start to learn immediately things on a 'craftsmanship' level, but because they lack these basic skills, they are not able to move any further. They are also very frequently not able to use the tools in a creative way. They are not able to create their *own* approaches to testing, either because they don't know how to do that (lack of 'foundations'), or because they don't have courage (lack of 'art'). Hence, they always rely on somebody else's solutions, frameworks and methods. This always limits our horizons, this kills our creativity, and we lose the chance to become a better test professional, who can perform really good and efficient testing.

---

[15]TMMi (Test Maturity Model integration) is a model designed for the test process improvement. It mimics the more general CMMI (Capability Maturity Model Integration) model for the process improvement.

If you think about our model as a tree—with roots being the 'foundations', trunk being the 'craftsmanship' and the forest canopy being an 'art' you may provide a nice analogy to the problem described above: the trunk is indispensable for transporting all the necessary ingredients from the soil, but in order to do this it needs to have solid roots. It is the only way it can develop its canopy. So, the middle level is very important, but you must also take care of the foundations. Only then you can become an artist in testing.

1.7   It's All About Communication

During one of the EuroStar conferences [38] the organizers asked some of the participants one simple question: what is the most important skill for a tester. There were many different answers (one of them was 'thinking'!), but there are two interesting things with this survey. First, almost all responses were related to the soft, not technical, skills. Second, the most frequent answer was 'it's communication skills'.

When you look at the testing in the context of the SDLC, this answer doesn't seem to be weird anymore. When you finally find a bug, the story doesn't end. In fact, it's just the beginning. First, you have to report this bug, that is—communicate to the developer, that something is wrong and that he has to fix it. You have to do it in a way that is:

- **precise enough**—so that the developer is able to find and fix the defect quickly,
- **convincing**—so that the developer agrees that it really is a bug, not a feature,
- **professional**—so that the developer won't take your statement personally.

No matter whether the statement is verbal or written, we can define several layers of our message. There is an interesting communication model by Friedemann Schulz von Thun [39], known as the 'four-sides' or 'four-ears' model. Von Thun says that each message has four layers:

- **the matter layer**—it contains the information that we want to communicate, related to the matter of data and facts;
- **the self-revealing layer**—it contains the information about the speaker: his motives, feelings, emotions, etc., which may be delivered consciously or may be not intended at all;
- **the relationship layer**—it contains the information on how the sender gets along with the receiver and what the speaker thinks about his interlocutor;
- **the appeal**—it contains the desire, advice, instruction and effects that the speaker is seeking; it reveals the sender's influence on the receiver.

One of the reasons for misunderstandings is that the sender wants to express some statement differently on different layers, but the receiver can understand this message differently on these layers. For example, a sender wants to put emphasis on the appeal layer, but the receiver understands the message only on the matter layer. Another reason is that some people may be 'deaf' on some layer, for example they may understand only the raw facts (the matter layer), but may be completely unable to 'hear' with the 'appeal' ear. In such situations the sender should modify his message in a way that the information on an intended layer is in fact given explicitly on the layer that is 'heard' by the receiver.

Example

Imagine the following situation in the workplace. A tester talks with the developer and says 'I found again this weird bug in your module'.

Sender (tester)

Matter layer: I found a bug in your module.

Self-revealing layer: I don't know why it happens.

Relationship layer: You are responsible for that and you should know why it happens.

Appeal layer: I'm angry, because it is the third time you do it.

Receiver (developer)

Matter layer: There is a bug in my module.

Self-revealing layer: You do not know why it happens and it makes you uncomfortable.

Relationship layer: You think my coding skills are poor.

Appeal layer: I should be more careful when writing the next part of this module.

The sender may just want to communicate that he found a bug (matter layer), but the receiver understands the message on a relationship layer. He thinks that the tester considers him as a poor programmer. This misunderstanding may worsen the relation between these two team members.

Von Thun says that when we communicate, in fact we speak with four different mouths and we listen with four different ears. To effectively use this model, when you are the sender, try to make sure that the receiver understands your message on a proper level. In the example above, maybe it would be better if you don't use the words 'again' and 'weird'. It may cause the receiver to understand your message on a relationship layer, which you absolutely don't want to use. On the other hand, if you are a receiver, try to understand from which 'mouth' the sender speaks. If you are not sure, you may ask the sender about it. In the example above, the developer might say: 'Yes, indeed, there is a bug. But what do you mean by saying it is weird?' or 'According to you, what is the reason that this bug is discovered again?'.

For a communication to be effective, it is also good to implement the following good practices:

- on a matter layer—speak directly, in a simple way, be logical;
- on a self-revealing layer—be authentic, try to sense the situation in which you are;
- on a relationship layer—be respectful of other persons, accept their right to make decisions independently;
- on an appeal layer—be open and honest.

Testers have the opportunity to use the effective communication on a daily basis. They communicate with the developers and they need to convince them that a bug is really a bug. They talk with managers and often need to convince the management that some decisions that are going to be made are risky, dangerous or ineffective. And that some other ideas are worth considering. They talk with the clients, who usually think that a tester reads their minds. Also, maintaining good relationships with our client and ensuring the mutual understanding results in effective cooperation and less problems in later SDLC phases, which gives us a very high return on investment. Practicing the communication skills is crucial for a professional tester.

1.8   Testing Process: Pure Abstraction or Tangible Reality?

We hear and use the word 'process' very often. We talk about the 'testing process', the 'quality processes in the company', the 'test process improvement'. We all know that we are a part of one or several processes. But what does it really mean? What *is* the testing process and why should we use this concept?

Formally, a process is a structured set of actions that take some input and transform it to some output. Grasping the nature of a test process is difficult, mainly because it is hard to see it as a whole. A process is an abstract notion, but related to a very concrete set of actions. Each tester, when working on some task, performs it in isolation from other tasks done by other people. Therefore, at one time we see only some small part of the whole thing. If we are able to see the 'big picture', the bird's-eye view, we may perceive some very interesting things.

Since a process is an abstraction, we may describe testing on different layers of abstraction. Figure 1.14 shows two different ways of representing the test process. The diagram on the left focuses on the phases and the relations between them. For example, after the test design phase, we may proceed with the test implementation,

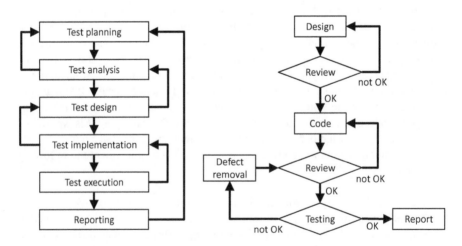

Fig. 1.14 Two different ways of representing the test process

but we also may go back to the test analysis phase. The diagram on the right focuses on the test activities performed for a given artifact (here, a piece of code). For example, when the review of a design is positive, a code may be written. Then, it is subjected to a code review. If it is positive, this part of the code can be tested, and so on.

The first representation shows the testing from the organizational point of view, so we may analyze this process from the organizational perspective. For example: is it natural in our company, that after the test execution we may go back to the test implementation, then to the test design, then to test analysis and finally, return to the planning phase? If it is possible, how should it be organized? Who decides on that? How many times can we do that? Should there be an intermediary phase between test execution and reporting? Why can't we go back directly from the test execution to, let's say, test planning? Is there any good reason for that?

The second representation is probably more natural for an engineer and gives us much more opportunities for the process improvements. It is important to remember that a process improvement is usually effective when we focus on the single activities within this process. In most cases the best strategy for a process improvement is bottom-up, not top-down. The reason is obvious: if you want to improve something, first you have to identify the problems and obstacles. They are usually related to particular activities or tasks defined in the process. For example, one problem could be a low effectiveness of the review process. Another one could be that testing or defect removal takes too much time. It is easier to measure the quality or effectiveness of a small, isolated task, than the whole process with many phases.

Of course, sometimes the serious organizational problems happen. In such cases, the best way is to look at them from the broader perspective. The process like the left-most one from Fig. 1.14 would probably be the best choice here.

There are many perspectives that can be used to perform a test process abstraction. For example:

- the organizational phases and relations between them,
- the life cycle of different artifacts, like: test case, piece of code, documentation, etc.,
- the communication between different stakeholders,
- the documents workflow.

When we want to describe the process in our organization, we should choose the abstraction layer that fits our purposes. Abstraction allows us to focus on a specific features or characteristics of a modeled object, ignoring the ones that are not important in a given situation.

Analysis of the processes described on the different abstraction layers can itself identify things that can be improved. For example, we may notice that there are some unnecessary, redundant or too long paths in the process. Fixing it helps to eliminate waste, which—in this example—is the time for performing unnecessary things.

1.9   Models in Testing

Many people think that models are superfluous, unnecessary and difficult to use theoretical constructs. However, it is exactly the opposite. Models are very helpful and most of them are really simple and intelligible. To see the benefits from using them, we first need to understand what a model is and what it can be used for. A model is an *abstraction* of something. It means that each model focuses on a particular part or characteristic of a modeled system. For example, when we use a control flow model, we are not interested in how the data is processed, but in what way the application control flow can be realized. The abstraction allows us to omit in the system description all things that are not important at this moment.

A good model should be consistent and unequivocal. This means that it cannot allow two contradictory system behaviors and that everyone should understand the model in the same way. Models can be formal, but sometimes it is better to use an informal one. For example, formal models can be used in the automatic test design and serve as the test oracles. Informal ones, on the other hand, can facilitate communication between a client and the dev team [40].

Example

Suppose we have to test a field that accepts a valid e-mail address and we focus on a data-driven approach only. This means that we just want to test whether the valid e-mails are accepted and the invalid ones are rejected. How to test it reasonably with a possibly small number of tests? We may use a model that defines the structure of a valid e-mail address in terms of a regular expression (RE) and then simulate different valid strings and different errors by manipulating the model, thus providing both positive and negative test cases. For the sake of simplicity, suppose that the RE describing the valid e-mail address is this:

$$a^{\{1-10\}}@\left(a^{\{1-10\}}\right)\left(.a^{\{1-10\}}\right)^{*}.b^{\{2-4\}}$$

where a denotes any letter or digit, b denotes letters only, $\{x-y\}$ denotes the allowed minimal and maximal number of occurrences (for example, $a^{\{2-3\}}$ describes a pattern that matches all two and three-letter sequences of the alphanumerical characters), $*$ denotes zero or more occurrences. Our RE says that a valid e-mail address needs to start with one to 10 letters or digits, followed by the @ sign, then again followed by one to 10 letters or digits, followed by zero or more occurrences of strings starting with a dot and followed by one to 10 letters or digits, and finally followed by the dot and two, three or four letters.

We may define the following strategy for generating the valid e-mails from this RE:

(continued)

- for any a pick a random symbol that matches a,
- for any $\{x - y\}$ take three tests: one with x occurrences, one with y and one with z, such that $x < z < y$; if $y = x + 1$ take just two tests, one for x and one for y,
- for any pattern of the form x^* take three tests: one that omits this fragment (takes it zero times), one that takes x (one repetition) and one that takes more than one repetition of x.

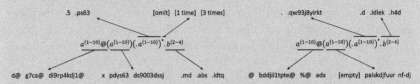

Fig. 1.15 Using a model for generating the test ideas

Figure 1.15 (left) shows how can we generate the test ideas for providing valid e-mail addresses by using the above-mentioned strategy. For every RE part we generate several strings, according to the rules given above. We may then combine them to provide the full e-mail addresses. Notice that we may apply different strategies here. For example, we may generate all combinations. One of them could be: 'd@' concatenated with 'pdys63', concatenated with '. ps63.5.5' (generated three times) and finally concatenated with '.idtq', giving the 'd@pdys63.ps63.5.5.idtq' e-mail address. Using the elementary combinatorics we may calculate the total number of such combinations, which is $3 \cdot 3 \cdot (0 + 3 + 3 \cdot 3 \cdot 3) \cdot 3 = 9 \cdot 30 \cdot 3 = 810$ test cases. It is probably too much for a manual testing, but these test cases could be designed, generated from the model and executed automatically. Notice that our model acts also as a test oracle: for every string it is able to tell us, whether this string matches the valid e-mail address pattern or not.

If 810 test cases are too many, we might loosen our criterion a little bit and assume that we want each version of each part of the RE model to appear in at least one test case. Such an approach is often called the 'Each Choice' approach. For example, for the first part of the model, we want at least one test with 'd@', at least one with 'g7ca@' and at least one with 'di9rp4kdj1@'. The table below is an example of the test suite that fulfills this criterion.

#	Test	Covered model elements				
		1st part	2nd part	3rd part	4th part	5th part
1	d@ds9003dssj.md	d@	ds9003dssj	–	[omit]	.md
2	di9rp4kdj1@pdys63. tt8ddksng4.idtq	di9rp4kdj1@	pdys63	. tt8ddksng4	[1 time]	.idtq
3	g7ca@x.5.ps63.5.abs	g7ca@	x	.5, .ps63	[3 times]	.abs

The next step is to generate the invalid strings. Here we may apply the following strategy:

- change every occurrence of a and b into an invalid symbol,
- for $\{x - y\}$ generate string with $x - 1$ and $y + 1$ occurrences (if possible).

Figure 1.15 (right) shows how can we generate the invalid e-mails. It is a good practice to define one test case for one invalid part, to avoid error masking. So, in our case, we would have 13 test cases. After generating the test cases it is important to check if it is indeed the invalid string, as it might happen that we accidentally generated a valid one. For example, for an RE in a form a^* @ a^* we might change '@' into 'x' (with intention to generate an invalid string), but for the first (resp. second) a we might randomly choose the string 'abc@d' (resp. 'bfd'), thus generating the valid e-mail address 'abc@dx. bfd'. Notice that checking whether we indeed generate the invalid e-mails is straightforward, because our model has the oracle property—matching strings to regular expressions is very easy.

The abstraction is a very important concept. It allows us to *deal with the complexity*. If we have to test a big, complicated system, we may define several test approaches, each of them related to some particular system feature or characteristic. Each approach can be realized with the use of a proper model. In this book, we introduce three important types of models and we show how they can be effectively used by a tester on a daily basis:

- **a software model**—a model that describes how the system works (see Sect. 5.3); such models are very useful for providing the test ideas for checking if the system does what it is supposed to do,
- **an error model**—a model that describes what can go wrong and how it may be noticed (see Sect. 5.6); such models are very useful in so-called 'dirty testing', when we want to perform a software attack, that is, to check if the system is able to handle some unexpected situation,
- **a 'creativity-boost' model**—a tool for improving our creativity; in Chap. 4 we describe the TQED model, which may increase the tester's creativity in providing good, effective tests.

1.10   A Bit of Philosophy: Problem of Universals from the Tester's Perspective

In previous sections we discussed two examples of two distinct approaches: exploratory testing and model-based testing. These are two examples of how the testing theory is used. In the exploratory testing we may actually not rely on any theory at all. The model-based approach, on the other hand, has solid theoretical foundations. The important question is: how much theory is needed and where/when should we use it to make our testing the most effective? How to combine in practice the two extreme approaches to testing: one, theoretical, driven by models and the other, pragmatic, using only the tester's intuition and experience?

We can find a nice analogy in the field of philosophy. In metaphysics there is a well-known problem, called 'the problem of universals', introduced formally by Boethius in the medieval times, although present in philosophy since the very beginning. The problem of universals refers to the question of the nature of *properties*: do properties really exist in the physical world, or are they just the abstract, theoretical entities?

There is a very famous painting by Raphael, The School of Athens (see the left part of Fig. 1.16), with all the greatest philosophers and scientists of the ancient ages. It uses the symbolic to show the philosophical views of the depicted characters. In particular, the painting shows two approaches to the problem of universals presented by two great ancient philosophers: Plato and Aristotle. On the right part of the figure we see the magnification of the central part of this painting, showing these two.

Plato is pointing his finger up, because he claims that the world we live in is merely a reflection, a shadow of the true reality, which is an eternal and unchanging property of the world. From the metaphysical point of view, the most important (or the truest) for Plato are the *ideas*, not 'a real world'. Aristotle, in turn, holds his hand down, pointing on earth. In his philosophy the only reality is the one that can be seen and experienced—the *reality* is more important than the abstract ideas.

In terms of software testing we could transform the dispute between Plato and Aristotle as follows. Plato would say that—as the reality just reflects the pure ideas— the most important things are: ideas about testing, abstract models and methodologies, notions, reports and communication. Aristotle would argue that the

Fig. 1.16 The School of Athens—a painting by Raphael (from commons.wikimedia.org)

main goal of our project is to deliver the solution to a concrete business problem, hence we just have to focus on this activity. We should do only what is necessary for achieving the client's satisfaction and—as the client and his problem are the real, tangible entities—we can do it by performing real, physical actions. The examples would be: performing the exploratory testing, executing the real tests, asking the client what, how and how much should we test.

Both these approaches have pros and cons. Hence, relying only on one of them usually will not be effective. This is because, in a sense, both these approaches are extremal—each of them focuses only on one particular aspect or philosophy of testing. So, each of them is necessarily self-limiting, as it does not benefit from the other approach. We have to find a sweet spot. The old truth says that the broader our look on a problem is, the more effectively we are able to solve it.

The important lesson from these considerations is that *a tester cannot be an ideologist*. Unfortunately, many testers, as well as developers and other IT people, are tempted by some temporal trends, ideas and fashions in the IT. In our community a good example may be the strife between supporters of a so-called 'context-driven school' and a 'classical', process-based approach. Both parties of this conflict frequently use non-substantial, irrelevant and ideological arguments. This obviously leads to nothing and does not bring any added value to the professional debate on testing. So, once again—a tester cannot be an ideologist—a tester needs to be *pragmatic*. Therefore, she needs to know both theoretical and practical approaches and no matter what her personal attitude is to these methods, concepts, and tools, she should be able to pick the ones that are the most effective in a given situation. Often it is necessary to blend two or more completely different approaches, to obtain an efficient and effective solution.

Testing Strategies: How to Become a Better Tester?

2

2.1 Introduction

In this chapter we discuss the testing strategies. Merriam-Webster dictionary defines *strategy* as a 'careful plan or method' or 'the art of devising or employing plans toward a goal'. We will focus on both these things, understanding the strategy as a plan and as the art of using this plan. The strategies we discuss here are defined on a high level. More detailed activities which could be called the *tactics*—namely, the testing techniques—will be described in the next chapter.

Testing can be seen as a *scientific method*, so we can apply the scientific paradigm to testing. This means that we build the hypotheses on defects and failures based on the error and software models, and we collect data to confirm or reject them. If our hypothesis is correct, we find a bug or a failure. If not, we need to redefine the hypothesis and try again. Therefore, it is convenient to treat each test (test case, test approach, test execution and so on) as a method for providing information about the software.

Hence, when designing a test or preparing a test execution it is very important to ask ourselves: what is the purpose of this test? What is it supposed to verify, confirm, validate? Asking such a question will save us a lot of time by not creating useless, weak or redundant tests. If we are not able to distinguish between the goals of two different tests, it means that it is pointless to execute both of them—they probably check the same thing. Testers often don't ask themselves this question, which results in producing useless, weak and poor, ineffective tests.

But where should we search for inspiration for the effective testing on a high-level, strategy-related approach? It may be surprising, but many good solutions may be found in the fields very different from computer science or engineering, like economy or philosophy. Also, a self-reflection in our mind from the psychological point of view may deliver us many important observations that we can benefit from during the testing. We discuss this in Sects 2.2 and 2.3.

There are also some generic rules, which I call 'methodological rules'. Because of their genericity, they allow us to act rationally in almost any situation, also related to

© Springer International Publishing AG 2018

A. Roman, *Thinking-Driven Testing*, https://doi.org/10.1007/978-3-319-73195-7_2

testing (Sect. 2.4). There are also so-called 'good practices' collected in the documents such as norms or standards—in Sect. 2.5 we discuss how we should use the standards effectively.

Testing—understood as bug hunting—can be viewed as searching the solution space in the computer games. Effective searching algorithms find optimal or suboptimal solutions using the heuristics and algorithms like alpha-beta pruning. In our case we cannot really prune any branch in the search tree, as defects can be everywhere. We may prioritize them using the error models (Sect. 2.6).

The last four chapters are devoted to other strategies: planning itself (Sect. 2.7), documentation (Sect. 2.8), estimation (Sect. 2.9) and simulations (Sect. 2.10). These strategies may not be so obvious and in fact they may seem to be completely irrelevant to testing. However, they are very efficient not only in bug searching, but also in test management (both in short and long-term). They fit well for a single project as well as for the optimization on the organizational level.

2.2   Be Inspired: What Can a Tester Learn from…

As testers, we can learn many things from different areas of science, technology and humanities. We may find surprising analogies between software testing and, for example, psychological or economic theories. Reading and analyzing works from such seemingly irrelevant fields as philosophy, mathematics or ergonomy enormously increases the tester's creativity. In this section we give some examples of how a tester can be inspired by different fields of science and humanities. In the latter part of this book we will utilize many ideas described in this section for providing better ways of testing the software.

The inspiration may led us to discover new, efficient approaches to testing. When a tester is able to design a *new* method for solving a certain test problem, it means that she reached the "art" level in the 'tester's development model' (see Fig. 1.13). To not leave the reader with the impression that this kind of acting is abstract, dull or useless, I give just a few concrete examples of how the inspiration from the different fields led people to invent many useful and practical methods, tools and approaches to testing:

- Whittaker in his book on exploratory testing [14] describes several exploratory testing techniques inspired by tourism and by the way the tourists visit and explore cities.
- Gregory Brown[1] gives a nice example of applying systems thinking in software development.
- Erik van Veenendaal, in his PRISMA method [41] designed for supporting the risk-based approach to testing, uses a statistical test (namely, the χ^2 test) to

---

[1]https://www.oreilly.com/ideas/the-critical-role-of-systems-thinking-in-software-development

encourage the stakeholder to use all the values in a value set for each risk factor when assessing the impact and/or likelihood.

- Search-based software engineering applies metaheuristic search techniques such as evolutionary algorithms, particle swarm optimization, A^* algorithm, etc. to software engineering problems defined as the optimization problems. In software testing the examples of such problems are: test suite prioritization (to detect bugs faster), test suite optimization (to reduce the test suite without reducing its ability to detect bugs), test data generation (to achieve a certain coverage level, for example in pair-wise testing) and so on [42, 43].
- Machine learning methods can be applied to generate test data of a good quality (see for example the KLEE tool [44]).

2.2.1   ... Philosophy

Philosophy studies fundamental problems about us, the world we live in, things like existence, truth, values, language, reason, mind, ethics. As testers, we may learn many important things from philosophy, for example:

- discipline in thinking—by carefully defining things, using the introduced notions precisely and understanding them correctly,
- questioning—by asking important and right questions, being critical about the things other people claim and the documents they create,
- discussing—by learning how to listen, making sure that we are on the same page as our interlocutor, avoiding fallacies and poor, inaccurate or false argumentation (for example, we may benefit from being aware of the eristic, which refers to argument that aims to successfully dispute another's argument, rather than searching for truth),
- argumentation—by conducting consistent, logical, clear and correct inference/ reasoning.

Some examples of using the philosophical approach were given in Sect. 1.2.2, where we discussed the *true nature* of testing and its consequences. In Sect. 1.10 we directly utilized some known philosophical concepts of Plato and Aristotle. In Sect. 1.2.3 we carefully defined two terms: quality control and quality assurance and we showed why it is very important to distinguish between them. These kinds of acting have the philosophical background and may led us to many interesting conclusions.

2.2.2   ... Psychology

Psychology is the study of mind and behavior. It studies such mental processes as: perception, cognition, attention, emotion, intelligence, motivation and personality. Knowing the psychological theories may—among others—help us, as the testers, in:

- self-development—by choosing the most effective way to learn and avoiding 'mental' obstacles during the learning process,
- better communication and improved persuasion—by understanding how and on what levels the communication process works,
- working effectively in the group—by being aware of how our acting affects other people and vice versa,
- better usability testing—by understanding the user and his behavior when using Graphical User Interface or interacting in any other way with the software.

Very often the tester needs to discuss a bug with a programmer and convince him that this is really a bug, not a feature. Or to convince the manager that we really should invest more money in some new tool or process. Psychology helps us to understand other people's intentions, desires and ways of acting, and utilize it to convince other people about what we say. We used a communication theory by von Thus in Sect. 1.7. This is an example of applying a psychological theory for improving the communication. In Sect. 2.3 we will discuss in detail the psychology of testing, taking as a starting point the considerations about the tester's mind.

2.2.3   ... Economy and Management

Economy deals with production and resource management in the world of producers and consumers. In the broadest sense, it is the study of human behavior in the surrounding world. The classical theory of economy assumes that the producers as well as the consumers are rational. Now we know that it is not true—people usually do not behave rationally. Being aware of that allows us to avoid making the irrational decisions. Management, on the other hand, helps us—in general—to deal with the complexity. It provides us tools and methods to embrace the complicated structure and relationships within an IT project.

Economy is considered as a social science, but some of its sub-disciplines are more of a scientific nature (for example econometry or game theory). Economy provides us many economic models that can be useful in a tester's work. The most obvious are the cost and risk models. We may use the economy and management theories to:

- check whether our actions will be economically justified—by performing the detailed profit and loss analysis,
- make 'what-if' simulations—that would show, for example, the relation between the quality and its cost,
- provide input to the decision process on when to stop testing,
- embrace the complexity of the testing process—by applying the management theories, tools and techniques.

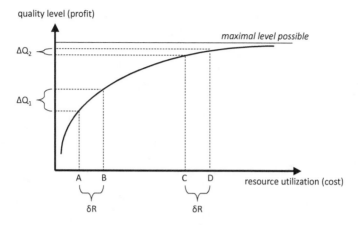

Fig. 2.1 Illustration of the Law of Diminishing Returns

Example

In economy, there is a very well-known law, called the Law of Diminishing Returns. We may use it to illustrate that there is some optimal moment of time after which our quality actions don't bring profit anymore and start to bring losses. It is a very instructive example, because it shows that forcing the 100% quality level is usually not profitable. It doesn't pay off to fight for the quality at any price! Figure 2.1 illustrates the Law of Diminishing Returns. Being at point A and investing δR we obtain ΔQ_1 increment in the quality level.[2] But as we achieve better and better quality, it requires more and more costs to achieve the same increment. For example, being at C, when we invest the same δR amount of resources as we did in A, we will achieve only ΔQ_2 increment in quality, which is much smaller than ΔQ_1.

Suppose that there are 1300 bugs in the code and they are found in consecutive weeks. Suppose also that:

- each week of the test team work costs us $15,000,
- in week n the test team is able to find $1000/n^{2.6}$ bugs,
- the cost of fixing each field defect (that is, a defect detected by the user after the release) is $1500,
- all field defects will be found by the users.

(continued)

---

[2]This quality level may be understood as a 'virtual' profit representing the avoidance of the loss that would have been caused by removing the defects found by the user after the software release. The value δR may be viewed as the cost of testing expressed in the number of man-hours work of the testers.

Table 2.1 An example of how Law of Diminishing Returns works

Week	1	2	3	4	5	6	7	8	9	10
# of bugs found	1000	165	57	27	15	9	6	4	3	3
Cost of testing	15,000	15,000	15,000	15,000	15,000	15,000	15,000	15,000	15,000	15,000
Cumulative cost of testing	15,000	30,000	45,000	60,000	75,000	90,000	105,000	120,000	135,000	150,000
# of field defects	300	135	78	51	36	27	21	17	14	11
Cost of field defects removal	450,000	202,500	117,000	76,500	54,000	40,500	31,500	25,500	21,000	16,500
Total cost	465,000	232,500	162,000	136,500	129,000	130,500	136,500	145,500	156,000	166,500

Table 2.1 shows the data from the first 10 weeks. Each column shows the actual costs assuming that the release is done in this week. The Law of Diminishing Returns works, because in each week we are able to find less bugs, but the cost of the field defect removal remains the same.

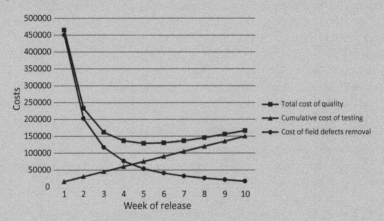

Fig. 2.2 Cost analysis and finding the optimal release date

Figure 2.2 shows graphically the three types of costs considered in our example: the cumulative cost of testing (which is linear, as the cost of testing is constant in each week), the cost of field defects removal (which is decreasing, as the number of field defects decreases each week) and the total cost, which is the sum of the two former costs. As we can see, from the 'quality cost' point of view, the optimal week for the release is week 5, with the total costs of $129,000.

(continued)

Of course, this simulation is *very* simplified and does not reflect the whole reality. For example: we do not consider here the loss of reputation because of the large number of field defects; we do not distinguish between the type or severity of the bugs found; we assumed that the number of bugs found follows a very simple formula which is a function of the number of week, etc. Nevertheless, the example illustrates well the Law of the Diminishing Returns, which usually results in the existence of some 'sweet spot'. This sweet spot represents the solution optimal in some sense, like the time (e.g., the best moment of release), resource allocation, cost minimization, work performed, etc. Usually it is very hard to find this optimum, but when the organization is able to measure accurately its own processes, it is usually possible to find at least the suboptimal solution, even if the simulation is performed under the very strict and unrealistic assumptions.

One must remember, though, that software/testing economy is a very difficult and complicated thing. To be honest, it is still not well understood by the researchers. We can still, though, use some classical economy tools to provide some valuable simulations and analyses related to the cost and quality of our product. Also, the language of the economy may make it easier to express and explain to the management the potential benefits from testing. One of the important concepts that can be used here is a profit understood as the avoidance of the virtual loss which would have happened if we didn't test the software.

2.2.4   . . . Mathematics and Logic

Mathematics deals with the deduction and reasoning based on the logical foundations. It can be useful for testers in at least two ways: first, as a general approach to problem solving, and second—as the set of tools and methods which can be applied directly during the testing. For example, many test design techniques are based on the formal logic and different math sub-disciplines: equivalence partitioning (algebra), decision tables and cause-effect graphs (logic), white-box techniques (logic, algebra and graph theory) and so on. A tester can benefit from mathematics and logic in many ways, among which there are:

- precision—in defining notions, expressing our statements, argumentation and reasoning,
- formalism—which helps us understand and effectively use the formal software models,
- modeling—which allows us to use the abstraction when describing different software characteristics, and also to use the different kinds of predictive tools, like defect prediction models,

- concrete tools and methods—taken directly from such math fields as logic, set theory, graph theory, discrete mathematics, algebra or probability, which can be directly applied in the tester's everyday work.

Math tools allows us also to analyze the requirements: their consistency, cohesion and correctness. But there are even much more distant analogies. For example, Dave Thomas in his brilliant talk on the concepts of 'agile' and 'agility' on a GOTO 2015 conference [45] gives the example of a PID controller[3]—a pure mathematic tool used for the optimal control of systems—as an analogy of the agility in the software development.

Example
In 2016 Poland experienced a very serious constitutional crisis. The Constitutional Tribunal, which is a constitutional court appointed for judging the consistency of legal acts with Constitution, had to evaluate the act describing the rules it has to follow when evaluating the acts. Many politicians claimed that the Constitutional Tribunal had to evaluate this act based on... itself. From the logical point of view this is absurd, because it leads to a logical contradiction. It is the same kind of problem as the problem of the statement that states about itself: is the sentence 'this statement is false' true or false? If true, then it says the truth, but it says it's false, so it's false—a contradiction. If it's false, it doesn't say the truth, so it's not true that it's false, hence it's true— we have a contradiction again. The problem is that the rules cannot be judged by themselves. It is like Baron Munchausen (a fictional character created by Rudolf Erich Raspe) who, swallowed by a giant fish, saves himself from drowning by pulling on his own hair. Knowing the logic foundations allows us to avoid such kinds of problems, leading to *logical* contradictions.

2.2.5 ... Probability and Statistics

Probability and statistics are considered to be the part of the 'applied math', as they are used in the real life and in the real, practical problems on a daily basis. The reason is that in the real life nothing is certain—especially in the IT projects. We never know how many bugs are there in the software under test, where we should search for them, how much it will cost us to fix them, how many bugs will be reported by the users, when the next failure will occur, and so on. Probability theory gives us a

---

[3]PID stands for 'proportional-integral-derivative'. A PID controller continuously calculates the error between the desired process value and the measured one and applies a correction based on proportional, integral and derivative terms. Proportionality represents the current error. Integration handles the history and derivative predicts the short-term future. Tuning these three parameters allows us to define the desired responsiveness to an error.

framework for describing, understanding and evaluating the uncertainty about the future events. Statistics, on the other hand, allows us to systematically compare different things and decide whether they are different because of some factor applied, or just because of the randomness. Probability and statistics can help us with:

- data understanding—especially with understanding the notion of variance,
- data presentation—which is useful when preparing different kinds of reports,
- data analysis—to interpret the gathered data, draw conclusions and make (optimal) decisions based on this analysis,
- formal verification of hypotheses—by using a statistical machinery,
- dealing with uncertainty—by applying a probabilistic approach.

We will write more about the data understanding in Sects. 6.2, 6.3 and 6.6 by analyzing the practical examples from the software testing area. It is very important, as people usually cannot properly interpret the data. People also have a tendency to draw conclusions based on single, incidental events. Also, when using the probability, most people do it wrong. Probability is not easy to learn and apply. It is full of paradoxes and unexpected phenomena, as shown in the following example.

Example
In the popular TV Show 'Let's Make a Deal' we're playing the following game. We are given the choice of three doors. Behind one of them is a valuable prize, behind the others, nothing. We pick a door (say, door no. 1) and the host, who knows where the prize is, opens another one (say door no. 2) with nothing behind it. We are now given the choice: either we stay with the previously chosen door (no. 1) or we can change our decision and pick the door no. 3. What should we do? It seems that it doesn't matter, but in fact—from the probability point of view—we should definitely change our mind and pick the door no. 3. When we stay with the door no. 1, our chance of winning the prize is 1/3. Changing our decision and picking the door no. 3 doubles this probability to 2/3!

There is a nice method for understanding the 'weird' things like the one from the example above. It can be called 'think big' or 'rescale' strategy and is very useful in understanding many phenomena. The strategy is simply redefining the original problem, but on a much bigger scale. In our example 'thinking big' would be multiplying the doors to, let's say, million. When we pick a door, our chance of winning is 1/1,000,000—almost zero. Now suppose the host opens *all* the doors except the one we have chosen and some other one. Behind all the opened doors is nothing. Now it should be clear, why we have to change our first choice.

2.2.6 ... Systems Science

Systems science studies the nature of systems—from very simple, to very complex. The systems may be of different forms: an ecosystem, a society, an organization. Systems science utilizes many scientific tools, like cybernetics or control theory in order to:

- take a holistic view of a system,
- study the relations and interactions between the different parts of a system,
- study the dynamic behavior of the system, which may be stable, but under certain boundary conditions can become unstable, chaotic or destructive.

The examples of how testers can benefit from the systems science are:

- the ability to analyze the system—by describing it, studying its parts and relations between them,
- the ability to design the system—by choosing the best architecture and optimal system component configurations (a good example may be the test process in the organization),
- understanding the system dynamics—by studying how a certain system stimulation in one place affects the other parts of the system,
- the ability to improve the system—by involving the three activities described above.

The so-called 'systems thinking' presented in Sect. 1.2.9 is an example of using the systems science. We analyzed there the impact of the feedback for the team on the overall quality of the product and process. We talk more about the systems thinking in Sect. 3.7.

2.2.7 ... Ergonomics

Merriam-Webster dictionary defines the ergonomics as 'an applied science concerned with designing and arranging things people use so that the people and things interact most effectively and safely'. People in Apple know very well what it is about. Apple doesn't excel their competition in software, hardware or technology—their products are comparable to the others in the market. Apple's success was founded on a very good product design and nice, intuitive user interfaces.

So, a tester can benefit from ergonomics mainly by designing things and testing the design. The most visible application of ergonomics is usability testing, which evaluates the product from the user's perspective. Some more concrete examples of ergonomics use are:

- **dialogue principles**—that is, the way the software communicates with a user,
- **software accessibility**—that is, the ease with which the disabled users are able to work with a software,
- **visual user interface**—that is, the way the interface is designed to be 'nice' and 'understandable' by a user,
- **error tolerance**—that is, the extent to which the software is able to handle unexpected, incorrect user (or environmental) actions.

2.3 The Tester's Mind: Psychology of Testing

As testing is an intellectual activity, it is always driven by a human mind. Therefore, it is important to understand what happens inside the testers' heads. In this section we shortly describe several psychological issues that may have impact on the testers' work.

2.3.1 Creativity

It is obvious that our tests should be effective in bug detection. We usually design them from what we could call the *test ideas*. These concepts tell us what could go wrong, if we use the software in a particular way. Test ideas may be derived from the plans and models, but we may also simply invent them. Good ideas require creativity. Surprisingly, it is not 'either you have it or you don't'. Creativity can be learned and there are some simple exercises for that:

- Try to make original associations, finding the inspiration in literally everything (the previous section may give you some hints on that, but your personal experience in different fields is crucial); a creative association brings out a new, refreshing perspective and changes our 'linear thinking' into more 'exploratory' approach.
- Listen, read, meet with people, talk to them—always be open for the new experiences.
- Become an expert in your field, which means that you need to possess a huge amount of knowledge. It is important, especially in the age of Internet, where it is very tempting not to learn anything, because 'we can always Google it'. If you have to interrupt your flow of creative work every time you need to look something up, you lose your focus and become ineffective.

A simple example of the creativity boosting is the so-called 'Gedanken experiments'. These thought experiments consider hypotheses, principles or theories for the purpose of thinking through their consequences. Let us return to the example of the ATM machine from Sect. 1.2.6 which was disbursing in one case twice as much cash as it should. Thinking of the potential results of the *negative* test results may lead us to some interesting test scenarios. If we are creative enough we may ask:

'what might cause the ATM to disburse twice as much cash as it should?'. This immediately brings to mind the idea about switching two cassettes with the banknotes and a test scenario for checking if such a situation is possible.

2.3.2 Cognitive Bias

A cognitive bias is defined as a systematic pattern of deviation from norm or rationality in judgement, whereby inferences about other people and situations may be drawn in an illogical fashion [46]. A cognitive bias may result in an irrational or very ineffective behavior. One of the sources of the cognitive bias may be the way we define a goal we want to reach. In software testing, especially in the test management, the way we define tasks and goals for other team members is a crucial success factor. It is because people are driven by their objectives and will simply adapt their acting to the imposed goal.

Here's the example. Suppose we have two different approaches to testing: first—to show that the program works correctly; second—to show that the program works incorrectly, has many bugs and cannot be released. It is very tempting to set our goal in the first manner, because this goal sounds nice and positive. People don't like bad news—they expect that everything will be just fine. But what are the consequences of such an approach?

Let's look at Fig. 2.3. It presents the consequences of both situations. When we define a 'nice', 'positive' goal, we will be subconsciously convinced that the program is free from bugs, before the testing has begun. This will result in designing weak tests that should 'confirm' our hypothesis about the good software quality. Weak tests won't find any bugs, so our belief in the high quality will be even greater, and will cause a positive feedback loop, which in turn will result in designing yet more weaker tests.

However, if we define the goal in a completely different way—that our software under test is full of bugs—from the very beginning we will try to confirm it. In a natural way, we will construct much better tests which will have better chance to discover the failures. Again, we have a positive feedback loop here: when we find a bug, our belief that the program is really very buggy will motivate us to create yet more stronger tests, which will probably find more faults.

Notice that just by *redefining the goal* we obtain a completely different situation in terms of its *effectiveness*. The word (goal definition) may impact the real efficacy of the testers. What is interesting here, is that in the second situation a tester may be biased as well—but here we actually take advantage on it. If a program is not buggy, strong tests will still be better than weak tests, because we are more convinced about the high quality when we're not able to detect bugs with stronger, not weaker tests.

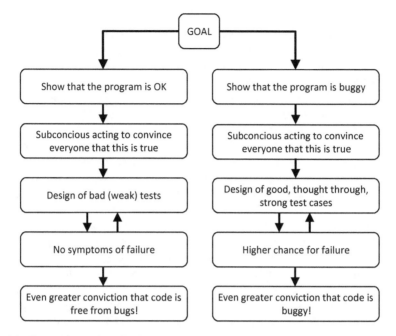

Fig. 2.3 The way we define a goal may result in a cognitive bias

2.3.3   Confirmation Bias and Wason Experiment: Software Testing as Hypothesis Testing

Confirmation bias is a type of the cognitive bias. It is also known as a selective collection of evidence. Confirmation bias is a person's tendency to favor information that confirms their assumptions, preconceptions or hypotheses whether these are actually and independently true or not [47]. There is a famous Wason experiment on this phenomenon [48]. In this study the subjects were asked to identify a rule that applies to sequences of three numbers. The rule was 'any ascending sequence'. The subjects were presented the sequence '2–4–6' and were told that it follows the rule. Then, they might construct any other sequences and the experimenter was telling them whether these sequences follow the rule or not.

Most participants tried sequences like '4–8–10', '6–8–12', '20–22–24' and so on. The feedback on them was of course positive. After a few more tries, the participants usually felt sure about their hypothesis, which was 'a sequence of even numbers'. But this hypothesis was wrong—it just covered a proper subset of all sequences that follows the true hypothesis 'any ascending sequence'.

Why did people behave this way? After presenting them the first sequence, most of them formed their hypothesis in their minds. The following sequences they asked about were to just confirm their initial hypothesis. As their initial guess was incidentally the subset of the true rule, all the following sequences were positive, so the subjects were yet more assured about their initial guess.

Figure 2.4 symbolically presents the different situations that may happen in hypothesis testing. The subjects' behavior from the Wason experiment corresponds to the situation (I), where the hypothesis was a strict subset of the true rule. The reason that subjects couldn't verify their hypothesis is—because of the confirmation bias—that they were constructing only the *positive tests*. Such tests give us only the uncertain confirmation: the reality agrees with our hypothesis, but this way we are not able to find the examples that agree with the true rule, but do not agree with our hypothesis (these tests are denoted by the black minus sign).

The Wason experiment is a very important lesson for the testers. We may consider testing as a process of verifying hypotheses about the different bugs in the SUT. But we have to use both positive and negative tests to verify our hypotheses effectively. Notice that in the ideal example (Fig. 2.4, IV) we may only have the *uncertain* confirmation about our positive and negative tests. We do not have any *strong* positive or negative falsification of our hypothesis, because it is true. If we use many 'different', positive and negative tests, and are not able to falsify (reject) our hypothesis, we may claim that the data confirms our theory and we may be more convinced that our theory is true (for example, that there is no certain type of a bug in a given part of the code).

The 'rejecting' tests, denoted by the black plus and minus signs in the figure, are very important, as they allow us to adjust our hypothesis. This is exactly the way the science works. We can never say that a scientific theory is true, only that the data strongly support it. But it is enough to provide one example that falsifies our hypothesis to say that the theory is certainly false. For example, the black plus signs denote the situations (experiments) that are aligned with our hypothesis, but do not occur in the reality.

In testing we apply exactly the same scientific method. The above-mentioned considerations on hypotheses testing are the reason why the tests should be diverse and non-redundant. The more diversity in tests, the higher the chance to construct the

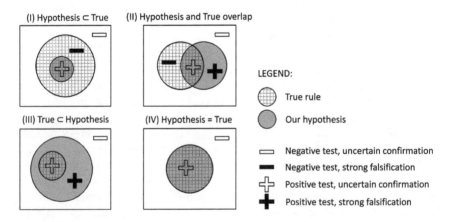

Fig. 2.4 Verification of hypotheses

correct hypothesis and the quicker the way to reject the false ones. The hypotheses should be tested in a way that allows us to gather as much information as possible.

Example

Suppose we are testing a new sorting algorithm. Our first hypothesis may be that it works only for positive numbers, so we may construct two tests, for example '3, 6, 2, 1' and '4, −4, −1, 7', to verify if it's true. If both tests pass, we have the negative test for the strong falsification (Fig. 2.4, I). We may then conjecture that the algorithm cannot handle sorted sequences and provide a test '3, 4, 7, 11, 11, 20, 21, 22'. If it passes, we may be quite sure at this moment that the algorithm works well for the negative numbers and sorted sequences.

So, we may think about other hypotheses, for example: if there is some 'divide and conquer' algorithm inside, does it work OK with the sequences of the length which is not the power of 2? A test '3, 1, 2' may check that. Notice, that we might test this hypothesis earlier, for example by replacing the former test '3, 6, 2, 1' with '3, 6, 2'. This way we reduce the number of tests, but we check the same set of hypotheses.

Another hypothesis: does the algorithm work well with only one element? Or with no elements? Or with a large number of constant numbers, like '4, 4, 4, …, 4, 4'? And so on. As you can see, each test confirms or falsifies some hypothesis about the algorithm and its potential bugs. If, for example, the one-element test '6' fails, we may interpret this as a positive test for the strong falsification (Fig. 2.4, II) and discover a bug: the algorithm does not work properly for one-element sequences, although it should.

2.3.4 Wason Selection Test: Why Is Language So Important?

Another famous experiment by Wason, called 'the selection test', is a logic puzzle used by the researcher in the study of deductive reasoning and its results are also very important from the tester's perspective. In the experiment, the subjects were presented four cards placed on a table, each of which had a number on one side and a letter on the other side. The visible faces of the cards were: 3, 8, A, F (see Fig. 2.5). The subjects were asked the following question: which cards must you necessarily turn over in order to test the truth of the following proposition: if a card shows an even number on one face, then there's a vowel on the opposite face.

Fig. 2.5 Wason selection test

In the Wason study over 90% of subjects were not able to solve this puzzle correctly. The correct answer is: we must turn over '8' and 'F'. We must turn '8', because according to the rule the opposite face should have a vowel. We must turn 'F', because there might be an even number on the opposite face, thus violating the rule. We do not need to turn '3', because it is not even, hence the card follows the rule, no matter what is on the other side. We do not need to turn 'A' either, because no matter what number is on the opposite face, the rule will hold.

In fact, this puzzle is just about validating the implication $p \Rightarrow q$, where p means 'there is an even number on one side' and q means 'there is a vowel on the other side'. This implication is equivalent to $\sim q \Rightarrow \sim p$, where $\sim$ is the negation (in logic it's called the contraposition rule). So, we have to check only if the rule holds for the assumptions p and $\sim q$, that is for even number and for the consonant.

This experiment itself may seem to be not so interesting. The really interesting thing is that Wason found that people were more able to solve the puzzle, when it was expressed in terms of the well-known social rule. When the numbers were switched to the 'age of a person', letters into 'water' and 'beer', and the rule into 'if a person is less than 18, she is not allowed to drink beer', the puzzle was much easier to solve for the subjects.[4]

What is the moral from this story? Well, the first one is that logic is sometimes not intuitive (!), but the computer programs *do* use logic, so a good tester must be familiar with it. The second one is that the language we use is very important. When talking to a client we should use the language as close to the business he works in as possible. The client won't understand any technical nomenclature. It is our, tester's, responsibility, to make the communication as effective as possible and to adjust our language and the way we communicate.

Example
Consider the following, very common example of a while loop:

```
x=0; i=1;
while (!(x==1 || i>=0)) {
   ...
}
```

where ! means 'not', || means 'or', == means 'is equal' and >= means 'greater or equal'. The while loop executes as long as the while condition is true. Will our loop execute at least once?

(continued)

---

[4]I replicated this experiment during the TestWarez 2015 conference in Poland on the group of ca. 60 testers. Of course, I was not able to conduct it in the laboratory conditions, but anyway, the results were very similar to the ones of Wason.

To execute the loop at least once, the while predicate must be true when its outcome is checked first time. It is the negation of the disjunction of two components. From De Morgan's Law we know that the negation of a disjunction is equivalent to the conjunction of negations of these components. Our predicate is hence equivalent to `(!(x==1)) && i>=0`, where `&&` stand for the conjunction. The conjunction is true if both components are true. So, `!(x==1)` must be true and `!(i>=0)` must be true. As $x \neq 1$, the first component is true. However, `i=1`, so it is not true that `i<0`. Hence, the whole predicate is false and the while loop will not execute.

Many people have problems with understanding logical expressions like the one in this example. This leads to many problems (for example, contradictory, wrong or missing requirements describing business rules). For a professional tester, proficiency in the elementary logic is a must.

2.3.5 Cognitive Dissonance

Cognitive dissonance is the psychological phenomenon of having a mental discomfort because of experiencing two or more contradictory beliefs, ideas or values. Leon Festinger [49] created a theory describing how people strive for internal consistency, when they experience this uncomfortable feeling. Its main assumption is that people always seek this consistency between their views and the reality. According to Festinger, when facing a cognitive dissonance, people may behave in several ways:

- change behavior or cognition,
- justify behavior or cognition by changing the conflicting cognition,
- justify behavior or cognition by adding new cognitions,
- ignore or deny any information that conflicts with existing beliefs.

Festinger claims that, in general, people tend to adjust the world view to their current condition, feelings and beliefs. In software testing the most obvious result of a cognitive dissonance may be recognizing a bug as a normal program operation. We may feel that the program should work fine and if something wrong happens, we rationalize it and convince ourselves that this is perfectly normal or—at least—nothing important. We may even 'adjust' the expected program behavior to the one that has just happened and report that the expected and observed results are identical, so everything is OK.

This is the crucial thing. At the heart of test execution lies comparing the observed results against the expected ones. The expected results—if possible—should be always defined *prior* to the test execution. The reason is exactly to avoid the cognitive dissonance. If the expected result is clearly defined, we will observe any discrepancy and report it as the test failure.

However, there are many situations in which we cannot really tell what should be the expected behavior. It is hard to express it in some number, string or some other simply defined output. Sometimes the expected result might be... 'the program works as expected', 'the program works fine', 'nothing wrong happens', 'there was no failure', etc. In such cases it is extremely important for a tester to be very attentive and inquisitive. Every strange situation should alarm us. A tester should *never* remain in his comfort zone. Even the slightest oddity should be investigated. Here are a few examples of the situations that might be classified as being strange:

- the program responds faster or slower than usually—this may suggest that the program did not perform the calculations that it should do, or that there is some inefficiency with the data processing,
- higher than usual processor/memory usage,
- an 'innocent' warning message—such message may foreshadow more serious problems,
- program behaves in a different way than before, for example does not return the same data as before or returns it in a different format.

2.3.6 Conway's Law

Conway's law states that organizations which design systems are constrained to produce designs which are copies of the communication structures of these organizations [50]. This phenomenon is usually explained in the following way: when different parts of an organization work on the design of the subsystems of some system, they need to communicate with each other. Therefore, the interfaces between these subsystems will reflect the social boundaries of the organization that produces it.

Conway talks about the *homomorphism* between two graphs: one that represents the organization structure, and another one that represents the system structure. In the first graph the graph itself, its subgraphs and edges represent system, subsystems and interfaces. We may map them into the second graph as committee, subcommittee and coordinator. As this mapping is often 1-to-1, the Conway's law follows.

How can we benefit from the observation by Conway? We may try to predict what kind of problems we can encounter or where we can possibly find them. For example, if we know that team A does not get along well with team B, and they work on two modules, say a and b, we may be quite sure that there will be some interface issues between these two modules.

We may also try to improve the software by improving processes within the organization. Improving team communication will always result in better software quality. We give another example (tools related) of applying the Conway's law in Sect. 6.9.

2.3.7   Csíkszentmihályi's Flow Model

In psychology, flow is defined as a mental state of being completely immersed in some activity. Csíkszentmihályi, a positive psychologist, describes it as

> being completely involved in an activity for its own sake. The ego falls away. Time flies. Every action, movement, and thought follows inevitably from the previous one, like playing jazz. Your whole being is involved, and you're using your skills to the utmost [51].

It should be obvious, that when we are in a flow, we are effective, we work efficiently and we are happy. It is therefore a desired level of acting. However, we cannot perform all activities in this way. Sometimes the problem is too hard (or too easy) and sometimes we simply lack skills.

Figure 2.6 presents the Csíkszentmihályi's Flow Model. It takes into account these two factors. For example, if we lack skills, but the problem is easy, when working on it we just feel an apathy. If the problem is a little bit complicated, we may feel worry, because we lack skills. For the same problem, when we have high skill level, we may feel relaxation. If we are given a difficult problem and we lack skills, we may feel anxiety or arousal. Only for challenging problems, when we have the proper skills, we are in the optimal mode of a flow.

The model is useful to assess our skills level and the problem challenge level just by observing our emotions. For example, if we feel boredom, probably we have to solve an easy problem being the experts in the field. It is not very challenging to us. The flow model is a useful tool for a test manager, to delegate tasks in a way that all (or as many as possible) team members are as fully immersed in their activities as possible.

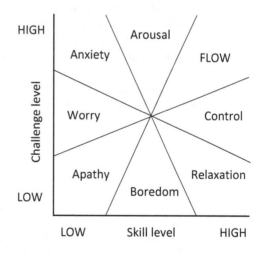

Fig. 2.6 Csíkszentmihályi's Flow Model

2.4 Useful Methodological Laws and Tools

In this section we present a few universal rules and tools, which may be handy in our everyday work as the testers. Some of them are very fundamental, methodological tools, and some are more concrete techniques. Being aware of them may significantly increase our efficiency.

2.4.1 Occam's Razor

Occam's razor is one of the most important methodological tools used in science and philosophy. It is named after William of Occam (1287–1347), an English Franciscan friar.[5] The simplest form of this rule says: 'don't multiply entities beyond necessity'. In a more formal way we can reformulate it as follows: 'among competing hypotheses, the one with the fewest assumptions should be selected'.

In science, this rule is used as a heuristic that allows scientists to build hypotheses, which explain *complex* things in terms of *simpler* causes. It is not an irrefutable principle of logic, more like an aesthetic criterion, because it is commonly accepted that scientific theories should be simple and elegant. And usually this works.

How can we use the Occam's razor in software testing? Here are a few examples:

- do not write the redundant tests that check exactly the same hypothesis,
- optimize the regression test suite so that it does not contain redundant tests,
- when searching for a bug,[6] use the scientific method like delta debugging [52],
- when measuring the process, use only a small, but sufficient set of metrics, which allows you to define and measure all the process characteristics you need,
- when defining documentation templates, define only the necessary (important) fields, that will allow you to use the documentation effectively (e.g., a bug report should allow us to replicate the failure easily),
- when building predictive models, use as few variables as possible (but not fewer!),
- when searching for the root cause, at the end limit yourself only to the crucial, important factors—usually there is only one or few reasons for the problem we try to solve.

---

[5]Occam did not formulate this rule. The term 'Occam's razor' first appeared in 1852 in the works of William Hamilton, who has noticed that Occam in fact used this rule frequently in his papers.

[6]To be precise, this is more debugging than testing, but it is a nice example of applying the Occam's razor.

2.4.2 Descartes' Doubt as Methodological Skepticism

Cartesian doubt, named after René Descartes (1596–1650), is a form of methodological skepticism. It first appeared in Descartes' famous work 'Discourse on the Method'. Descartes wanted to find the genuine, reliable sources of the truth, so that they might become the foundation of his reasoning about the world. He rejected everything that might result in precipitancy and prejudice and the only thing that was left, was doubt. But we cannot doubt that something has to be there to do the doubting (this is the famous Cartesian saying 'I think, therefore I am'). Descartes' method includes the following rules:

1. Accept only information we know to be true.
2. When facing difficulties under examination, break them down into as many parts as possible, and as might be necessary for its adequate solution.
3. Solve things in order, starting from the simplest and easiest, and then ascend to the knowledge of more complex things.
4. Make complete lists of further problems.

There are many situations in software testing, where the Cartesian's doubt should be applied, for example:

- doubt if the client thought exactly what he said,
- doubt if the requirements really reflect the client's needs,
- doubt if the documentation is correct and complete,
- doubt if the data says the truth,
- doubt if our peers say the truth and if we are on the same page,
- doubt if the accepted test strategy will give us exactly what we expect.

A professional tester is a *constantly doubtful expert*. She is always suspicious, she always asks questions and she always makes sure two or three times if everyone understands things in the same way, as this is the most frequent root cause for most problems in the project.

2.4.3 Optimization and Prioritization: Pareto 80-20 Principle

The Pareto principle says that a small fraction of causes results in a large fraction of effects. Sometimes the principle is given in 'numerical' manner: roughly 80% of the effects come from 20% of the causes. Joseph Juran named this principle after Italian economist Vilfredo Pareto, who noted this phenomenon when examining the ownership of the land in Italy. He observed that approximately 80% of the land in Italy was owned by 20% of the population.

The Pareto principle is surprisingly common: 80% of the sales come from 20% of clients; 80% of the wealth is owned by 20% of the richest people; 80% of the bugs are hidden in 20% of the modules, and so on. In software testing we may use the Pareto principle mainly for optimizing our efforts and for prioritization, for example:

- if we know the distribution of the bugs found so far in the software modules, focus first on the 20% of the most buggy modules—you will probably find ca. 80% of the total bugs,
- focus first on the 20% of the most frequent bug types—you will probably find ca. 80% of the total bugs,
- if you want to cover as many code as you can, start with 20% of the most covering tests—they will cover ca. 80% of the code.

2.4.4 Time Management: Parkinson's Law

Parkinson's Law first appeared in Cyril Parkinson's humorous essay in The Economist [53]. It states that 'work expands so as to fill the time available for its completion'. It's not a formal theorem, but despite its comicality, each of us experiences it all the time. In corporations, the most visible realization of the Parkinson's law is during the meetings. For example, if a 1-h meeting is devoted only to one simple thing, people will talk 1 h about it. But if at the same meeting people have to solve several different problems, the task will be done magically in exactly 1 h.

Having Parkinson's Law in mind we may optimize the work of our team. If we know what is the expected, *real* time for solving a given problem (or at least we have some reasonable estimation), we should give our team exactly this amount of time. If we are to organize a 1-h meeting, we should discuss there only the problems people are able to solve in total in 1 h.

2.4.5 Burch's Four Stages of Competence

The 'four stages' model was developed by Noel Burch, an employee of the Gordon Training International. The model describes the changes in the competence of a person who gathers experience (Fig. 2.7, left part):

- **stage 1 (unconscious incompetence)**: we don't know what we don't know—we are unable to learn independently, we need help from more experienced colleagues,
- **stage 2 (conscious incompetence)**: we know what we don't know—so we are able to learn consciously,
- **stage 3 (conscious competence)**: we know how to use our skills—we try it out, experiment, practice, but we need think and work hard to do this,
- **stage 4 (unconscious competence)**: the skills we have are natural for us, we use them unconsciously—we achieved the mastery in the field.

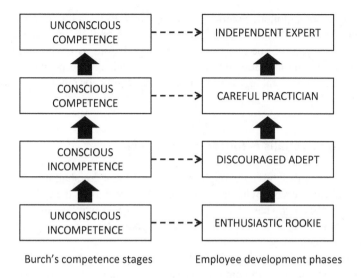

Fig. 2.7 Burch's four stages of competence and employee development phases

Burch's model may be very useful for both the management and their subordinates to develop their skills effectively. The right part of Fig. 2.7 describes figuratively the person on a given competence stage.

Knowing on which stage we are (or the people we manage), we are able to push ourselves (or other people) in the right direction, so that we (or others) are able to develop the desired skills in the way that is the most appropriate for a given level of our (or their) competence. For example:

- **enthusiastic rookie** needs guidance and training from the manager and more experienced peers; at this level it is crucial to balance between giving the freedom and being instructive, so that the enthusiastic rookie won't become discouraged; the management should take the 'teacher' approach,
- **discouraged adept** still needs some form of a guidance and training, but should be given more freedom, as well as opportunities to experiment and to make mistakes; the management should take the 'empathic listening' approach,
- **careful practicians** know what to do and the management should let them do it; the management role moves to the supportive one,
- **independent experts** use their skills almost unconsciously; the management should take the role of the active listener and fully equiponderant partner.

In section "What Is This Book About?" we gave four examples of the tester's awareness—they may be well mapped onto Burch's model. In order to become a professional in testing, we need to go through all four levels. At the beginning of our journey we need to teach a lot and other people may guide us in the right direction.

Then, being more and more experienced, we are able to learn on our own. Finally, we become the experts in the field. The goal of this book is to help you in this journey, so that you will be aware of many things before its beginning, therefore making it easier and more effective. In this context Chap. 3 is especially important, as it gives you the general and very important framework for rational and effective proceeding.

2.4.6 More Eyeballs Is Better: Linus's Law

Linus's Law says that 'given enough eyeballs, all bugs are shallow'. It is a very practical hint for everyone who needs to find bugs, not only in the code, but also in our own tests. When you have difficulties in writing a well-working test, or if you are not able to find a bug in our code, it is always a good idea to ask your colleague or colleagues for help.

You might experience many times the situation, in which you lost much time trying to solve your problem without success. And then, when you ask someone for help, she or he was usually able to solve it in the twinkling of an eye. This is because the 'other pair of eyeballs' have a different, often fresh, view on the problem you work on for a long time. This is also the reason why pair programming works. Another, even more effective activity from the testing point of view is a modified pair programming, where one person is a programmer and the other one the tester. If we can only afford it, we should definitely use such forms of programming.

However, there is one issue with Linus's Law: it works only when people are willing to help other team members. In many teams there are persons, usually very talented, who are reluctant to share their knowledge with other people. This is dangerous because of several reasons:

- knowledge sharing allows us to keep the knowledge within an organization, when people quit the job—in such a case other people can take over their responsibilities; when there's no knowledge sharing, the knowledge disappears with the team members that quit,
- it is the simplest way to worsen the relations between the team members, which of course results in poor effectiveness, and—finally—in poor quality of the final product,
- having and tolerating 'stars in the team' is a clear signal for all the team members that we don't care about the common responsibility for quality, so people will not feel this responsibility.

2.4.7 Legacy Code: Eagleson's Law

Eagleson's Law states that 'any code of your own that you haven't looked at for six or more months might as well have been written by someone else'. This is a law that each programmer is well familiar with. Testers participate in code review, so they

Table 2.2   Defect potentials by application size (from [28])

Application size in Function Points	10	100	1000	10,000	100,000
Defects per Function Point	7.05	9.20	11.30	13.00	14.45

should put emphasis on the good practices of writing a clean code. But even more important is that this code should be *testable*. Developers must understand that they do not write code for themselves. Their code will be tested by other people, either directly or indirectly. It will also be modified by other developers, so there must be set some standards on how to write clean, testable and maintainable code.

There are several good practices for doing that, see for example [54] or [55]. This knowledge is mainly addressed to developers, but testers should be well aware of these practices. Here are some examples of how the code should be written to be testable and maintainable:

- units of code (modules, classes, functions, procedures) should be short and simple, having at most 15 lines and at most four decision points,
- code should not be duplicated; where possible write reusable code and execute existing methods,
- keep unit interfaces small; functions should have at most four parameters,
- separate responsibilities in modules; avoid large modules with high coupling and low cohesion,
- keep architecture components balanced; there should be a small number of equally large and complex components on every abstraction layer,
- keep the codebase small—the larger the repository is, the more problems it causes and the harder it is to maintain it (see Table 2.2 for concrete industrial data),
- use meaningful names of variables, constants, classes and functions,
- comment your code in an informative way; avoid redundant, misleading comments,
- follow the code formatting standards approved and applied in your organization,
- use proper error handling (exceptions rather than return codes).

Notice that although the tester doesn't need to be a professional developer, it is desirable that she is at least able to read and understand the code.

2.4.8   How to Hire New People: Peter Principle

The Peter Principle says that 'the selection of a candidate for a position is based on the candidate's performance in their current role, rather than on abilities relevant to the intended role'. It is sometimes formulated in the following way: 'managers rise to the level of their incompetence'. It means that when a manger works well, he gets more responsibility and more difficult tasks to perform. But finally, at some level, the task will be too difficult for him—he won't be able to perform it and will fail.

The Peter Principle is quite useful when hiring new testers. At the job interviews candidates are often evaluated by their past performance. Hiring managers forget that they hire a new team member for a certain reason, which usually has nothing to do with the candidate's previous jobs. It is therefore important to evaluate candidates having in mind their future responsibilities.

This requires the proper preparation to the job interview: constructing the right questions, creating the puzzles and other tasks that we expect the candidate to be able to solve and so on. It takes time and often people don't want to 'waste their time' for such preparation. This is a big mistake, as hiring a new tester is a very important investment in the project quality. If we hire the wrong person, the software quality may be heavily damaged because of his incompetence. We will not only spend money on the requirement process, but also on cleaning after such an incompetent tester!

2.4.9 Meeting Facilitation: Sayre's Law

Professional testing emphasizes static testing methods, such as reviews or inspections. A tester usually participates in many meetings and frequently these meetings are ineffective. For not wasting time and making the meetings beneficial, it is important to moderate them in the right way.

Sayre's Law, a bit humoristic, says that 'in any dispute the intensity of feeling is inversely proportional to the value of the issues at stake'. It is a very handy indicator of the importance of the discussed matter. If we see an intensive argument between participants, probably they argue about meaningless or not so important things. We may then cut off this debate and move on.

2.4.10 Data Centralization: Ellison's Law of Data

The Law of Data, named after Lawrence Ellison, a co-founder of Oracle Corporation, states that 'once the business data have been centralized and integrated, the value of the database is greater than the sum of the preexisting parts'. This law is extremely important in analytics for at least several reasons:

- centralized data is easier to maintain than distributed data,
- it is easier to generate different kinds of reports, especially the ones that aggregate different types of data from different sources,
- it is easier to assure consistency and data quality,
- it is easier to compare and correct the same data coming from two or more different sources.

As testers gather, store and use different kinds of metrics, the single data repository is beneficial to the quality processes. Data centralization may be one of the tasks of the software process improvement. Data centralization usually goes together with implementation of automatic data gathering which protects us from negative 'human factors', like discretionary data interpretation or human errors.

2.4.11 False Sense of Security: Spafford's Law of False Alerts

Spafford's Law states that 'as the rate of erroneous alerts increases, operator reliance, or belief, in subsequent warnings decreases'. This phenomenon, if it happens, has very serious impact on the final product quality.

We should consider two things the law is talking about. The first one is the rate of the erroneous alert. The sole fact that it increases should be disquieting. We should proactively try to mitigate this risk, by for example:

- better tests design,
- detailed analysis of the test execution results,
- fixing the defects/closing the incidents as quickly as possible, but not in a careless way.

All these activities, when performed well, should decrease the rate of the false positive alerts. The second thing we should consider is the weakening of vigilance. It is hard to eliminate it in case of a high rate of false alerts. But nevertheless, a professional tester needs to be aware that each and every alert should be carefully investigated. Otherwise, a very serious bug might be unnoticed just because the symptoms looked like the symptoms of dozens of the previous false alarms.

2.4.12 Beizer's Pesticide Paradox

The Pesticide Paradox was defined by Boris Beizer [17] in the following way: 'every method you use to prevent or find bugs leaves a residue of subtler bugs against which those methods are ineffectual'. Another popular version of this 'paradox' says that 'a set of tests will become less effective as developers learn to avoid making mistakes that trigger the tests'.

I quoted the word 'paradox', because, in fact, there is absolutely nothing paradoxical in these statements! When our tests show some failures and the corresponding defects will be fixed, it is *natural*, not paradoxical, that there will be less defects in the code. Hence, it will be harder for our tests to detect other defects.

The name 'pesticide' was taken from the original, agricultural version of the pesticide paradox, which states that 'by applying pesticide to a pest, one may in fact increase its abundance. This happens when the pesticide upsets natural predator-prey dynamics in the ecosystem'. The dynamics infringement happens when there exists a natural enemy of the predator in the ecosystem. The pesticides that kill the bugs (predators), at the same time kill this natural predator's enemy, so increase the predators abundance—and this really *is* a paradox.

Summarizing, there's nothing paradoxical in the software version of the 'paradox'. It has nothing to do with the original one—there's no reasonable analogy between them, because in software testing setting there is no analogy of a predator's enemy. Instead of the Beizer's Pesticide Paradox we may use the following, simple and obvious rule: as every bug is different, we need a diverse set of tests to be effective in bug detection. We should not rely on a sole method or technique.

2.5   Standards and Norms: Best Practices or Pure Evil?

A standard is an established norm or set of requirements. Standards may refer to different fields of science and engineering. Some well-known standards related to software testing and quality are:

- IEEE 829—a standard for test documentation, containing templates for many test-related documents,
- IEEE 1008—a standard for software unit testing,
- IEEE 1028—a standard for software reviews and audits,
- IEEE 1044—standard classification for software anomalies, describing among others the incident life cycle,
- ISO 9126—software quality model,
- ISO 25000—a set of standards on software quality, replacing the old ISO 9126 norm,
- ISO 29119 Software Testing Standard—a set of five standards on software testing (Part 1: Concepts & Definitions, Part 2: Test Processes, Part 3: Test Documentation, Part 4: Test Techniques, Part 5: Keyword-Driven Testing), built on IEEE 829 and British Standard BS 7925.

As standards are usually written by a group of experts in the field, they contain different views on a given issue and are based on the so-called good practices, that is—activities that were proved to be beneficial in the real projects. Following the rules the standard describes may protect us from making many costly mistakes. On the other hand, by definition, standards and norms also impose some procedures or ways of acting regardless of the type of the project we work in. You might have often heard that a certain company or its processes are compliant with some standard (probably the most popular one is ISO 9001). Does it really help and does it really impact the final product quality?

The fundamental question from the tester's point of view is this: how should we treat standards? If they are created by the experts, shouldn't we accept the content they impose, treat it as carved in stone and follow it blindly? Or maybe use the norms only as some handy guidelines that we may, but don't necessarily have to follow? The latter sounds reasonable when we perceive that a standard is a result of many different experiences and hence is not universal for all types of projects.

Some people say that there are only good, but not best practices. One may argue with that, for example washing and disinfecting hands by a surgeon before an operation is definitely the *best* practice, not just a good one. Nevertheless, for sure there is one essential and universal best practice: you should always *think* before you act. Having said that, the most reasonable use of standards seems to be as follows: we should not treat norms and standards as infallible sources of truth, but rather as the set of suggestions and ideas that *may* be advantageous.

The idea is simple: use the useful, skip/ignore the irrelevant. However, things get complicated when standards are introduced at the organizational level and we do not have any impact on how and to what extent a given norm will be used in our company. But when it comes to the team level, we usually have more opportunities to influence the management and convince it to use technical norms and standards wisely.

In recent years (2014–2015) the testing community debated intensively on the introduction of an ISO 29119 standard. It was quite an argument. There was even a petition for suspending its publication. In the debate on ISO 29119 many reasons against the standard were given, for example:

- testing is a young discipline and it is definitely too early for standardizing it,
- testing is a creative action and therefore cannot be subject to standards: training testers to use standards frames and narrows their thinking—rather than using their creativity to solve problems, they seek to choose from a set of ready-made solutions that may just not apply to a given situation,
- although standards make sense in manufacturing (acting in the same way minimizes variability between produced parts), it does not apply to services or software, which are characterized by high variability and uniqueness,
- the standards are just the money-making tools for organizations that 'certify' other organizations, not bringing any real added-value.

Some of these arguments make their point, some are disputable (for example, one may argue that standards do not standardize creativity, but processes). Nevertheless, the wise tester should be 'professionally neutral' in such situations. Remember that professional testers call themselves 'quality *engineers*' for a reason. An engineer is a thinking person, who maximizes the work effectiveness while minimizing the costs. Therefore, if someone defines and publishes a standard on software testing—good for him. We may read it and see if there's something of our interest. If so, we may adopt it. If not—we won't do this. It's as simple as that. The same is with any book, blog, website or conference talk. Some of them are inspirational for us, and some aren't. We are offered a pile of ideas, methods, techniques and practices and we just cherry-pick—there's no big deal about it.

We compared earlier testing to a scientific method and this analogy is still valid regarding the standards. Notice that there is no standard on how to do science. You cannot standardize science. There are paradigms in science, but they change. Every time it happens, we talk about the revolution in science. The examples may be Newtonian physics, Copernican revolution or Einstein's theory of relativity. The scientific theories are verified by data and observations. The progress in science is because of refutations, that is, rebuttal of erroneous theories and replacing them by the new ones.

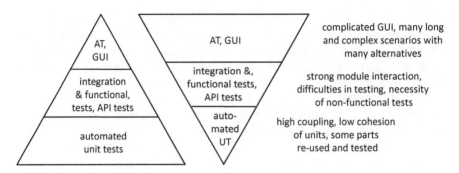

Fig. 2.8 Agile test pyramid and why it is wrong

However, there indeed *are* the best practices which could be understood as some kinds of the standards in science. For example, the procedure of verifying the statistical hypotheses follows the set of very clearly defined rules. Popper's falsifiability criterion [56] may be also viewed as a standard—the Basic Scientific Principle—which describes the formal requirements a theory must fulfill to be called scientific.[7] The same thing is with software testing. Some processes or techniques may be subjected to some kinds of standards or regulations, but thinking—the essence of testing—cannot be standardized.

The last thing I want to discuss are the standards and models that are potentially harmful or at least methodologically incorrect. If the statements they contain are not supported by data, their value may be questionable. One of the examples of such a model is the well-known test pyramid, very popular in the agile framework, introduced by Cohn in [57].

The test pyramid model is shown on the left part of Fig. 2.8. The essential point of the model is that we should have more low-level unit tests than high-level end-to-end tests running through a GUI. The problem with this model is that it imposes the relations between the number of different types of tests. It is obviously irrational, as every project is different and there are hundreds of factors that impact the test strategy. For example, the right part of Fig. 2.8 shows an example of a project, for which the strategy that fits best is exactly the opposite—a 'reversed' pyramid.

According to Fowler [58] 'If you get a failure in a high-level test, not just do you have a bug in your functional code, you also have a missing or incorrect unit test.' This statement, evidently claimed by a programmer, not a tester, suggests that good unit tests should be enough, which is obviously not true—some software characteristics can be checked only in end-to-end systems, when it is possible to realize full business scenarios. Sole unit tests will never detect defects in the high-level business logic.

---

[7]According to Popper, a scientific theory must be falsifiable. It means that it must be inherently disprovable. For example, the existence of God is not a scientific theory, because such a hypothesis cannot be disproved.

Fig. 2.9 Door slide bolt lock

> **Example**
> Figure 2.9 shows a typical door slide bolt lock. We may perform thorough unit
> tests of this lock, check that it fits to the door, it is robust and resistant, can be
> moved easily and so on. We may also perform thorough unit tests of the door.
> But all these tests will never be useful if the lock is mounted on the sliding
> door. . . This failure will, on the other hand, be trivial to detect on the integra-
> tion or system test level.

Unit tests are usually done by developers. The tester's kingdom is system- and
acceptance-level tests. Each test type detects different types of bugs and failures,
therefore we should never restrict ourselves to just one type of test.

The above-mentioned problems with the Test Pyramid model might result from
the fact that people like Cohn and Fowler have background in development rather
than in testing, and they consider testing from the developer's perspective. Of
course, the Test Pyramid may work well for many projects, but prior to using any
standard or model, we should definitely evaluate its correctness and credibility.

2.6   Models of Software Errors and Why We Should Use Them

The idea of the software error model is crucial to testing, although testers often use it
subconsciously. In Sect. 1.2.2 we noticed that the main direct goal of testing is to find
bugs. When can we claim that we have found a bug? When the actual results are
different than the expected ones. The only way to check this is by observing the
deviation from the normal behavior through the error model.

There are at least three types of error models:

- direct error models (given directly),
- error models defined within software models,
- indirect error models.

Direct error models are usually utilized in dirty testing, when we seek for
abnormal program behavior under 'weird' conditions, caused for example by the

improper use of a software or by performing a software attack. These models usually define the possible bugs/failures explicitly, for example:

- force all error messages to occur,
- overflow input buffers,
- force invalid outputs,
- force the screen to refresh,
- try to violate data constraints,
- perform SQL injection.

A very good source of such error models, defined as the software attacks, can be found in the books of Whittaker, Thompson and Andrews [59–61]. These attacks can be directly applied in any project. There also exist different defect taxonomies that may be helpful, for example Beizer's [17] or Kaner, Falk and Nguyen's [62]. Binder [63] gives the taxonomy for object-oriented systems.

Error models defined within software models define errors as the deviations from the expected behavior of some aspect of a SUT. For example, when a tester uses a finite state machine as a model of software behavior, she may test if it is possible to extort an incorrect transition while being in some state. If we are able to do this, we discover a bug related to the incorrect transition. Each software model is constructed in a way that allows us to discover a certain type of failure. The examples are given in Table 2.3. More on software testing techniques can be found in [10], [14], [15–18].

Indirect error models are usually used in confirmation testing, where we want to check if the software works exactly as it is expected, or to test so-called 'happy paths', that is, the desired user behavior. The example of such models may be the use cases or high-level scenarios and requirements used in user acceptance tests. In such situations, we do not have any specific bugs or failures in mind—we just check if the software works as it should. If something wrong happens, we discover a bug, but prior to that we are not able to tell what type of bugs we are searching for. Usually, during the high-level tests we are more likely to make sure that everything works OK than expect to discover a large number of bugs.

Error models play a significant role in practical software testing. Testing is always more effective, if we know what we are searching for. It also gives more confidence, if we seek for a certain type of bug/failure and we are not able to find it. If we do this systematically, for many types of bugs, we may be quite sure that these defects should not occur in the operation.

Error models can be used formally, in a written form, being contained in the test plans. But they may also be used only as the ideas that a tester has in his head. The important thing is to be aware of them when testing the software. In fact, every sane testing is driven by some kind of an error model, because in such an approach the derived tests have more chance to detect bugs. We do not grope for errors—we know what we are looking for, so our actions can be planned, rational and effective.

From the practical point of view, it is also important to remember that some defects may be latent. For example, a defect may cause the data constraint violation

Table 2.3 Software models and corresponding error models

Software model	Model elements to test	Possible types of bugs
Equivalence Partition, Domain Analysis	Equivalence class	Wrong behavior of a SUT for a given type (class) of data
Boundary Value Analysis	Boundary values	Wrong behavior of a SUT for a given value of data
Decision Table, Cause-Effect Graph	Table columns, paths in C–E graphs	Wrong behavior of a SUT for a given combination of conditions
Finite State Machine	States, transitions, paths, etc.	Wrong behavior of a SUT while changing its state
Combinatorial models (Classification Tree, pair-wise testing, etc.)	Combinations of features	Wrong behavior of a SUT for a given configuration setting
Control flow graph	Statements	Wrong behavior of a SUT because of executing a certain buggy code instruction
Control flow graph	Decisions, conditions, Modified C/D, etc.	Wrong behavior of a SUT because of an incorrect control flow (incorrect logic)
Data flow graph	Du-paths	Wrong behavior of a SUT because of incorrect handling of defining and using the data
CRUD	Sequences of operations on the data	Wrong behavior of a SUT because of incorrect operations on the data

in the database, but we won't observe any visible effect. If we know that such a defect may occur, we should not only look for the visible results, but also check, for example, the data consistency in a database.

Example

Consider the following method, which counts the numbers of zeros in an array given as its input.

```
public static int numZero(int[] x) {
  //Effects: if x==null throw
  //NullPointerException, else return
  //the number of occurence of 0 in x
  int count = 0;
  for (int i=1; i<x.length; i++)
  {
    if (x[i]==0)
```

(continued)

```
    {
        count++;
    }
  }
  return count;
}
```

Notice that the loop iterator i starts with 1, but arrays in Java are indexed from 0. So during the searching process we will never analyze the first array element, $x[0]$. If this element does not contain 0, no test will detect this error. But if we are aware about this type of error (often called an 'error by 1'), we may design a test for which $x[0]=0$ and thus prove that the algorithm does not work correctly in this case—it returns a value one less than the expected result. Notice, that we may detect this error without source code analysis: we may assume that there must be some iteration over the input array, and apply an 'error by one' model.

2.7   'Plans Are Useless, But Planning Is Indispensible'

The title statement is by Dwight Eisenhower, a general and later president of the USA. It is a very wise saying and should be promoted especially in the IT community, because of its huge incomprehension about the planning. The whole misunderstanding is about the objective of the planning activity. Many people think that planning is a long and costly process that ends up with a detailed document describing the detailed actions written out in the detailed schedule, which will perfectly reflect the actual project activities.

This reflection of the actual future actions is considered as the main goal of creating the plan. Such thinking seems to be rational: if we have a detailed plan, what could possibly go wrong? Having this document done we feel safe. Not only have we the sense of controlling the project, but also the sense of controlling the future. Unfortunately, according to reports like the Chaos Report published regularly by Standish Group, we know well that merely one third of the projects end up successfully (delivered on time, on budget and with requested functions and features). But we had so perfect plans! Why is it so?

Well, it is because no matter what the plan looks like, how much time we spent on it and what sophisticated methods we used to construct it, we will never be able to predict the future. The only constant thing is change. So, things will change. So, what's the point in creating the plans? The answer is this: it is not about the plan itself—it is about the *activity of planning*.

The most important thing in planning is the opportunity to better understand the problem we are working on and to anticipate possible problems that may occur in the future. This is the great value of the planning, and yet, surprisingly, so many people don't get it. Good planning takes advantage on the fact that *when we plan, the planned actions have not yet occurred*. The planned piece of code has not yet been written; the planned test suite has not yet been implemented and executed; and so on. The fact that we do not have yet these final artifacts allows us to avoid the bias that we would have experienced if we had actually been working on them. Because they do not exist, our minds are clear and unbiased, so we see much more interesting things and hence, we may plan our actions better. At the end of this section we give a tangible example that should explain better the above-mentioned theses.

Of course, the planning thing applies to testing as well. Here, the planning may be understood as the modeling or designing the tests. The main advantage of such test planning is the perception of the potential design errors. This type of error is hard to detect in the development or high-level testing phases. However, it is easily detected earlier, either during some static activities (requirement, code & design reviews) or during the planning. For example, Harry Robinson reported that much of the bug-finding happens while doing the modeling, well before the automated tests are coded [64].

One of the most obvious forms of planning is TDD (Test-Driven Development)—a technique in which first we write a test, and then the piece of code that should pass this test. It is said that tests drive the design. There is a strong critique of this approach, see for example [65]. However, the critics focus on the arguments that 'TDD is bad, because writing tests is a waste of time', but they do not see the most important benefit of a TDD: the *opportunity to plan*. Creating the tests is just a by-product. The crucial thing in TDD is that when we are about to write the test, we are forced to think first: what exactly should this test check? Sometimes, during this analysis, many interesting and important design-related questions appears, even before we actually implement and run the test itself. The following is a good example on that.

Example

Suppose we have to program a parking gate controller.[8] The gate has three sensors (see Fig. 2.10):

- *gatePosition*—with three possible values, 'top', 'middle' and 'bottom', signifying the position of the arm of the parking gate,
- *carAtGate*—'true' if a car is waiting to come through the gate and 'false' otherwise,

(continued)

---

[8]This example is based on the material for the MIT course 'Introduction to Electrical Engineering and Computer Science', https://ocw.mit.edu/courses/electrical-engineering-and-computer-science/6-01sc-introduction-to-electrical-engineering-and-computer-science-i-spring-2011/unit-1-soft ware-engineering/state-machines/MIT6_01SCS11_chap04.pdf

- *carJustExited*—'true' if a car has just passed through the gate; it is true for only one step before resetting to 'false'.

The gate has three possible outputs (think of them as controls to the motors for the gate arm): 'raise', 'lower' and 'nop' (no operation). The requirements for the gate behavior are as follows:

1. If a car wants to come through, the gate needs to raise the arm until it is at the top position.
2. Once the gate is at the top position, it has to stay there until the car has driven through the gate.
3. After the car has driven through the gate, it needs to lower the arm until it reaches the bottom position.

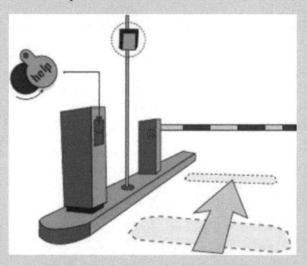

Fig. 2.10 A parking gate with sensors (from: parking.mcmaster.ca)

Suppose we follow the TDD approach and we are before the implementation step. The first thing we have to do is to implement the test. We want it to verify the proper parking gate behavior, according to Requirements 1–3 given above. The preconditions are:

- *gatePosition* = bottom
- *carAtGate* = false
- *carJustExited* = false

Once the preconditions are fulfilled, we may execute the test case. After the execution, the postconditions should be exactly the same as the preconditions given above. So, how should we design our test?

(continued)

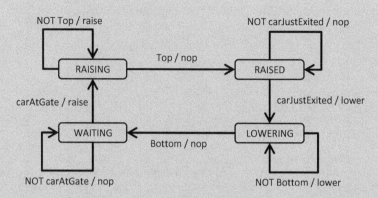

Fig. 2.11 A finite state model for the parking gate controller

Figure 2.11 shows the model for our controller. It is a finite state machine with states representing the gate movement. The arrows denote possible state transitions. Each arrow is labeled by X/Y, where X is the event that may occur and Y is the action the controller does. For example, when we are in the 'Waiting' state and we receive *carAtGate* signal, an action 'raise' is taken, which results in raising the gate, and we switch to the 'Raising' state.

Based on this model we may construct our first test case, that will check if the whole process goes as it should, according to Requirements 1–3. The sequence of actions in this test follows the whole cycle from the state 'Waiting' to itself:

```
preCondition();
send(carAtGate); assertIf(raise);
waitUntil(Top); assertIf(nop); wait(10); assertIf(nop);
send(carJustExited); assertIf(lower);
waitUntil(Bottom); assertIf(nop);
assertIf(PostCondition)
```

This is a pseudo-code, because our intention here is not to show the exact code, but an advantage of the rational planning. The 'send' command simulates a signal from the sensor. The 'wait' command freezes the algorithm for a given time. The 'assertIf' command returns true if a given assertion holds, and false otherwise.

Now, let us analyze our model in a more detailed way. This is a real-time system, so there may occur some unexpected sequence of events. For example, what happens, if we are in the 'Raising' state, *gatePosition* is 'middle' and suddenly we have just received a signal from the sensor behind the parking gate, that is *carJustExited* is 'True'? Notice, that this may physically happen: while a gate is raising, the car does not need to wait until the gate reaches its top position

(continued)

and drive through the gate earlier. This violates the third requirement, because the gate will remain in the top position until the next car drives through the gate.

Being aware of this issue we may document it by writing the following test:

```
preCondition();
send(carAtGate); assertIf(raise);
wait(10); send(carJustExited);
waitUntil(Top); waitUntil(Bottom);
assertIf(PostCondition)
```

Now we might write a piece of code that passes both tests. The code might look like this (the while loop is an infinite one, as the controller should work incessantly):

```
PreConditions();
while(1) {
  while (not carAtGate) {};
  while (not (gatePosition==Top | carJustExited)) raise();
  if (!carJustExited) { while (not carJustExited) {}; }
  while (not gatePosition==Bottom) lower();
}
```

But before we write it, we may plan and analyze a little bit more. The gate controller is a real-time system. If a signal comes from a sensor, how does the software handle it? Is it a constant signal that lasts some period of time? If so, there may be a problem with receiving it, because of the timing issues with the algorithm: for example, when we check the condition *carJustExited*, we do this in the loop. The signal may occur just after one checking and cease just before the next checking. Hence, we may miss the signal.

How to solve this problem? One, very natural, way is to represent signals as raising and lowering the flags. For example, when a signal appears, it is represented by raising a corresponding flag, which is lowered after its first checking. This way, we solve the problem of missing signals. Our code may therefore be simplified and correspond directly to the finite state machine model of our controller:

```
PreConditions();
while(1) {
  while (not carAtGate) {};
  while (not gatePosition==Top) raise();
  while (not carJustExited) {};
  while (not gatePosition==Bottom) lower();
}
```

(continued)

Notice that in this example planning and treating TDD as the opportunity to analyze the system that is going to be built, allowed us to find an *architectural solution*. We discovered the best way to represent and handle signals in the system. We did it before any line of code was written and before any architecture was defined. This simple example shows the power of planning. The sole plan (model) of the system, shown in Fig. 2.11, was only a starting point for the more thorough analysis that resulted in finding the optimal design.

2.8   The Eternal Problem of Documentation

The opinions about the documentation vary. Some people say it is extremely important, some—quite contrary—claim that it is superfluous and that many projects, especially the agile ones, can perfectly go without any documentation. The truth, as usually, lies somewhere in the middle.

When deciding on how, when, and how much documentation should be done, it is very important to approach the problem rationally. It means that creation of each and every document should be sufficiently justified. The best way is to imagine a situation, in which a given document may be useful and used. We should ask ourselves questions like: who will benefit from reading this documentation? Will it be necessary for someone to read this documentation? Will reading it bring any added value to the process, project, quality, etc.?

There may be different reasons for creating the documentation, for example:

- documentation may play an instructional role, when a new employee is joining our team and should familiarize himself with the system, processes and so on,
- a test will be executed by a tester who is not the author of this test, so comments included in the test, describing what exactly this test does and what its purpose is, may be very helpful for other testers to better understand the test and execute it smoothly,
- an incident history, containing the symptoms, screenshots, investigation, root cause analysis, description of how it was fixed, forms a priceless database of knowledge on incidents and defects that we have encountered so far; such a database helps us in dealing with new incidents and problems, if they reoccur or are similar to the previous ones; fixing them is faster and more efficient,
- test case documentation, in more complex situations, may have an educational value for new testers who may learn how to write effective test cases, using good practices, design patterns, etc.,
- graphical models of the system, its architecture and so on, may be helpful when communicating with a client, but also as the base for the reviews, which are able

to detect many design errors, hard to detect at later phases, when we test the
implemented software,

- any document that may be reused facilitates work on future projects and protects
  us from making the same mistakes again,
- documents often contain different types of data that may be gathered, aggregated
  and used in analyses and predictive modeling (for example: data on team effectiveness, defect distribution, reliability expressed in terms of consecutive
  timestamps of software failures, data on how fast defects were fixed, data on
  how much do different quality activities cost and so on).

If we know in advance, that a given document will never be read by anyone, we
just don't write it. It would be a waste of time and resources. Every single document
should bring a concrete added value, although this value doesn't need to be visible
immediately. We also must remember about the maintenance costs. The documentation should be easily modifiable in case of some change and the necessity for
updating the related documents.

Another issue is the test cases themselves. Should we document them or not? The
problem is that it is hard to provide a unified, general definition of a test case, so it is
also in the case of test case documentation. Nevertheless, it is very practical to use
test cases themselves as a form of a so-called living documentation. This approach is
used in methods such as ATDD (Acceptance Test-Driven Development), EDT
(Example-Driven Development), BDD (Behavior-Driven Development), or user
story testing. Gojko Adzic [66] refers to this technique as 'specification by example'
and claims that it is very beneficial, because:

- it ensures the discipline of specifications and tests,
- it improves communication between stakeholders and team members,
- it reduces the number of unnecessary remakes and fixes.

When the specification is executable we have the true 'living' documentation. In
case of any change in the requirements we are forced to change the specification,
therefore the documentation is always up to date. The same refers to automatic tests
acting as a form of the system documentation.

2.9   Underestimated Estimation, Unpredicted Prediction and Measures Not Measured

In everyday work we often need to measure or estimate something. For example, we
want to know the workload for a given task, how much it will take to finish our
testing project, how much it will cost to perform the system and acceptance tests for a
new release and so on. There are also some more advanced techniques that allow us
to do predictions. For example, we may predict the number of defects in the software
after release. If this prediction is more or less correct, we may better organize the

work of the support team, because we know in advance, approximately, what will be the rate of raising the bugs by clients.

So, estimations, predictions and measures are very useful, but also very dangerous when used in an improper or irrational way. Some people claim that estimates are a waste, are unnecessary or wrong. However, the devil is in the details. The problem is that a wise use of these tools requires—apart from the obvious things like ability of analytical thinking—some mathematical and statistical background, which managers usually lack. The irony is that this advanced math knowledge sometimes allows us to decide that the optimal strategy for estimation or prediction should *not* involve the advanced scientific machinery! But to know that, you need to gain and understand this knowledge first.

Let's look at the exemplary case study. In [67] two Microsoft employees described their approach to optimize the work of their team that maintained over 80 applications for internal use. The tasks were mainly small change requests, often bug fixes. The backlog of work was exceeding capacity five times and it was growing every month. They introduced the estimation phase, which was done by one developer and one tester for every change request. The estimation was a 'ROM'—Rough Order of Magnitude—and its role was to allow us to prioritize the tasks. This process took in total one day per change request.

It turned out that the estimation activity was a waste of time, since it took too long. This time could be effectively spent on the development work. If 'rough order of magnitude' was an acceptable approximation, spending the whole day on it was absurd. It would be enough to organize a meeting with several subject matter experts and spend literally 15 min on providing a rough estimation using techniques like planning poker, Wideband Delphi or something similar.

How can we decide what level of estimation is optimal? To do this, we need to understand two fundamental things: first, that the estimation process takes time (which might be used for doing something else), and second, that estimations have different errors. A small error makes the estimation reliable, but a big error makes it useless and is often costly. We could symbolically write this in a form of the following equation:

$$TC = C_{est} + C_{work} + C_{error},$$

where:

- TC is the total cost of all our activities,
- C_{est} is the cost of estimation of the future effort,
- C_{work} is the cost of work performed according to estimated parameters,
- C_{error} is the cost of the effort due to estimation error.

Example

Suppose we need to perform the system tests for a new commercial off-the-shelf application. We need to estimate the workload, because we are also involved in other projects and need to organize our work efficiently. We estimate (on a 1-day meeting) that it will take 40 days to remove about 90% of all bugs. In the next 40 days we found 45 critical errors that were fixed. However, our estimation was rough and so had a large error. After the release the clients discovered 15 more critical bugs. Their fixing was very expensive and took 50 days of developers' work. Our company lost it reputation, which is even hard to express in money. In this example we have $C_{est} = 1 \cdot E$, $C_{work} = 40 \cdot W$, $C_{error} = 50 \cdot M$, where E, W and M are the costs of one-day effort on estimation, development and maintenance teams respectively.

Now suppose we use some more sophisticated estimation method, taking into account more factors, analyzing more data and inviting more experts on the estimation meeting. It may take 3 days and because of involving more people may be four or five times more expensive than the previous one-day meeting. But the estimations we made may be more accurate. Suppose we say that we need 50 days to remove 90% of all bugs, and we found 55 critical bugs. After the release, clients have found five more, which were fixed in 5 days. The estimation costs were higher, but the maintenance costs much lower, because we provided fixes in 5 days, not in 50. We saved 45 days of developers' work. In this example we have $C_{est} = 3E$, $C_{work} = 50W$, $C_{error} = 5M$.

Another approach might be to obtain very rough estimates, but in a short time. For example, we invite four subject matter experts for 15 min meeting and they estimate that we need 50 days for finding 90% of all the bugs. In these 50 days we may find 56 bugs, and four others are fixed in 3 days. Here the estimation cost was almost 0, maintenance cost also lower than in the previous case, but the estimated time for testing was much longer. We have $C_{est} \approx 0$, $C_{work} = 50W$, $C_{error} = 3M$.

In our example the third approach is better than the second no matter what the values are of E, W, M. When comparing the first and the third one, or the first and the second one, the results depend heavily on these values.

From the above example we see that it is nice if we know the costs of efforts on developing, testing, analyzing, maintenance and so on. It is always good to *measure* the process parameters related to such activities. The more accurate data we have, the better our estimations will be. Much of this data can be taken from different reporting and bug-management tools like Jira.[9] However, it is always good to think before, if all the data we need are available. If not, we should set up a process for gathering them (which also takes some time and cost!).

---

[9] www.jira.atlassian.com

It may seem that estimation based on the expert knowledge (as in the Delphi method) is very inexact. However, it is surprisingly accurate, especially when the participants are really experienced experts in the field, having different views on the problem subject to estimation. This is because the error ε has the distribution with zero mean value: $E[\varepsilon] = 0$. Therefore, each expert will make some error. One will estimate too much, another one too little. But the *mean* value of the accumulated error will tend to 0 with the increasing number of participants.

This phenomenon, called 'wisdom of crowds', was observed—according to an anecdote—by Francis Galton[10] at the beginning of the twentieth century. He noticed that the crowd at a country fair was able to accurately guess the weight of an ox, when their individual guesses were averaged. The mean estimation was closer to the ox's true weight than the particular estimates of most crowd members. Why? Let $x_i = \mu + \varepsilon_i$ denote the ith crowd member guess, where μ is the true weight and ε_i is the error made by the crowd member. Let X be the mean value of all x_i. Then, we have

$$E[X] = E\left[\frac{1}{n}\sum_i x_i\right] = \frac{1}{n}\sum_i E[x_i] = \frac{1}{n}\sum_i E[\mu + \varepsilon_i]$$
$$= \frac{1}{n}\sum_i (E[\mu] + E[\varepsilon_i]) = \left(\frac{1}{n}\right) \times (n\mu + n \cdot 0\,) = \mu.$$

The averaged value is equal to the true weight μ. Of course, the bigger the sample size n is, the closer is $\frac{1}{n}\sum_i x_i$ to the real value μ.

Predictions are more advanced tools, as they require the advanced knowledge on math, statistics and modeling. These issues are beyond the scope of this book. The recommended further literature on this topic is [68] or any other textbook on predictive modeling.

2.10   Simulations: Your Manager Loves Them

The problem with estimations is that we need some input values for our model and the most fundamental inputs are not known—we have to make an (educated) guess. The estimations are usually needed by our management, who want to know, for example, how long a given task will take, or how much it will cost. When we prepare the requested report containing all the calculations and estimations, there is always a risk that someone will criticize us for choosing bad input values, and undermine our analysis.

There is one nice solution for avoiding such a situation. Instead of providing the final report with all calculations done, we may prepare a *simulation* which can be used by managers to perform a so-called 'what-if' analysis. We only create the model, but we leave freedom for choosing the input values. In Excel it can be easily done with the use of scroll bars. It looks nice, is easy to use, and managers love it.

---

[10]Sir Francis Galton (1822–1911) was an English statistician, known from his concept of correlation. Also, he was the first mathematician who applied statistical methods to the study of human differences. He introduced questionnaires and surveys for collecting statistical data.

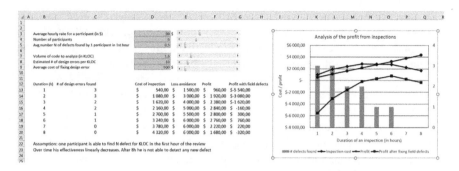

Fig. 2.12   An example of the simulation for calculating the profit from inspections

Of course, the simulation won't be 100% exact, because its result depends on the quality of the model and the input values. But it still may have a cognitive value to the management. From simulations we may learn the trends or the nature of dependencies of different factors. For example, we may learn that the function we want to maximize is unimodal, that is, it has one maximum. Or we may notice that this function is increasing or decreasing. This is also a very important information— we don't need to predict the exact values, which is impossible anyway.

Figure 2.12 presents the sample simulation for computing the profit from reviews. There are six input values that can be dynamically changed by the use of scroll bars:

- average hourly rate for a participant (D3),
- number of participants (D4),
- average number of defects found by one participant in the first hour of an inspection (D5),
- volume of code to analyze (D7),
- estimated number of design errors per KLOC (D8),
- average cost of fixing design error that escaped to the production and was raised by a client (D9).

The simulation assumes that the participant effectiveness decreases linearly from 100% in the first hour to 0% in the eighth hour. Number of design errors found (column C) is hence calculated as number of participants (D4) multiplied by the effectiveness (D5) proportional to the duration of the inspection. Inspection cost (column E) is calculated as number of participants multiplied by number of hours multiplied by the average hour rate. Loss avoidance is the virtual profit we have because of detecting the design errors and is computed as the cumulative number of defects found multiplied by the average cost of fixing (D9). Profit (column F) is the difference between columns E and D. The last column, G, represents the total profit, including the real costs of fixing the design defects that escaped from the inspection phase into production. It equals $profit - D9 \cdot (D7 \cdot D8 - \text{\# of defects found})$.

The trends from columns C, D, F and G are plotted on the graph on the right. When a user manipulates the input by moving the scroll bars, the chart is automatically updated. From the simulation shown in Fig. 2.12 we see, for example, that both profit and final profit are unimodal, that is, have one maximum. For the profit maximization the inspection process should take 4 h. For the final profit maximization, the inspection should take 6 h.

Of course, the exact numbers may not be accurate—our model is quite simple, it uses several assumptions (like the linear decreasing in effectiveness), and the input values may not correspond to the real ones. But the interesting thing from the analysis is that the optimal inspection duration may be different for the two types of profits. This is a nice result that we were able to obtain by performing the simulation. It shows that we shouldn't extend the inspection time, but the optimal time is not necessarily determined by the 'local' criterion—we should also take into account the costs of fixing the field defects. The optimal inspection time depends on the relation between these costs and the costs of inspection and loss avoidance.

The simulation will be more credible, if:

- there is a good data quality,
- the data is accurate (for example based on historical observations),
- the underlying model corresponds to the reality as much as possible.

The simulation from Fig. 2.12, in a form of the Excel chart, is available online: www.ii.uj.edu.pl/~roman/TDT. Remember, that it is much better when you provide to the management simulations, not the final reports with static data. Simulations allow us to play with numbers and observe different trends and behaviors. By producing such nice, graphical simulations you will not only create an effective decision supporting tool, but also gain more respect from the people in your organization.

Thinking-Driven Testing: A Universal Testing Framework

3

3.1 Introduction

After describing the fundamentals of software testing and general strategies for boosting our creativity and inspiration, in this chapter we introduce TDT (Thinking-Driven Testing)—a universal framework, or approach, to testing. The TDT framework primarily puts emphasis on thinking. There are different types of thinking and all of them should be used in our everyday work. These are:

- **analytical thinking**—the ability to define and model the problem, identify, construct and evaluate arguments, solve problems systematically,
- **critical thinking**—the ability to think clearly and rationally about our past, present and future actions, to evaluate the relevance and importance of ideas, to reflect on the justification of one's own views and opinions,
- **logical thinking**—the ability to conduct a valid, deductive reasoning,
- **systems thinking**—the ability to see the 'big picture', to understand the relations between different concepts, ideas, actions, perceiving the impact of one of them on all the others.

We show how to apply these concepts in software testing. In Sect. 2 we introduce the main ideas of TDT in a form of the manifesto. Section 3 is devoted to universal rules and practices that should be followed by every tester regardless of the project type he or she is involved in. Section 4 focuses particularly on test automation, as this has been a hot topic since a few years and it is therefore worthwhile to discuss it separately, because people still make fundamental mistakes when automating their processes. In Sect. 5 we give the exemplary, practical application of one of the universal rules from Sect. 3—'know, where you are'. We do it by introducing the reasonable way of measuring our testing in a way that brings as much benefit as possible.

© Springer International Publishing AG 2018
A. Roman, *Thinking-Driven Testing*, https://doi.org/10.1007/978-3-319-73195-7_3

Sections 6 and 7 are devoted to critical and systems thinking.[1] In Sect. 8 we give some hints on how to professionally develop your career as a software tester. In Sect. 9 we discuss the so-called design thinking, which is said to be an effective way of designing things. We do this to show that often some well-known ideas, beneficial to the test process, are sold under a new name. We end with Sect. 10, where we discuss an extremely important topic, which is systematically overlooked at different test conferences: how to study testing effectively on our own.

3.2   TDT Manifesto

When we think about the testing process, we often have a feeling that this abstract concept emerges in different organizational areas and somehow 'controls' or 'leads' our work. This is why people trust the process so much. They think that it is something 'official', and well-defined, and therefore must be infallible. So, they often follow it blindly, with no reflection, hoping that these well-defined rules and procedures will ensure that everything will go just fine.

Unfortunately, it's not true. Of course, well-designed and implemented processes are very helpful, but *processes don't think*. It's people who do this. We must remember that every task we perform originates from the conscious thought. This *human* thought is the most important success factor of everything we do. Living in the era of tools we almost forgot that machines won't do all our work. The most important thing they cannot do is this conscious thinking. It is, and will probably always be, the realm of humans. So is the *creativity*—one of the most important skills that a good tester should possess. It is crucial in test design, different types of analysis (like risk analysis) or process improvement.

The progress in specialization of almost all human activities is incredible. There is a joke saying that soon we will have two separate specializations in ophthalmology: right-eye and left-eye oculists. The same is in IT. In Fig. 3.1 we present just a small fragment of different test activities that have begun to be performed by completely different specialists. We have security testers, performance test engineers, UX specialists and so on. And this is just testing, which exists within a much bigger and complicated environment. Therefore, testers not only need to be aware of people like: developers, business analysts, database engineers, project managers, product owners, documentalists and so on. They need to understand them and work with them proactively to deliver the highest possible quality.

This is why professional testers should not have the phrase 'comfort zone' in their dictionary. They cannot sit somewhere in the corner, in a complete isolation from all the others, and just do their work. Not only must they communicate with all the others, but also *understand the complexity* of the whole development process and the relations within it.

---

[1] As for the analytical thinking, see the TQED framework described in Chap. 4.

Fig. 3.1 Specializations in testing

Functioning in such a complex environment is very difficult, but yet more challenging is introducing the change. A professional tester, by definition, is usually the one *who initiates the idea of a change* that should result in some process or product improvement. Sometimes these changes require process modifications, hence, dealing with people as well, as they typically do not like any changes at all.

Putting together the above-mentioned considerations, we may formulate the TDT manifesto, similarly to the Agile Manifesto:

Thinking-Driven Testing Manifesto
A professional tester values:

- critical thinking *over* procedures and rules,
- skills *over* tools,
- creativeness *over* following the process,
- systems thinking *over* working in isolation,

(continued)

- initiative and courage to change *over* 'business as usual'.

   That is, while there is value in the items on the right, a professional tester values the items on the left more.

We should value the left items more, because there are unceasing problems with the right ones:

- Following the procedures and rules usually means following them blindly. A procedure is often focused on one, isolated aspect of the whole process. Following it just ensures us that we do something in the way it was expected—nothing more. Of course, this is very important, but it does not bring any added value in the sense of tester's creativity. Also, following the process won't help if something unexpected occurs.
- Tools are important, but the overconfidence in tools kills the creativity. We discuss this issue in more detail in Sect. 6.9.
- Working in isolation kills communication, which is a crucial project success factor. Any software development project is done by a *team* of people. If they do not communicate, they will not be able to utilize their skills diversity to work effectively.
- Business as usual brings boredom and false sense of security. If people do not take initiative, if they do not stimulate their minds by new, fresh ideas, they will fall in stagnation. This will immediately result in the decrease of their engagement and effectiveness. The management in the organization should create the open environment, in which all ideas are friendly welcome.

TDT is a specific process in at least several ways:

- TDT is based on a system approach. Our profession is not only about testing the code, but testing everything and everywhere, including software development and software testing processes. It is about constant improvement of everything, everywhere. It is about educating, proposing beneficial changes and encouraging other team members to do that as well. TDT requires the ability to see the big picture, that is all the subtle and complicated relationships between the elements of the puzzle called 'software engineering'.
- TDT encourages us to use root cause analysis, so that we can eliminate the sources, not the symptoms. This practice is often underestimated and not respected, which results in the occurrence of the same problems all the time. Such an approach is contradictory to the TDT approach which focuses on rational process improvements and effective actions that bring added, not subtracted, value.

- TDT emphasizes the role and importance of the professional knowledge and the ability to use the abstract models in real situations.
- TDT promotes a balance between an engineering and a 'soft' approach. In some situations an engineering approach works just fine, but in others the soft skills will be much more beneficial. This is especially true when dealing with people, organization, processes, introducing the change, improving something, etc. Here, the pure engineering approach will almost certainly fail.

Let us be clear on one thing: TDT itself isn't any revolutionary approach. When you study the rest of the book you will notice that it just uses or creatively combines many other, well-known methods. Some of them are just fitted to the domain of software testing and quality. The most important thing is to be aware of them and to convince ourselves that these methods just work. It just requires a bit of courage to go away from the usual, hackneyed ways of doing things. In many cases they simply don't work or at least are very ineffective. Sometimes the reason is that people use these techniques unthinkingly. The primary role of the TDT approach is *to change your thinking*. Once you do this, you will take the first step to achieve the mastery in testing.

3.3 Universal Rules

In the testing profession there is no silver bullet and no snake oil. Each and every project we are working on is completely different from all the others, even if they look very similar. You always need to approach them individually. Each project will require its own analysis, test approach and selection of tools and techniques. The real tester's wisdom is to know exactly *what and when to do in given circumstances*. However, regardless of the problem you are working on, there are some universal rules that apply to all testing projects. Here they are:

1. Know your client's needs.
2. Know where you are.
3. Know your enemies (faults).
4. Be reasonable and professional.
5. Be optimal.
6. Don't give up.
7. Think!

3.3.1 Know Your Client's Needs

You test for your client, not for yourself. Remember that from the customer point of view the software you are testing is just a tool. The software itself has absolutely no value for a client—his *business goal* has. Your real aim is not a software without bugs, but a client satisfaction obtained by reaching his business goal. The system thinking skills, promoted by the TDT manifesto, allow us to understand deeply the relations between the client's expectations, software development processes and the final software quality. They help us to relate the quality to the level of the client's needs fulfillment. Initiative and courage—another TDT manifesto postulate—allows us to maintain the good relations with the clients and developers. Such an approach makes them feel that we attend individually to their needs and expectations.

For discovering the client's needs the teams usually follow the process of the requirements acquisition and specification. But instead of starting with asking the client about the consecutive functionalities he needs, a way much better idea is to ask him first the following questions:

- what is the business problem?
- what are the reasons that he's not able to solve this problem on his own?
- how would an ideal solution look and in what way would it be beneficial to the customer?
- are there any potential solutions that already exist (for example, owned by the competitors)?

The first question allows us to get to the root cause of the whole project. We should discover the real, business need. Only then we may start to collect more detailed requirements. When we understand the business goal, we will be able to provide good system and acceptance tests. Of course, the requirements are gathered by the requirements engineers, but the tester needs to understand them, because only then she understands the real business need the client has. The tester also needs to look at the requirements critically, because they are also subject to a quality control.

The second question forces the client to justify the reason he wants to use software for solving his problem. Sometimes it may happen that the problem lies somewhere else and has nothing to do with software or automating things. Talking about this issue may allow us to gather non-functional requirements as well. Instead of asking 'what should be the maximal allowed time for performing function X', which is a very abstract and hard to answer question, we may talk—using a business language—and discover such needs indirectly.

The third question creates the opportunity for a client to be creative and tell us about the ideal product. This vision should then be the definition of perfection that we should strive for. Of course, in most cases it will be impossible to build an ideal software, but at least we will have a clearly defined goal. From a tester's point of view, it may also help to define the quality measures as the differences between the real and the ideal product characteristics.

The last question helps the client to express his needs. If there already is a competitive product in the market, we may ask our client to what extent it fulfills his needs and expectations, what is missing and what is redundant. It is always easier for a client to refer to the existing, real product, than to plans, prototypes and models. This competitive product may act as a kind of a prototype, except that we don't need to waste time and money on building it. Also, the client may precisely tell us which of its parts, functions and characteristics may be adapted in our product, which should be modified and in which way and so on.

Having discussed the above-mentioned issues, it is much easier to define and model both functional and non-functional requirements for the product. We may even already have some quality metrics defined. When there's no particular client identified (for example, we create a commercial off-the-shelf product) the situation is more complicated. In such a case, it is good to have a sample of potential product clients and discuss all the above questions with them. The only difference is that it is we who define (in a general way) the business goal for these potential clients.

Example

A restaurant wants us to create for them an e-order application, so that their clients may order food on the Internet.

The business need: to make the order process simpler and more reliable (for now it's done by phone, which takes the restaurant's employees time; also many errors happen, for example the person that takes orders misunderstands the address or the dishes ordered); another goal is to minimize costs of the delivery.

The reasons that the restaurant is not able to do it on their own: they need software so that their application is easily accessible and may be used on different devices: desktop computers, smartphones or tablets. With the application it will also be easier to manage all the promotions, discounts and loyalty programs.

The ideal solution: a client logs in to the app, his address is known, as the client provided it during the registration, so he doesn't need to waste time for entering it (there is always an option to send the order to a different address). After logging in the client sees the menu and current offers, discounts and promotions. All promotions are calculated automatically. A dish is ordered by clicking on it. At the bottom of the page there's a 'finalize order' button. After pushing it the client gets the message that his order has been sent and is now processed. There is a possibility to cancel the order within 1 min after placing the order.

Sample conclusions: the business goal suggests that the application should be simple, usable, easy to learn and available for as many different devices as possible. So we expect to be asked for the thorough usability and combinatorial tests (different models of different devices). The important business goal is to minimize the ordering process and delivery time. Hence, it will be extremely important to test well the module for defining and optimizing the caterer's routes. Also, as the application will be the main way of communication with the restaurant, it should be reliable and safe—the company image heavily depends on this. So, we will have to focus as well on the security and reliability testing.

3.3.2 Know Where You Are

The professional tester always knows where she is in the testing process. It is easy to verify: whenever we ask her the following questions, she should always give us a satisfying, reasonable answer. The example questions are:

- why are you testing this function now (and why not earlier or later)?
- what exactly are you testing (what is the primary reason of the test actions)?
- why are you using this particular testing technique?
- what should not be tested and why?
- what are your available resources for this task?
- how much time do you have for performing this activity and how much time you expect to spend on it?
- what exactly are your responsibilities now in this area?
- how does the testing environment look and why is it necessary?
- is there any documentation, design, software model that could be used in your analysis and test case design?

A good tester is able to explain and justify every single action she undertakes, which requires a very strong critical thinking and system thinking skills mentioned in the TDT manifesto. It is extremely important, because conscious, logically related actions are more effective than unplanned, ad-hoc undertaken activities. Also, knowing where we are allows us to estimate the current quality level and other project-related metrics, like: expected time to completion, expected effort, estimated number of residual defects and so on. Of course, this quantitative process description is possible only when we are able to gather metrics about the product and the test activities. We expand this topic in Sect. 5.

Another important thing that helps us to 'know where we are' is the business domain knowledge which the SUT is working in. This makes it easier to understand *why* we test. And knowing 'why' we also know 'how' we should test. The same problem may require completely different test approaches, when the business circumstances are different.

> **Example**
> Recall the e-order system from the previous subsection. Imagine now that this is a 'diet box' restaurant, where a client receives several meals on a daily basis, according to a predefined diet. Now, it is obvious that this is a completely different system than the normal restaurant. The clients have to be registered, as they stay in the system for a long time—they do not order meals occasionally. The system should be more client-focused. Also, the reliability will have a lower priority, as the system requests will happen less frequently: after registering and setting up his own diet, a client receives his meals every day

(continued)

without any interaction with the system. The application may also have a much more complicated interface: a client will use the app only once, but will spend much time defining his own diet program. Much attention should be paid to the date/time issues: the clients may prefer different delivery time. This should be taken into account when testing the module for the caterer's route optimization. The testing activities will therefore have different priorities and intensiveness than in the former e-order application.

3.3.3 Know Your Enemies (Faults)

Before you act, create a fault model (even if it is only in your mind and even if it is very general) and follow it. It is much easier to find something when you know what you are searching for. Having the beforehand defined error model allows us also to work in a more methodic manner and to provide stronger, non-redundant tests. Creativeness, promoted by the TDT manifesto, may help you in providing better, more realistic models.

In Sect. 2.6 we indicated three typical sources of error model: direct models (describing the error itself), error models defined within software models, and indirect error models resulting from specification and expected software behavior. We will show now their practical use.

Example
Recall the e-order shop from Sect. 3.1. Here are a few examples of the direct error models:

1. Force all possible error messages to occur.
2. Improper handling of a non-standard character set.
3. Input buffer overflow.
4. Force abnormal interruption and check if system is able to recover.

When using the first model, we may search for all exceptions that are implemented (or documented) and try to induce them to occur. We may check if they are handled correctly. For the second model, we may use 'weird' or special characters for the form fields, as well as in the text files (including their naming) processed by the SUT. In case of the third error model we should try to exceed allowed sizes of different structures (length, numerical value, physical object size, etc.), like form fields. The fourth model may be applied by closing the website when logged, and opening it again. This way

(continued)

we may check if the session is restored properly when an abnormal termination occurs.

As for the indirect models, we should first define the expected SUT behavior for different scenarios. The scenarios may emerge from the functional specification. The general, coarse-grained scenarios may be refined, or more detailed sub-scenarios may be derived from a high-level scenario. For example, we may define and refine the following high-level scenarios for our e-order system:

1. Registration process (client).
   (a) Registering a new client living in the admissible area.
   (b) Registering a new client living in the non-admissible area.
2. Ordering process (client).
   (a) Simple order without any discounts and promotions.
   (b) More complicated order with a discount/promotion.
3. Client data processing (operator).
   (a) Blacklisting the client.
   (b) Sending a promotional e-mail message.

For each scenario, we may check the 'happy path', that is, if the system works as expected for a given use case. This way we check if there are any process-level errors. An example of such a test case for the case 2a above may look like as follows:

1. Log in as a valid user [this may be the separate test case, 'logging in'].
2. Check if all dishes are available in the menu.
3. Pick one dish twice. Check the total price.
4. Remove both items from the basket. Check if the total price = 0.
5. Pick another dish twice. Check the total price.
6. Pick another dish. Check the total price.
7. Place order. Check if the confirmation message appears and if the order is processed by the restaurant.

Notice that the above, 'happy path' scenario checks several things. First, it ensures us that we are able to use the login function. Second, that the menu is available and is up to date. Third, that we may order more than one item of a given dish. Fourth, that it is possible to empty the basket. Fifth, that it is possible to order two different dishes with different cardinalities. Sixth, that we are allowed to perform a sequence of different actions on a basket.

The third type of error model is the one that lies within a software model. For example, a model may describe the business logic of calculating the discount. It may be a simple model in a form of a decision table, but it may

(continued)

also be a much more complicated model. Suppose it is defined in a textual way as follows:

For every tenth order a client gets 5% discount from the total price. Additionally, if the total price (after applying the possible 5% discount) exceeds $100, the client gets $8 for the next order. When calculating the total discount, this value is subtracted from the total price first, before the 5% discount is applied. If a discount exceeds the total price, the total price is set to $0.

How can we use this requirement for deriving the possible error models when checking discount evaluation functionality in the SUT? The first thing we can do as the testers, is to think of how the discount is calculated in the system. We may imagine that it looks like the process shown in Fig. 3.2. *TotalPrice* is the total value of the order before any discount rules are applied. The value *T*, at the end of the process (gray rectangle) gives the actual price with all possible discounts applied.

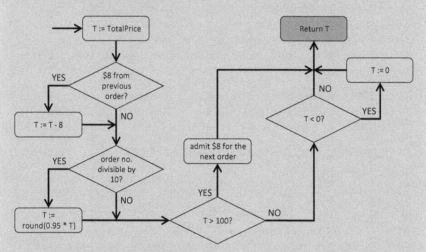

Fig. 3.2 Flowchart for discount evaluation

Notice, that in practice the algorithm may be realized in many different ways. There may be a different control flow, there may be other variables used and so on. Nevertheless, our model abstracts from the implementation details and focuses only on the *logic* of the whole procedure. No matter how the algorithm is implemented, it should follow the logic described by our model. How should we derive the tests from this model, so that each of them will check some type of a possible error in the business logic? We may put it in another way: how should we check, if the SUT conforms to the model, that is, works exactly as the model says?

The first idea may be to check all possible paths from the beginning to the end. As we have four decisions going from the beginning to the decision

(continued)

'$T > 100$?', and each of them may be extended in three different ways ($T > 100$, $T \leq 100$ and $T < 0$, $T \leq 100$ and $T \geq 0$), we have $4 \times 3 = 12$ different paths. The two last decisions deal with the numerical value of a variable T, so we may also, at the same time, check the boundary values. That is, for the decision $T > 100$ we will try to provide two test cases: in the first one, when checking this decision, the T value will be $100 (the largest value for which the condition does not hold), and in the second one—$100.01 (the smallest value for which the condition holds). Similarly, for the decision $T < 0$ we should provide test cases with values $T = -0.01$ and $T = 0$. Such 'boundary value' errors happen surprisingly often.

To calculate these values we need to perform a 'reverse analysis'. For example, if we want $T = 100$ in the decision $T > 100$, and we assume that both $8 and 5% discounts were applied, the *TotalPrice* should be such that $round((TotalPrice - 8) \cdot 0.95) = 100$, where *round* rounds the argument to the nearest number with two decimal digits, as the smallest currency value is $0.01. Also, the number of the order should be divisible by 10, because only then the 5% discount is applied. From the equation we have that *TotalPrice* = $113.26. In a similar way we can calculate the input value for the other cases.

Table 3.1 Test cases derived from the discount calculation model

No.	TotalPrice	$8 used?	5% used?	T after discounts	T > 100?	T < 0?	Returned T	$8 for the next order?
1	0	NO	NO	**0**	NO	NO	0	NO
2	-4.12 (?)	NO	NO	-4.12 (?)	NO	YES	0 (?)	NO
3	123.57	NO	NO	123.57	YES	NO	123.57	YES
4	105.26	NO	YES	**100.00**	NO	NO	100	NO
5	-200 (?)	NO	YES	(?)	NO	YES	(?)	NO
6	105.27	NO	YES	**100.01**	YES	NO	100.01	YES
7	8	YES	NO	**0**	NO	NO	0	NO
8	7.99	YES	NO	**-0.01**	NO	YES	0	NO
9	108.01	YES	NO	**100.01**	YES	NO	100.01	YES
10	113.26	YES	YES	**100.00**	NO	NO	100	NO
11	7.98	YES	YES	**-0.01**	NO	YES	0	NO
12	1008	YES	YES	950	YES	NO	950	YES

Table 3.1 presents all 12 test cases. The bolded numbers in the central column denote the boundary values for the conditions $T > 100$ and $T < 0$. We may not be able to perform tests 2 and 5, because the application may not allow us to force the negative total price before applying the discounts.

So, we might end up with these 12 (or 10) test cases. But we can further analyze the problem. First, under some conditions, the application gives $8 for

(continued)

the next order. We should definitely check this, so we should design a test scenario composed with two test cases: the first one should end up with $8 admission, and the second one should check, if this discount is applied. Notice, that here we want to *isolate* the $8 discount: we are not interested in 5% discount. This isolation is important—imagine that the following error may happen: $8 discount does not occur, but 5% is wrongly applied, and the final price is correct. It may happen if $TotalPrice - 8 = 0.95 \cdot TotalPrice$, that is, if $TotalPrice = \$160$. Such a situation is called *fault masking*—one fault (incorrect applying of 5% discount) is masked by another one (not applying $8 discount). In result, we are not be able to tell which discount was applied, if only one of them was used. Therefore, to avoid such a situation, for this test scenario we have to choose *TotalPrice* different than 160!

Another question is about the ordering of discount application. Usually the different order in applying $8 and 5% discounts gives different results. But is there a *TotalPrice* value for which the ordering does not affect the final result? A quick calculation shows, that it is impossible, because $(x - 8) \cdot 0.95 \neq x \cdot 0.95 - 8$ for all x. So we don't have to take care about this issue.

Suppose now that 12 test cases from Table 3.1 is too much: tests run slowly and we don't have time for executing all of them. Formal test design techniques provide us a wide variety of so-called coverage criteria for the models. They usually form a reasonable trade-off between the number of test cases and the power of the test case suite. For example, in our model we may require to cover not all the paths, but only all decision outcomes. We have four decisions in our control flow: '$8 from previous order?', 'order no. divisible by 10?', '$T > 100?$' and '$T < 0?$'. Only two tests are enough for covering all these decisions outcomes, for example tests 6 and 8 from Table 3.1. Notice, however, the trade-off here: we reduced the test case suite to only two tests, but, for example, we are not able to check all the boundary values for decisions '$T > 100?$' and '$T < 0?$'.

The above example shows how the formal test design techniques allow us to derive error models (here, related to the computational logic for discount calculation) and systematically cover all of them by using a formal coverage criterion. Remember, however, that formal test design techniques, although being a very strong tool, provide very specific and limited error models. You shouldn't rely *solely* on these techniques. A good tester knows exactly where he will benefit from the formal techniques, and when they will be only an obstacle.

Of course, we may blend the strategies and combine all three above-mentioned error models. For example, we may take a given scenario, like 'place an order' (indirect error model), refine it regarding a given software model, like the discount calculation model in a form of the control-flow described above, and finally use a model error, like 'force boundary value errors', by applying inputs that force different boundary values in the internal decisions of the control flow.

3.3.4   Be Reasonable and Professional

Although testing may seem to be an art rather than technical craft, it has strong scientific foundations. Also, it is a part of software engineering. Therefore, good testing requires an engineering approach. This means that you have to be *reasonable* in what you are doing. Of course, there are situations in which we have to utilize our experience, imagination or even gut feeling. But even these actions need to be rationally explainable.

Do something only when you understand what you are doing and why you are doing this. You should always be able to answer questions like 'what is the purpose of this thing you have just done?' and explain it in a professional, comprehensible way. If someone asks you to do something, and you don't understand why should you do this, ask about it. If you hesitate, discuss the issue with your colleagues. You must always be convinced that what you are doing makes sense. Only then you will be effective.

Below we give a few, more specific suggestions for testers that endeavor to become professionals in the field. They fit well in the 'skills over tools' part of the TDT manifesto.

- communicate in professional way—do not attack personally other people, do not use *argumentum ad personam*—it always ends in a war;
- base your opinions on pure facts, data and numbers, but be human in the way you communicate your statements;
- use logical thinking—it is surprising that many people don't do this; if you don't feel comfortable in this area, you may read some great books on this topic (for example [69], where the author also discusses many popular logical fallacies in reasoning);
- think outside the box and don't just follow the crowd—the fact that almost everyone automates everything doesn't mean that it will always be beneficial in your project;
- remember that effectiveness is much more important than forms and ceremonies, but remember also that sometimes forms and ceremonies support effectiveness!

3.3.5   Be Optimal and Always Bring Added Value

Do only things that bring added value to the product's quality. Your time is valuable—don't waste it. There are some crucial areas in which the eagerness for optimality may bring a huge benefit, but making a mistake may cause a serious harm to the project or people involved in it. These are:

- documentation,
- automation,
- test optimization.

The problem with documentation was described in detail in Sect. 2.8. It is very important to remember that the documentation is useful, when it is constantly used. Every document that will be read only by its author is useless and creating it is just a waste of time.

Automation is usually associated with a lot of both initial and recurring work (setting up the environment, buying tools, writing and maintaining scripts and so on). Introducing the automation to the project is a serious decision and should be preceded by a very detailed analysis. The analysis should answer the following questions:

- what areas of the process are about to be automated?
- what are the initial costs of introducing the automation project?
- what are the recurring costs of automation?
- how often will we use the automated tests?
- will the quality of the automated tests be lower/the same/greater than in the case of the manual tests?
- will we need additional manual tests, or will the automated suite be just enough?
- what is the ROI (Return on Investment) of the automation project and when will the gains outrank the costs?

All authors say that the automation should relieve testers of doing tedious, repetitive work. This is of course a trivial observation. But there is a thing way more important to realize: *the time we save should not be spent completely on maintaining the automation process.* This time should be spent for additional, manual testing and analytical work done by testers. Automated tests are 'stupid' in the sense that they always check the same thing. They usually form the regression test suite. But as the product evolves, there is a need for new analyses and new, efficient tests.

Test optimization may be performed on different levels:

- **single test optimization**—designing the tests such that a small number of them is able to test many different characteristics and aspects of the SUT;
- **test suite reduction**—reducing the number of executed tests (especially the regression suites that tend to grow very fast) while keeping the trade-off between the test set size and the ability of this set to detect defects;
- **process-level optimization**—by eliminating the redundant, unnecessary or useless steps and activities within a process (for example: does the regular status meeting bring any added value to the project? Are there documents/process in the organization with the high cost in maintainability, which are not used by anyone?, etc.).

Example

The simplest way to check if introducing the automation is a good idea, is to perform a ROI (Return On Investment) analysis. The general formula for the ROI is

$$ROI = \frac{benefit}{costs} = \frac{gain - costs}{costs}.$$

To calculate ROI properly we need to express both gain and costs in terms of the same unit (usually it's money). The factors that should be considered when calculating ROI are:

- test efficiency—the number of tests that can be executed in a given unit of time; the gain here comes from saving money by not executing these tests manually,
- test effectiveness—the rate of finding bugs; the more bugs found by tests, the lower the costs of fixing the field defects,
- time-to-market—the faster the product is delivered, the faster we will make money on the product,
- time spent on writing and maintaining scripts—expressed in terms of the man-days costs,
- time spent on solving technical problems—expressed in terms of the man-days costs,
- costs of the automated test execution (usually close to 0),
- initial and recurring costs related to tools—tool acquisition, license costs, trainings, etc.

One of the important gains, frequently omitted by publications describing the ROI analysis for the test automation, is the fact that automation gives testers the time that can be spent on performing manual tests, but *different than the tests they would execute if there was no automation*. Without automation, the testers would just execute the same tests that are subject to automation. However, when we automate them, testers have time to perform *other* tests. This time may be spent not only on additional manual tests, exploratory sessions and other experience-based techniques, but also on additional documentation analysis, more careful test design or even on introducing new forms and paradigms of testing, like model-based testing or mutation testing.

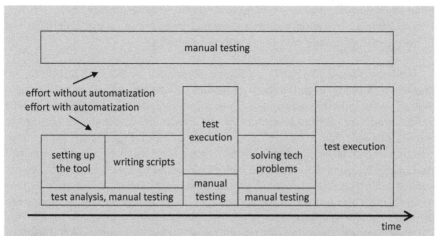

Fig. 3.3 Symbolic comparison between automated and purely manual testing process

Figure 3.3 symbolically presents the ROI analysis for an automation project. It compares the effort with and without test automation. The height of the gray rectangles represents the number of executed tests. As we can see, the automation project inherently requires some costs not present in manual testing, but it may be beneficial if the above-mentioned gains outperform these costs.

3.3.6 Ask the Right Questions and Don't Be Afraid of Asking

The ability to ask the right questions is far from being trivial. It requires experience, but also a deep understanding of where we are and what we are doing. A 'right' question is one such that answering it requires a conscious and critical analysis. Such questions are usually unobvious and posing them often leads to inspirational discussions and finding new, effective solutions.

There is another benefit of asking the right questions. It is similar to the so-called rubber duck debugging, where the programmer debugs the code by explaining every step to the rubber duck. The sole act of explaining, even if done to the inanimate object, often leads to hitting upon the solution. Asking the other team member with a good question is the similar 'trigger' of creative and critical thinking.

There are different types of 'right questions'. Here are some examples:

- a question for knowledge acquisition—just to get some knowledge from somebody else,
- a question for understanding something,
- a Socratic question—to probe someone's thinking, to help others to distinguish between what they know from what they don't know, to convince someone that he made a mistake in reasoning

- an inspirational question—to unleash creativity, critical thinking, etc.
- a 'confirming' question—to make sure that everyone is on the same page and everyone understands things in exactly the same way.

The tester should also have the courage—promoted by the TDT manifesto—to question everything, even the 'holy methodics', if she has any doubt on the effectiveness of the criticized matter. The big problem in the IT world is the 'fashionable trends', which are uncritically accepted by the community. For example, there are no convincing, scientific evidences that a stand-up meeting in Scrum is the most effective when it takes *exactly* 15 min. Maybe for some teams 20 min will be better? And maybe rejecting the idea of these meetings would be even a better idea? Every team and every project is unique. A professional tester knows that *in quality there is no snake oil*. There is no universal approach to testing and never will be. And, since the tester's role is to ensure the best possible product quality, this is the reason why she must question everything that may be the obstacle to achieving the full success. Even if this is a well-defined, widely used technique or so-called 'best-practice'. The only way to check if something is good for the project, is the recognition in battle: if it works, it's good. If not, it should be replaced by something else. As simple as that. For a tester, nothing is sacred (except the quality!).

3.3.7 Don't Give Up

Never give up. Remember that every problem has a solution. Use all the available tools, methods and techniques that can be applied in a given situation. If you can't solve the problem by yourself, search in the literature. If you cannot find the solution in the literature, ask other people to help you. If no one is able to help you, organize a brainstorming session, seminar, etc. Such meetings boost up the creativity in the team and probably the solution, later or earlier, will emerge.

The concept of never giving up should be also applied to the task of bug finding: you should never give up when searching for a bug. It is important to remember that if a tester doesn't find any bug, he fails. Professional testers almost always find at least one bug in a testing session. This is because they are not only creative, but they also know many different testing techniques and can apply them efficiently. That's why a constant education and self-development is so important. We talk a little bit more about this in Sects. 8 and 10, where we give simple, practical hints on how to effectively learn the tester profession.

3.3.8 Think

'THINK' is a slogan first coined by Thomas J. Watson in 1911. Three years later he brought it with him to IBM, which, by the way, still uses it as its trademark. When asked about what he meant by the slogan, Watson replied: 'By THINK I mean take everything into consideration' [70].

This motto perfectly fits the professional tester's mindset. Testers should always take every possible factor into consideration. To discover the possibly hidden ones, testers should use their communication skills, 'trust no one' attitude and 'asking the right questions' skills. The problem is that usually there are many factors that impact quality. Hence, testers need to use thinking skills again (in this case—analytical thinking) in order to reduce and prioritize the tests. Finally, when executing the tests, testers need to be able to distinguish between correct and incorrect SUT behavior, which often is far from being trivial.

Taking everything into consideration can be also interpreted in the following way: before you start solving the problem, think about it. Analyze it. Consider different approaches, their pros and cons. Think about all possible consequences of your future decisions. As an academic teacher I often observe the students, who were just given the problem, immediately go to the computer and start coding. They don't do any plans, they don't think about the problem. They don't *abstract* it, which might help them to find the optimal solution. The effect is usually a poor, not very effective solution (if any!). Students (and also the employees) make this fundamental mistake: they want to take a shortcut. They start with the problem formulation, omit the analytical part of the problem solving process, and immediately start the implementation phase. Such an approach is a sure way to failure.

Apple's motto till 2002 was 'Think different'. Some people say it was referring to IBM's slogan. Nevertheless, this is another good motivational example: when designing tests, testers should think out-of-the-box. The more creative they are, the more 'different' thinking in their minds is, the more effective their job is.

The big problem is that acting is visible, and thinking is not. This may be the reason why the management likes so much the concrete effects of our work (reports, scripts, pieces of code and so on) and underestimates the analytical part of the process. Every responsible and reliable test/QA manager should convince the management that if they want to achieve a *really* good product quality, thinking is indispensable.

3.4   There's No Such Thing as 'Automation Tester'

Labels like 'software engineer in test', 'agile tester', 'test automation engineer', 'test developer' suggest that there are different 'kinds of testing'. But there is only one testing. The labels just describe a particular technique, skill, or put the testing in the SDLC context ('agile tester').

The emphasis that nowadays is put on test automation does harm to the testing craft. There is a serious problem with this issue. Don't get me wrong—test automation skills are very important and every tester should be familiar with them. But we cannot restrict test activities only to automation. When you look at the testing conferences programmes, or when you read blogs, web pages or professional literature on testing, you may have an impression that testing=automating. And many candidates to the testing profession think that testing is about writing automated tests.

Of course, this is wrong. The most important thing in testing is *thinking, analyzing and creating good, effective tests*. It always works in the same way, no matter what

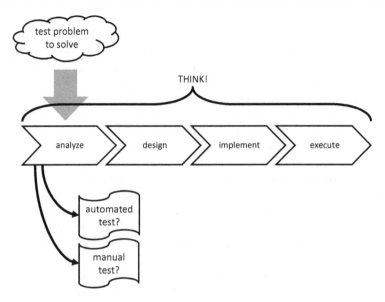

Fig. 3.4 The correct sequence of test creation process

development process we are following and what type of the tools we are using. Of course, some tests will be more effective when automated, but the correct sequence of action, depicted in Fig. 3.4, is: think, analyze, design, and finally implement and execute—not the other way around! The decision about whether to automate anything (remember that we can automate not only test execution, but also test data generation, test implementation and, in some cases, even the test design!) should be a result of the analysis. It should never blindly follow the arbitrary ideology.

Quality people like to distinguish between 'manual' and 'automated' tester. Notice that programmers don't say that they are 'automatic developers'—they are just 'developers'. Coding is just their work, and the programming language is their tool, not a *role*. Programming is an intellectual work and a piece of code is just the record of this process. The same is with testers—they are not 'manual testers' or 'automatic testers'—they are just *testers*. No matter whether the testers write scripts or perform manual tests, this is just the record of the intellectual process, and prior to the execution, the test had to be *thought* by a human. There is absolutely no reason for distinguishing between scripting skills—we could as well speak about 'static technique testers' and 'dynamic testers'; 'integration testers', 'system testers' and 'acceptance testers'; and so on. It just makes no sense.

The whole problem with automation comes probably from the fact, that the testing profession is still not 'formalized'. There is no one, typical career path (studies, courses, etc.) for a person who wants to become a tester. Testers come from many different areas and they graduate from many different fields: science, humanities, engineering. Probably, in the future the software testing studies will become more popular. The curriculum will obviously cover not only the testing theory, test design techniques, and software engineering fundamentals, but also the courses in programming. Then, the artificial and nonsensical split between 'manual' and 'automatic' will finally disappear.

The moral from this story is very simple: learn tools, learn how to write scripts and automate tests, but remember what is the essence of the testing craft. It's thinking, not coding.

3.5   Dimensions of Testing and Process Measurement

Testing can be performed in an infinite number of ways. However, we want to choose the best one, because we want our test process to be as effective as possible. It is impossible to guess or to infer the optimal approach. Of course, analytical thinking is a big support here, but we still need to proceed in a trial-and-error manner in order to find, if not the best one, at least some suboptimal solution.

When we look at the process improvement methods like Six Sigma [71], DRIVE,[2] etc., we can easily notice that all of them are just different versions of the simple, standard, iterative PDCA cycle, also known as Deming or Shewhart cycle (see the left part of Fig. 3.5).

The concept of PDCA cycle is based on the scientific method, where we make some hypothesis, do the experiment, collect data, and validate our claim. If it's supported by the data, the hypothesis becomes a theory. The theory should be able to predict future behavior of the system. If the data does not support our hypothesis, it may be refuted or modified, to fit better to the observed data. The whole process is repeated in a cycle, which enables us to constantly improve our theory.

Testing is not an exception here. In order to evaluate any theory about the testing process—its effectiveness, economic profitability, etc.—we need to do some measurements. Analysis of the metrics allows us to evaluate the current state of the process, our approach to testing, and also to show the possible ways of its improvement.

The metric-related activities in the PDCA cycle are shown in the right part of Fig. 3.5. In the 'Plan' phase we define the metrics that should be tracked, and we may also define their baselines, that is—their acceptable values. This is important, because the process should be *controlled*. When we compare the real value to the expected one, we see if we are on track or if there are any problems within the process. In the 'Do' phase we just measure what was previously planned to measure. In the 'Check' phase we analyze the results. This part requires the most our analytical skills. Based on the results of our analysis, we introduce the improvements, eliminate root causes of the problems, design new, better solutions and approaches. Finally, in the 'Act' phase, these conclusions are implemented in the process. They may require a modification of the current baselines, but also the introduction of new metrics, which will be done in the next cycle in the 'Do' phase.

---

[2]DRIVE stands for Define, Review, Identify, Verify and Execute. It is a simple and useful technique for problem solving and analysis.

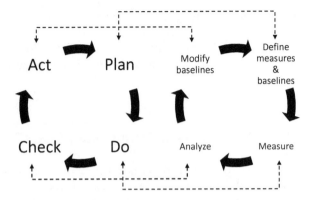

Fig. 3.5 Standard process improvement cycle and its reflection in metrics

The testing process is a very complicated system. How to choose wisely what to measure? There is a simple and effective approach, called 'Goal-Question-Metric' which may help us with this issue. First, we have to define our goal, for example: 'evaluate the effectiveness of system tests', 'are the code reviews effective?', 'investigate the relation between code coverage and the final quality', etc. Having it precisely defined we think of the questions that should be answered to reach the goal. Next, for each of them we define one or more metrics that should be measured in order to answer the question.

Figure 3.6 presents the general view on the testing project dimensions. It may be helpful for understanding the relations between different parts of the project and for choosing the right metrics. It is important to choose only a small set of metrics, that will allow us to reach the predefined goal. We shouldn't measure everything that is possible, because it takes time, it costs and it is hard to do any meaningful analyses when we have available thousands of metrics.

The model presented in Fig. 3.6 describes two main project entities (the team and the product) crossed with three measurable characteristics (progress, quality and project-related issues). For each entity and characteristic some sample metrics are given. For example, team progress may be represented by the number of tests implemented; product quality may be evaluated through coverage and defect metrics.

The most difficult part of the process/product measurement is the analysis of the results. Many engineers and managers perform something that could be called 'one-dimensional analysis'. For example, they take a report that presents the number of bugs found in the function of time, and reason about the product quality from this report. However, this is just scraping the surface. The reality is *much more* complicated and in order to make valuable and beneficial analyses, we have to dive much deeper. Also, the data analysis is a very slippery slope—see Sects. 6.2, 6.3 and 6.6 for a few examples of data analysis pitfalls.

Every analyst must remember the following basic rules:

- it is impossible to describe the whole process, project or quality by just one metric,

	Progress	Quality	Project related
PRODUCT	product size, requirements implemented, tests executed	test coverage, reqs coverage, # field bugs, risks, MTTF, MTBF, types of bugs	Mean Time To Repair, cost of defect fixing
TEAM	tests designed/ implemented/ passed/failed/ blocked	test effectiveness (#bugs/#tests, #cov/#tests) etc.	effort (man-hour), cost of work, resource availability

Fig. 3.6 Dimensions of testing project and sample metrics

- metrics are related to each other,
- some phenomena can be properly understood only by analyzing the interactions of the metrics.

There does not exist one, universal metric that could tell us if everything goes OK or not. This is not only because the processes are very complex, but also because many ideas (abstract, like quality or even prosaic such as test progress) are multidimensional. For example, risk level is described usually by two components: likelihood and impact.

Relation between metrics may be very simple. It may come from the fact that one metric directly depends on the others (for example, defect density (DD) is a function of number of defects (ND) and the product size (PS) and is represented as the ratio of the two last ones: $DD = ND/PS$. But this relationship may also be indirect and much more subtle. Let us consider some of the metrics from Fig. 3.6. The relations between them are presented in Fig. 3.7.

A declining chart denotes the negative correlation. This means that the growth of one metric causes an increase of the other. Increasing chart denotes the positive correlation: the growth of one metric causes the growth of the other. For example, the larger number of tests designed requires larger team effort. Better test effectiveness results in lower number of field bugs. Some relations are denoted by both types of correlation, because the proper type depends on how we understand a given metric. Costs and field bugs are correlated positively, when by costs we understand the bug fixing costs. On the other hand, the correlation would be negative, when costs mean prevention and appraisal costs.

But things are even more complicated. The relations from Fig. 3.7 are very simple. They hold caeteris paribus, which means 'with other factors unchanged'. For example, increase of the number of tests may cause the decline in test effectiveness, because tests may be redundant, they may require a long time to execute, there

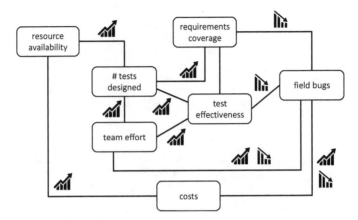

Fig. 3.7 Complicated relationships between metrics

may be many blocking tests and so on. So it is very frequent that the change of one metric may be caused by the interaction of two or more other metrics. Moreover, the relations between metrics are not linear—they may be more complicated.

We may try to investigate these complicated relations, however this requires the knowledge of statistics and mathematical modeling, which is not very common in the typical IT companies. The statistical analysis may show us the exact relations, correlations and interactions between different metrics. We can even build predictive models, which are able to predict the future value of a given metric based on the past values of other metrics. This goes out of the scope of this book, but it is important to realize that advanced math modeling is able to show us much more interesting things than just the surface scratched by simple one-dimensional analyses.

Good testers should be able to represent the overall condition of the process (including the current product quality level) based on the set of metrics. The analysis of different kinds of reports allows us also to perform different types of analysis, including a root cause analysis, for example:

- the distribution of defects split by defect type allows us to optimize the regression test suite and focus on the most error-prone areas of the software,
- the number of defects found may be more helpful, when we analyze it together with coverage metrics and the trend in time,
- the less number of designed tests may be quite normal, when the tests are more complicated and therefore stronger and time consuming, but may indicate a problem, when the test effectiveness remains on the same level,
- the correlation between test coverage, number of defects found and effort may sow a sweet spot that realizes a trade-off between effort and quality.

Example

A test team creates 12 test cases in a week. On average, such a 12-element test suite finds six bugs in the code. The test manager wants the test team to find more bugs. In order to increase the team effectiveness, he sets up a target: increase the productivity and achieve the level of 20 test cases in a week. To mobilize the team, the test manager decides that the bonus will depend on achieving this target. Two weeks later the test manager checks the reports and sees that the target was even exceeded—the test team created 24 test cases for a new code. Unfortunately, this suite found only four bugs. The problem is that people adjust to the measures they are measured by. The test team had to create more tests in the same time and they did it, necessarily sacrificing the test quality. If we want to evaluate the test team, the goal we set for a team must be aligned with the goal we want to achieve in the project. For example, it may be related to the final product quality, test effectiveness, etc.

3.6 Critical Thinking

Peter Facione in his report [72] presents the following consensus statement regarding critical thinking (CT) and the ideal critical thinker:

We understand critical thinking to be purposeful, self-regulatory judgment which results in interpretation, analysis, evaluation, and inference, as well as explanation of the evidential, conceptual, methodological, criteriological, or contextual considerations upon which that judgment is based. CT is essential as a tool of inquiry (...) The ideal critical thinker is habitually inquisitive, well-informed, trustful of reason, open-minded, flexible, fair-minded in evaluation, honest in facing personal biases, prudent in making judgements, willing to reconsider, clear about issues, orderly in complex matters, diligent in seeking relevant information, reasonable in the selection of criteria, focused in inquiry, and persistent in seeking results which are as precise as the subject and the circumstances of inquiry permit.

It is clear that all these features describe an ideal tester, for example:

- **habitual inquisitiveness**—a professional tester always asks questions like 'what can go wrong here?', 'how exactly does it work?', 'why is this piece of software designed this way and not the other?', etc.; the more he knows, the more added value he can bring to the testing process,
- being **well-informed**—a professional tester needs to see the big picture of the software development process and to understand complicated relations between its parts, as well as between the physical parts of the software being developed,
- being **trustful of reason**—software testing is an engineering discipline and all decisions the professional tester makes need to be based upon rational analysis, logic, facts, data and numbers, not our vague beliefs or other kinds of wishful-thinking,

Fig. 3.8 Chart with a plateau for cumulative number of defects found

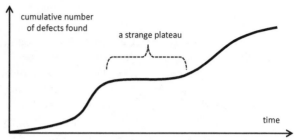

- being **clear about issues**—a professional tester needs to make clear statements, be able to describe the problems and the solutions in a clear, comprehensible way, so that he is understood by other stakeholders.

Let's see how does the critical thinking work in practice. The typical approach to thinking critically about the arguments looks as follows:

1. Recognize the argument—making sure, if there really *is* a problem. Some issues are the apparent problems and do not require any actions to be taken and any problem solving skills involved. For example, if we analyze the chart presenting the cumulative number of defects found and we observe a plateau (see Fig. 3.8) we may immediately start to drill down the data and try to find the root cause that resulted in this phenomenon. But when we recall that the corresponding period of time was... a bank holiday, the 'problem' is immediately solved.
2. Analyze the argument—if there is a problem, why is it so? This part of the process usually requires some analytical skills and often resembles detective work. A tester needs to associate facts, analyze different reports, maybe talk to some people. In result, we should be able to reveal the cause (or, if possible, root cause) of the problem.
3. Evaluate the argument—how serious is the problem? Can it cause a significant risk putting in danger the product, process or project? This part of the analysis allows us to prioritize problems and divide them into the serious ones that should be handled immediately, and the less important that may be left over.
4. Reasoning that should lead us to the solution. There are two main types of reasoning: inductive and deductive.

Deductive reasoning is a 'top-down' approach, where we work from the more general to the more specific. It is a standard, scientific method used to test hypotheses. We start with a general statement (theory) and then we make predictions of its consequences. So, we predict what the observations should be if the theory were correct.

Inductive reasoning is a 'bottom-up' approach. We begin with some specific observations, detect some patterns, basing on them we formulate the hypotheses that can be explored and finally we develop a theory.

Example

There is a general theory in the software quality engineering that the distribution in time of the defects found follows a so-called Rayleigh distribution (see Fig. 3.9). Using this model we predict the number of defects that will be found in the consecutive iterations. Knowing the release date, we may estimate the number of defect fields. This is an example of a deductive reasoning.

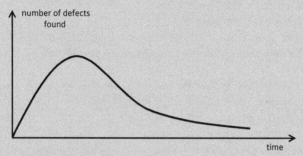

Fig. 3.9 Rayleigh distribution

We gather data on defects from different modules and we see that their distribution is not uniform: the vast majority of defects is concentrated in a low number of modules. The same situation is observed in several other projects. Analyzing this data we state a theory that the defect distribution across the modules follows the Pareto-like distribution (see Fig. 3.10). This is an example of an inductive reasoning.

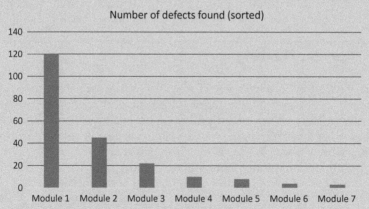

Fig. 3.10 Pareto distribution of the number of defects found

Critical thinking may help us in increasing the test process effectiveness. For example, we may apply the inductive reasoning to the following problem: we have a very large regression test suite which runs for a very long time. Can we reduce the test suite (and therefore make its run-time shorter) without sacrificing the test suite ability to detect bugs? Analyzing the data and the bug reports we may observe that some types of tests, when passed once, pass all the time. We may now apply several strategies:

- remove these tests from the test suite,
- set the lower priority for these tests,
- exclude these tests from the test suite, but execute them less frequently, for example, instead of on a daily basis, execute them once in a week.

Choosing the strategy should be based on the risk level and also taking into account the economic analysis. Critical thinking allows us to approach the problem in a systematic, rational way by clearly defining the problem, the factors that influence the software quality and economy and so on. We make the decision based on data, facts and numbers, having a very clearly defined goal in mind. We also should develop a way to validate our approach, so that our strategies can be evaluated.

Finally, let us notice one very important thing. In Sect. 1.3 we discussed the role and the meaning of a test case. Having discussed the issues on critical thinking we should notice that a *test case may be a formal procedure for critical evaluation*, since it represents the recording of the tester's rational activities aiming to check some aspect of a system. Designing and implementing test cases is a realization of a critical thinking activity, where we ask a question 'what should go wrong with this part of a system?' and answer it by executing the test case.

3.7   Systems Thinking

Systems thinking is a particular way of reasoning, where special attention is put on the analysis of the system as a set of subsystems and relations between them. Understanding the complex, and often non-trivial, relationships within the system allows us to act in an efficient way more than in the case of solving the problems restricting ourselves only to a local, small part of a system.

Smith [73] defines systems thinking in the following way:

Systems Thinking is really just a set of tools, concepts and ideas that can be applied to dealing with messy complex systems. Note that it is not a magic wand or something that solves all of your problems for you. But with a better understanding and discipline of Systems Thinking you will be well equipped to navigate and drive the system in a more aware, intelligent and genuine way in order to achieve a desired outcome and know how you got there.

Systems thinking is a crucial skill for a tester, since the modern way of developing and testing software is very complicated. Many testers, when approaching any kind of test problem, usually find the solution which is 'locally optimal'. The ability to see a big picture of a system allows the tester to find the 'globally optimal' solution and avoid future problems caused by the present actions.

System thinking is one of the most important aspects of Thinking-Driven Testing. It helps us in understanding the purposefulness of many different actions, behaviors and practices. We may analyze them through the system analysis and answer these vital questions: *why* are we doing this? What *real* benefits does it give us? How does it impact other parts of the process? Is it a positive or negative impact? Is the effort-to-effects ratio gainful? If we see that our actions make sense, we stay attached to them. If not, we may abandon the practice and forget it with no regrets.

As we show in Sect. 7.2, thinking is much more important than senseless following of different kinds of 'rules' (methods, procedures, models). A professional tester is not only suspicious about the code and its quality, but questions the very rules as well. Of course, it should be done in a professional way—we cannot criticize something just because. We criticize when we have good, rational arguments against a given idea. We have to be supported by facts, data, logic and reasoning. Systems thinking is one type of rational reasoning.

3.7.1 Eleven Laws of Systems Thinking

Peter Senge in his splendid book 'The Fifth Discipline' [13] defined 11 laws of systems thinking. Let's go through them and see how they may apply to the practical situations that every tester stumbles upon in her everyday work.

1. Today's Problems Come from Yesterday's Solutions When we solve a problem, we interact with the system by introducing some change into it. This change impacts different parts of the system, which may cause other problems that we will have to solve in the future. The solution may result not only in intended, but also unintended consequences. For example, when we always are short on time with our testing and we decide to solve this problem by automating our tests, this may result in the following future issues:

- the test scripts will have to be maintained, which costs and takes time and effort,
- a team may have a false sense of security, believing that the system is tested well, just because the tests are automated, so they won't be motivated to write good, effective manual tests,
- the automated regression test suite will grow over time and at some point it may happen that we don't have time to run all the tests.

2. The Harder You Push, the Harder the System Pushes Back In the language of the systems thinking this phenomenon is called the 'compensating feedback'. The more effort we put in doing something, the stronger the system's reaction. For example, suppose you treat very seriously your quality assurance activities. You want to measure many parameters of the process in order to improve it. Hence, developers and other team members need to fill many additional documents. But they probably won't like it and they will be very reluctant to do that. But even if you make them do this, it may turn out that the time they spent on filling the reports might be much better utilized when used for writing code.

3. Behavior Grows Better Before It Grows Worse It takes some time before the compensating feedback occurs. For example, take the classical situation in testing. You need to execute some number of tests, but due to the tight schedule you are not able to run them all. Hence, you reduce the test suite and do not run some tests. This solution is effective in a short term, because you fit in time. But the tests you did not run might detect some bugs. These bugs may reveal themselves later, causing serious problems.

Another classical problem related to this rule is the so-called 'technical debt'. Quick fixes and ad-hoc created workarounds work pretty well in a short time. But when it comes to the maintenance, suddenly a lot of problems arise.

When we understand this law and apply it in our systems thinking approach, we will be much more willing to bear higher costs for the particular activities in the initial stages of the process. It will just pay off in a long term.

4. The Easy Way Out Usually Leads Back In It is very tempting to use well-known, popular approaches and ways to solve problems. But the reality is much more complicated. Especially in software quality engineering, there are no universal rules, techniques or methods of testing. If there were such, all testing projects would always be successful. There is a nice saying (due to Maslow) illustrating this rule: 'if all you have is hammer, everything looks like a nail'.

To overcome the problem of 'easy ways out' we need to move away from our comfort zone. We also need to change our way of thinking. It is amazing how many managers think in a very naïve, 'one-dimensional' way. They think that improving one parameter in the system will directly translate in the process overall improvement. Their way of thinking represents the left part of Fig. 3.11. The reality is much more complicated (right part of the figure).

A good example illustrating the naïve thinking is the automation project. Managers tend to think this way: 'let's buy tools—we will automate most of the work, be able to fire some testers and save much money'. After acquisition of the tool it turns out that—what a surprise—it must be operated by someone! So, instead of firing, they need to hire another tester. Writing scripts takes some time. Testers are not very familiar with programming, so they need to be trained. It takes time and it

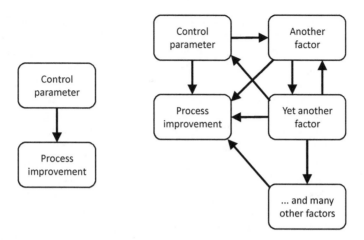

Fig. 3.11 Naïve and real representation of the relations between process parameters

costs. When they study, they don't test. The tool maintenance also isn't for free. And tech support. And the licenses. And so on, and so on. At the end of the day, it turns out that we bear much higher costs than before the automation project. Managers who think linearly: 'higher automation = better testing' don't notice many other factors that influence the team effectiveness.

Another example is related to formal test design techniques. Because they are formal and described in many academic textbooks, they seem to be important, wise, universal and effective. When we see code like this:

```
if (isValid(x) and x.age > 20) then
     doSometing()
else
     doSomethingElse()
```

and we think about the ways we could test this piece of code, many testers familiar with formal test design techniques involuntarily think about things like statement coverage. The resulting solution is something like "we need two tests for this code: one should execute the 'doSomething' part and another one 'doSomethingElse'". Testers with more advanced knowledge may wish to apply a more sophisticated technique, for example decision coverage or path coverage.

However, wouldn't it make sense to ask about the semantics of the code before designing any tests? Shouldn't the tester know what this code is for, what it really does and so on? What if this is some critical part of the software that needs to work fast, but computing the `isValid()` function takes more time than it should? What if there should not be the 'doSomethingElse' part, because the documentation was just wrong about it? Surprisingly, many testers, when asked about the problem like this, don't even ask *any* question to clarify the problem—they immediately apply a known white-box technique, just because the problem involves a source code.

5. The Cure Can Be Worse than the Disease The cure may be quite harmful, when we apply the simple solution and then get addicted to it. A good example may be hiring consultants instead of training the managers to face the problems by themselves. Hiring a specialist that is able to solve our problem is very tempting. It's easy, it's effective and it's not our responsibility anymore. The result is that the company hires consultants even for simple problems that could be solved by the company's employees at hand. The organization indeed gets addicted to consultants. There is absolutely no know-how in the company, team members don't have an opportunity to learn new things and to gain experience by solving the real problems.

Another example concerns the concept of coverage. Suppose the code coverage by our tests is around 70%. The management wants to increase the effectiveness of the testing process, that is, they want more bugs to be detected. They decide that this may be achieved by setting a 90% code coverage goal. Achieving this level of coverage may be not only difficult (so time consuming), but also purposeless. The code parts that are not covered may be related to some weird and not important exception handling, the fragments that are very difficult to reach (thus, they will probably never be executed after the release) or even the dead code. Testers may spend a lot of time trying to increase the coverage, but the effect will be only a set of weak, unnecessary tests. This time might be consumed for creating really important tests for other parts/characteristics of the system. The result? More field bugs and more problems.

6. Faster Is Slower Every process has its own, optimal tempo. Testing is a very good example here. Testing detects bugs which are often caused by developers who were in a rush. When people work under pressure, they are stressed and make mistakes. So, if we want to detect bugs, we cannot do it in a rush—careless testing just won't find them.

The story below is a literal confirmation of this rule.

Example
The story comes from http://darwinawards.com/darwin/darwin1995-04.html:

> The Arizona Highway Patrol were mystified when they came upon a pile of smoldering wreckage embedded in the side of a cliff rising above the road at the apex of a curve. The metal debris resembled the site of an airplane crash, but it turned out to be the vaporized remains of an automobile. The make of the vehicle was unidentifiable at the scene. (. . .) It seems that a former Air Force sergeant had somehow got hold of a JATO (Jet Assisted Take-Off) unit. JATO units are solid fuel rockets used to give heavy military transport airplanes an extra push for take-off from short airfields. Dried desert lakebeds are the location of choice for breaking the world ground vehicle speed record. The sergeant took the JATO unit into the Arizona desert and found a long, straight stretch of road. He attached the JATO unit to his car, jumped in, accelerated to a high speed, and fired off the rocket. (. . .)

(continued)

The operator was driving a 1967 Chevy Impala. He ignited the JATO unit approximately 3.9 miles from the crash site. This was established by the location of a prominently scorched and melted strip of asphalt. The vehicle quickly reached a speed of between 250 and 300 mph and continued at that speed, under full power, for an additional 20–25 s. The soon-to-be pilot experienced G-forces usually reserved for dog-fighting F-14 jocks under full afterburners. The Chevy remained on the straight highway for approximately 2.6 miles (15–20 s) before the driver applied the brakes, completely melting them, blowing the tires, and leaving thick rubber marks on the road surface. The vehicle then became airborne for an additional 1.3 miles, impacted the cliff face at a height of 125 feet, and left a blackened crater 3 feet deep in the rock. Most of the driver's remains were not recovered; however, small fragments of bone, teeth, and hair were extracted from the crater, and fingernail and bone shards were removed from a piece of debris believed to be a portion of the steering wheel.

Ironically a still-legible bumper sticker was found, reading 'How do you like my driving? Dial 1-800-EAT-SHIT.'

7. Cause and Effect Are Not Closely Related in Time and Space People tend to assume that effect occurs immediately after a cause happens. Unfortunately, in most cases this is not true. Therefore, when we want to improve the process, we have to be patient and we need to bear in mind that there will be some delay before the results of our actions will be visible.

The same mechanism works when a problem occurs and we want to find the cause. There are different techniques for performing a root cause analysis. For example, in a '5 whys' technique we ask the 'why' question until we won't be able to reasonably answer another 'why' question, and the last answer probably indicates a root cause. Consider the following scenario: QA department reports that there is a very high defect density in a code. We apply the '5 whys' technique:

- Why there is a high defect density in a code? Because the programmers write bad code.
- Why the programmers write bad code? Because no one tells them it is bad.
- Why no one tells them it is bad? Because it is not identified as a bad code.
- Why it is not identified as a bad code? Because testers don't do static analysis.
- Why don't they do static analysis? Because they are not experienced in it.
- Why are they inexperienced? Because we didn't check this skill in the recruitment process.
- Why didn't we check this? Because the recruitment process is careless.

Actually, we asked 'why' more than 5 times. But we discovered at least one possible (and very unobvious) root cause of the high defect density in a code: a problem with the recruitment process. Notice that if it is really the true root cause, its effects (high defect density) appeared long time after the first tester was hired. It is therefore not so easy to detect the root cause immediately.

8. Small Changes Can Produce Big Results—But the Areas of Highest Leverage Are Often the Least Obvious The following excerpt comes from a Jason Fell's article [74] and describes a well-known history of how Steve Jobs saved Apple:

> When Steve Jobs returned to Apple in 1997, the tech company he co-founded more than two decades earlier was on the brink of failure. During the final quarter of 1996, Apple's sales plummeted by 30 percent. Microsoft was the dominant computer company in the market. (. . .)
>
> Fresh off a partnership deal with Microsoft that injected Apple with $150 million, one of Jobs' first goals as CEO was to review the company's sprawling product line. What he found out was that Apple had been producing multiple versions of the same product to satisfy requests from retailers. For instance, the company was selling a dozen varied versions of the Macintosh computer.
>
> Unable to explain why so many products were necessary, Jobs asked his team of top managers, 'Which ones do I tell my friends to buy?' When he didn't get a simple answer, Jobs got to work reducing the number of Apple products by 70 percent. Among the casualties was the Newton digital personal assistant. Unfortunately, the cut-backs also resulted, in part, in a workforce reduction of about 3000 employees.
>
> 'Deciding what not to do is as important as deciding what to do,' Jobs says in the book. 'It's true for companies, and it's true for products.'
>
> Moving forward, Jobs' strategy was to produce only four products: one desktop and one portable device aimed at both consumers and professionals. For professionals, Apple created the Power Macintosh G3 desktop and the PowerBook G3 portable computer. For consumers, there was the iMac desktop and iBook portable computer.
>
> The move to a smaller product line and a greater focus on quality and innovation paid off. During Jobs' first fiscal year after his return, ending in September 1997, Apple lost $1.04 billion and was '90 days from being insolvent,' Jobs says in the book. One year later, the company turned a $309 million profit.

One simple decision—reducing the number of different products offered by Apple allowed the company to get back in the game. Notice that the decision wasn't very obvious. In fact, it was counter-intuitive, because we intuitively feel that the more the company offers, the better it is for the business. In this case, it turned out it's not.

Here are a few other simple examples of actions or changes that may have a big impact on process improvement:

- Organizing the meetings with clients, but inviting more than one client representative. You may be surprised how effective such meetings may be. Usually client's representatives will have different points of view on the system being developed. When a discussion about the product, its functionalities and requirements starts, the clients quickly start. . . discussing with each other. The meeting will help to clarify many things, issues and ambiguities.
- Just asking 'why are we doing this?' Sometimes people undertake actions automatically, without really thinking if it makes any sense. For example, if we have

to fill a report which seems not to be used by anyone, or contains things that don't bring any added value, we should ask the management: what is the purpose of this report? If management is not able to give a concrete, precise answer, we have an argument against wasting time for useless bureaucracy.

- Introducing a short code review for critical parts of the code. This will not only help to quickly discover many bugs (including the design ones, which are the most difficult to be detected early and are probably the most expensive ones to fix), but also to improve the developers' skills. Better developers means better code, and better code means less quality issues.

9. You Can Have Your Cake and Eat It Too—But Not At Once When about to make a decision, people usually think in the 'either/or' mode. They think that their decisions are inevitably related to some kind of a trade-off: we need to sacrifice something in order to get something else. This is because people think about things as if they need to occur in one moment of time. In such a case, indeed, usually a trade-off will occur. But systems thinking encourages us to look at the whole process not only in space, but also in time dimension.

When we abandon the static style of thinking, it turns out that most of the trade-offs vanish. We *can* have a cake and eat it—just not in the same time. Of course, this takes some time and, usually, some costs. In many cases this also requires a change in thinking about our process and work we do. For example:

- You cannot increase test coverage without writing more tests. But when you train your testers to write better tests, you will obtain higher coverage with the same number of tests.
- You cannot do effective testing, documenting it and maintaining the documentation in the same time. But when you introduce techniques like 'specification by example' [66] and start treating your tests as specification, you will have good tests *and* good documentation at the same time.
- You cannot increase your quality without increasing your costs. But when you introduce practices like 'pair programming' where the pair consists of a developer and a tester, this may result in much less number of defects in the code, so lower costs and higher quality at the same time.

Notice, that in all the above-mentioned cases you need some time to achieve both goals. The solutions seem to be obvious and easy to implement, but usually it's not true. They always require a change—in procedures, processes, people's ways of thinking. Sometimes it also requires more detailed analysis. For example, when we introduce the 'pair programming' practice, during the whole period of time, when tester sits next to developer, he should be as effective as when he was testing in a 'normal' mode. He may observe the implementation process and detect bugs 'on-line'. But also, being inspired by the developer's work, at the same time he may plan the higher-level test scenarios that will be performed later.

10. Dividing an Elephant in Half Does Not Produce Two Small Elephants This rule resembles one of the most important things in systems thinking: look at the system as a whole. We frequently get some task to be done and we focus on it intensively, forgetting about the surroundings. Suppose we have to test a new functionality in a web page of a bank system, which allows us to generate reports. Of course, we will check if the reports are produced correctly, under different conditions and in different client account configurations. But when we understand that a report functionality is a part of the whole ecosystem, and that it is designed for a client who must have a particular business need when he uses this function, some other test ideas may come to our minds. For example:

- the reports will be used by the clients from all over the world—is it possible to generate the report in different languages and are there no issues with this?
- the reports take data from the database server—is the performance OK? Will it be OK when 10,000 clients will generate the report at the same time?
- the report module needs to communicate with the account module—does the integration between these two modules work fine?
- the report format will probably evolve in time—is it easy, from an architectural point of view, to change the report format? How will it affect our automated tests? Does the architectural design envision this?

11. There Is No Blame People, especially in large organizations, like to blame and point fingers about almost every situation, problem or mistake. Systems thinking teaches us that errors and mistakes are inevitable. They are a natural part of the system. We should stop blaming others (because it will never bring any positive effect) and, instead, start learning from our mistakes. The thorough and rational analysis of our wrong decisions, or just simply the errors we made, when done with intention of the constant improvement, may lead us to many ideas about how to avoid such problems in the future. The analysis may also result in valuable ideas about process, product or personal improvement.

Code reviews are a good example. Some people are very satisfied, if they have an opportunity to publicly point out developers' errors. But the idea of code reviews is to find bugs, not punish their authors. Code review may be very stressful for an author. If the team understands well the main reason for which they conduct such inspections, no one will blame anyone.

It is manager's role to make all the team members understand that their primary and common responsibility is the quality of the work products. When this is achieved, code reviews will have another, very positive aspect. They will be a nice opportunity for less experienced developers to learn from senior team members how to write good, clean code, how to use design patterns and so on. This will have the overall impact on both process and product quality.

3.7.2 Systems Thinking and Software Development Models

We have to be very careful with models we use in our everyday work. Usually, strictly following the process kills creativity and narrows our perspective. It gives a false sense of security: we have a very well defined scope of our work, so we just do our job, without taking care of other people's work. We also don't feel responsible for process improvement, because 'there's a methodology we follow, and the methodology assures that everything will go just fine if we only apply it exactly as it is required'.

This is a classic example of a death march. No methodology can help us in achieving the success. How can an abstract idea do that? Success is achieved by people, not tools. Methodology may be a good source of general ideas of how the process should be set up, but it always needs to be tuned, because each project is different.

The classic example is agile. According to the 'Agile Manifesto' this methodology values 'working software over comprehensive documentation' [75]. Many agile evangelists say that writing code is much more important than documenting it. Let's apply some simple system analysis to this problem.

Figure 3.12 represents the so-called system diagram for the development process. Arrows denote the relations between factors. An unlabeled arrow says that factors move in the same way—for example, when quality of tests grows, so does the code quality. Arrows labeled with 'O' represent relationships working in the opposite way—for example, the higher the code quality is, the less time is needed for debugging. Arrows can form cycles, called feedback loops. A loop means that the change of one factor impacts another, which will then affect the first. There are two types of the feedback loops:

- Balancing loops—represent situations, where a change of one factor results in the opposed trend. For example, higher code quality results in less time spent on the

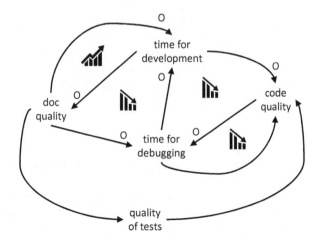

Fig. 3.12 System diagram for software development process

debugging. But when we debug less, the code quality may get worse. Balancing loops have an odd number of 'O' arrows in their cycle.

- Reinforcing loops—represent situations, where a change of one factor reinforces this change. For example, spending more time on documentation results in lower amount of time for coding, which may lead to yet more time spent on documentation. Reinforcing loops have no 'O' arrows or an even number of them.

Let's study our diagram. If we spend more time on documentation to improve its quality, we have less time for development. We write less code, so it's easier to keep its quality. When code quality increases, we need less time for debugging, which results in more time for development. However, when we debug less, the code quality decreases. Higher quality of documentation results in better, stronger tests. This, in turn, increases the code quality.

Now, let's analyze the 'development time' factor and see how it impacts itself through different feedback loops in our system. We have a reinforcing loop 'time for development' → 'doc quality', but also two balancing loops: 'time for development' → 'doc quality' → 'time for debugging' and 'time for development' → 'code quality' → 'time for debugging'. So, we have indeed some reinforcement, but, on the other hand, we also have balancing loops, which means that trying to spend more time on coding may result in... less time for this activity.

As we see, it's not so trivial—we cannot push the 'dev time' to the limits, because—as the second law of systems thinking says—'the harder you push, the harder the system pushes back'. Forcing all developers to spend 100% their time on pure coding may result in problems that in the future will have to take their time. So, not only they will code less, but also the quality may decrease. We have to find a sweet spot in the proportion between 'coding time' and 'doc time', because documentation quality improves the code quality, which results in lower number of problems, which in turn allows developers to spend more time on coding. However, if they code too much, they will have to sacrifice the documentation quality, which will result in quality decrease...

The moral is that we shouldn't blindly follow any methodology, because the world is much more complicated than the idealized model says. Systems thinking is a great tool to perceive these subtle relations between different process factors and draw some non-trivial and often surprising conclusions. The analyses like the one we have just performed may be a great trigger for a team to have more courage in introducing the change into the process (in this case, by appreciating the role of a documentation of high quality).

3.8   Personal Development in Software Testing

The IT world changes with an unbelievable pace. To be up to date, IT specialists—including testers—need to constantly develop their skills. There are many options for educating ourselves. Here are some of the most recommended ones:

- **Books**. It is always useful to read some good, old-fashioned, paper books. The only problem is to distinguish between the good and the bad books. Typically—although this is not a general rule—the worthy books are published by the reputable publishing houses. There are also the books considered as the classics (see the list below) and every tester should know them. When you don't know the author of the book that seems to be interesting, you can use Google to find out some more information about her. Is she a respected figure in the testing community? What is her publication record? What is her background and experience? Are the reviews of her papers positive? Is she a frequent speaker at different conferences?

- **Conferences**. They are a great opportunity to meet (in real!) other professionals in testing and hear about how they deal with the problems that we probably also stumbled upon in our work. Becoming a speaker at the conference is also a very good way to develop our skills. First, you master your skills in describing the problem in the way that is intelligible for other people. Second, you polish your presentation skills. Third, you have the opportunity to discuss your solution with other testers—they may challenge it, criticize it or propose some other approaches; some of them will share with you the experiences they had in the past with the same problem. Finally, conferences are fun and allow you to build your professional network of contacts: you can meet many new, interesting people and interact with them. Below you will find the list of the international testing conferences considered as the best in their category.

- **Studies**. Some universities offer postgraduate studies in software testing or quality assurance. Their curricula focus on the quality topics, so undertaking such studies is a good idea to gather a lot of valuable knowledge in a relatively short period of time. Undergraduate and graduate programmes usually do not focus on testing and quality, but more broad areas, like computer science or quality management. However, every good education is valuable and gives us a certain way of thinking, which may be helpful in developing even the tester's creativeness.

- **Blogs**. There are many of them. Reading the blogs is the easiest way to constantly update your knowledge—blogs do not have a long publication release cycle, so blog's authors can share their ideas immediately. The only problem—as in the case of books—is to be able to distinguish between the good and the bad blogs. This will come with practice. If you feel you don't have enough experience, you can always ask more experienced colleagues what do they read and do they recommend any, valuable in their opinion, blogs. Learning from the best professionals is always a good idea.

- **Meetups**. Meetup (www.meetup.com) is an online social networking portal that facilitates offline group meetings in various places all over the world. The web page allows you to both organize a meeting, or search for an interesting one and sign up. Recently, meetups became very popular and you may find a meeting in your neighborhood in almost any topic you imagine.

- **Talking to experts**. If you work as a tester or attend different conferences or meetups, you meet a lot of people. Some of them are the experts in their fields.

Use such occasions and talk to these people. Ask them about their experiences, what did their career path look like, what practices they use to learn (yes, the masters don't know everything and they need to learn like anyone else!). Discussion with people more experienced than you is extremely beneficial and may boost your development in testing. The more people you meet, the more different perspectives on testing you get. You can experiment with them and choose the ones you find most effective, valuable or convenient for you.

- **Practice**. The best way to learn is to practice, make mistakes, learn from them and gather experience. All the above activities won't help much if you don't put into practice things you have learned.

When learning new stuff, it is crucial to not restrict ourselves to testing only. A wise tester draws inspiration also from other disciplines—see Sect. 2.2 for some examples. Another important thing is to be systematic. As the Queen of Harts says in 'Alice in Wonderland' [76]: 'My dear, here we must run as fast as we can, just to stay in place. And if you wish to go anywhere you must run twice as fast as that.' This sentence applies especially to the IT industry!

Life-long learning develops and strengthens qualities like curiosity, critical thinking, imagination, creativity. It also allows us, after some time, to almost imperceptibly achieve the state of the unconscious competence (see Burch's stages of competence in Sect. 2.4.5)

Classic Books on Software Testing

- **Glenford J. Myers—'The Art of Software Testing'**. One of the most well-known books on software testing. With the first edition being published in 1979 (!), the book has stood the test of time. The third edition was published in 2011, 34 years later. This says quite a lot about how universal the content of this book is. It is because Myer doesn't focus on transient topics on technology and tools, but presents a solid, philosophical framework and a rational approach to testing. The newest edition addresses topics that were not yet topics when Myers wrote the first edition (agile, web programming, etc.).
- **Boris Beizer—'Black-Box Testing. Techniques for Functional Testing of Software and Systems'**. A classical book on test techniques, written by one of the most respected experts in the field of software testing. First published in 1995, the book covers the methods of testing, based on a solid, formal background. The technique selection was guided by the feedback of Beizer's students, who were asked by the author which techniques will be the most useful for them and which do they use. The book describes some control-flow testing techniques, but focuses on the black-box approach: equivalence partitions, Boundary Value Analysis, domain testing, transaction-flow testing, syntax-based testing, finite-state testing.
- **James A. Whittaker—'How to Break Software: A Practical Guide to Testing'**, **'How to Break Web Software: Functional and Security Testing of Web Applications and Web Services'**, **'How to Break Software Security'** (the last one co-authored by Herbert H. Thompson). An excellent series of three books that

are a sort of 'testing cook-books'. The books present a huge catalogue of very concrete techniques for performing different types of software attacks. These very ingenious (and effective!) methods can be directly applied by any tester in his everyday work.

- **Paul C. Jorgensen—Software Testing. A Craftsman's Approach**. The book applies mathematic techniques (discrete mathematics and graph theory) to a coherent treatment of model-based testing for both structure-based (white-box) and specification-based (black-box) testing. It covers the techniques like: equivalence partitioning, Boundary Value Analysis, decision tables, path testing (including the beautiful theory of McCabe's basis path method), data flow testing. The book covers also topics like: integration testing, system testing, model-based testing, object-oriented testing, software complexity, exploratory testing, Test-Driven Development, combinatorial testing and software technical reviews.

Of course, there are many other excellent books on testing. Some of them try to be more universal and technology-independent, some of them focus on particular tools. Just Google the phrase 'recommended books on software testing' and enjoy.

Conferences on Software Testing

There is plethora of software testing conferences, but here we will mention just the ones considered the most important and respected in the community. We don't include in the list the scientific conferences, restricting it just to the conferences for practitioners.

- **STAR Testing Conferences**—a series of periodical conferences (Star East, Star West, Star Canada) organized by TechWell.
- **EuroSTAR**—the longest-running (since 1993), biggest and probably the most prestigious periodical software testing conference in Europe.
- **Google Test Automation Conference**—first held in 2006, the conference focuses on the latest technologies and strategies in test automation.

3.9   Design Thinking or Good, Ol' Fashioned Requirements Analysis?

Tim Brown, CEO of the IDEO, a global design company, says that 'Design thinking is a system that uses the designer's sensibility and methods to match people's needs with what is technologically feasible and what a viable business can convert into consumer value and market opportunity'. In recent years, 'design thinking' became quite a buzzword. It is claimed to be a method for creating the innovative products and services based on a deep understanding of user problems and needs.

The assumptions of the design thinking are: be user-focused (to understand his both conscious and unconscious needs), have an interdisciplinary team (to get the

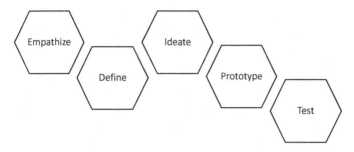

Fig. 3.13 Stanford Design Thinking Process

widest possible perspective of a problem) and experiment and hypotheses test
(to base our actions on the past experience). According to the Stanford Design
Thinking Model,[3] the design thinking process has five steps, as shown in Fig. 3.13.

We might have asked: why a thing such as design thinking, which is supposed to
boost creativity, is shaped into a formal process? Doesn't it *kill* creativity instead of
reinforcing it? The problem is that creative thinking is very difficult, if impossible, to
formalize, because of... its very nature. But let's think rationally, let's give a chance
to this approach and let's investigate what it may offer to the testers. After all, the
method promises to be useful in tackling complex, ill-defined problems. What an
accurate description of software testing!

The first obvious area in which an approach like design thinking might be useful,
is test design. We would like to be able to provide—for a given SUT—a set of
strong, effective tests, that would be able to detect all existent failures with very high
probability. In Table 3.2 we present the five steps of a design thinking process,
together with the exemplary applications of these activities in testing. We also put
some remarks about the particular well-known tools and methods that may be useful
in performing these steps.

Notice that the design thinking process overlaps the standard test process. It is
nothing strange—the design thinking process' steps are generic, natural stages of all
problem-solving approaches. You can see that from the last column in the table.
Each design thinking activity, applied to the testing domain, has a corresponding
group of well-known tools and methods that are used for years.

The conclusion is this: for a novice tester, a design thinking process may be
helpful in learning the way in which rationally thinking people solve (difficult and
complex) problems. For more advanced testers it is probably of less value, as they
are already experienced in this kind of activity. Probably they may benefit more from
books like [77], where one can find a plethora of handy tools and methods for quality
control and quality assurance. Another tool that may also be very handy is the TQED
model described in Chap. 4. Because of its genericity, it may be easily applied to
many different types of problems encountered by testers. It is also a nice tool for
increasing the creativity and generating many new, fresh test ideas.

---

[3]https://dschool-old.stanford.edu/groups/k12/wiki/17cff/steps_in_a_design_thinking_process.html

Table 3.2 Design thinking stages and their application to testing

Step	Description	Application in testing	Known tools/approaches
Emphatize	Gaining an empathic understanding of the problem, people experiences and motivations, etc.	Understanding the client needs from the quality point of view	Brainstorming sessions, Nominal Group Technique, Joint Application Development, interviews, active observations
Define	Defining the problem using the knowledge gathered in the 'Empathize' step	Analyzig the requirements	Requirements validation, risk analysis
Ideate	Having a human-centered problem, generate ideas to identify solutions	Preparing the test ideas and test scenarios, performing the test case design	Test design techniques, out-of-the-box thinking
Prototype	Produce a number of inexpensive prototypes to empirically verify if they are able to solve the problem	Effective test case implementation	Script languages, tools for test implementation, automation framework like keyword-driven testing, data-driven testing, etc.
Test	Testing the complete product using the best solutions identified in the 'Prototype' phase	Test execution, measuring the test effectiveness, number of false positive tests, the criticality of the bugs found	Test execution tools, Coverage tools, defect reports, metrics for test, risks, requirements, functions coverage

As Don Norman said about design thinking, "when we examine the process in detail, what is being labeled as 'design thinking' is what creative people in all disciplines have always done". Design thinking is just thinking.

However, some ideas from the design thinking approach may be directly mapped into testing practices. For example, design thinking recognizes two ways of thinking: analysis and synthesis. Analysis breaks down a structure into parts or components. Synthesis is the opposite: it combines separate components to form a coherent whole. Analysis is applied when we perform things like Work Breakdown Structure or when we analyze the requirements, models, etc. to provide a set of strong test cases. Synthesis is applied when we do not rely on formal models, for example during the exploratory testing sessions. By observing the application and how it reacts to our actions we collect data which are subject to the synthesis. Putting all the known facts together we may either induce a failure or understand and localize the causes of a possible failure.

Synthesis and analysis always go hand in hand: synthesis is built upon the results of a preceding analysis, which requires a subsequent analysis to verify the correctness of its results [78]. Translating this observation into the testing domain, we may, for example, improve our exploratory testing process. It should be planned and related to a single, well-defined goal (analysis) and performed by a tester (synthesis). Its results should be subjected to another analysis, which may direct us to estimate a subsequent, rational goal for another exploratory testing session.

3.10   Why Study Software Testing?

Many people, when they finally get their job as a tester, think: 'Finally! I don't have to study anymore—I moved from my student's life to an adult's life. Now I have to work and earn money. I don't need any education now'. But after some time, the same people start to feel frustration, tiredness and the sense of 'regression in development'. There are at least two reasons for that, both of which support the need of studying the field in which we work:

- IT develops incredibly fast and everything—methods, tools, approaches—changes almost in the blink of an eye. If you don't acquire this new knowledge, you regress. You will not be able to use the new tools, it will be more and more difficult to communicate with other experts in the field. The lack of progress may even result in being fired and when it happens, it may be very hard to find a new job due to our unacquaintance of the modern approach to testing.
- Remaining on the constant level of proficiency means that we are able only to do the same job again and again. Repeatability is boring and tiredness causes frustration. Moreover, repeatability successfully kills tester's creativity.

To avoid these problems, but also to work on our self-improvement, we should study. There are two ways of learning: to learn how to do things and to learn how to learn. The first one is indispensable for an IT professional who wants to stay on track. The second one is much more subtle and results—as an educational process—in creating a new person. Good education first makes you confused, angry and upset. It undermines all your actual beliefs about the world, other people, or—in our case—testing. It destroys almost everything you knew (or imagined) about testing. When you are emptied of all this stuff, you are ready to be filled with a new knowledge that will change you completely.

When you are new to testing, it is obvious that you need to learn the craft, so probably you will spend some time on training for the business, that is—learning some elementary things a tester needs in his work. But for the longer period of time, you will notice that training for the business does not work, because you learn old stuff that is out of date when you finish the training and go to work—education is useless here. Such training can be done at work. It is important to learn the fundamentals of the testing craft. Theory has this nice feature that it doesn't so easily outdate.

The danger here is that students, who are by definition inexperienced, may not understand it and treat theoretical knowledge as some useless stuff. This results in the lack of basic education and, later, in difficulties in understanding different testing techniques. Uneducated testers often lack the independent thinking and do not understand *why* the methods they use actually work. In result, they are not able to analyze and solve test problems effectively.

The main benefit of the educational process is not the better job and higher salary (although, this is also a nice side effect), but *the way you look at the world and the way you understand it*. You will do things differently and treat other people differently. But, what is the most important, *you will test differently*. And in the testing world there is one important rule: the more the creativity and diversity in approaches, the better the tests, stronger the test suites and higher the probability of detecting more bugs.

Once you are an experienced tester, continuing your education will also bring a great value. Maybe it will not destroy your world completely, and maybe won't confuse you as much as in the case of a beginner, but it will encourage you to make deeper reflection about your work, the methods you use, the way you think, analyze, solve problems. At this stage of your career it is very important to learn not only technical things, but also some more advanced theoretical fundamentals of software testing. Moreover, it is important to expand our horizons in other areas, not only for direct inspiration (see Sect. 2.2), but also to be precipitated out of the rut of thinking. Sometimes reading a completely non-technical book (like a philosophical essay or a good novel) may inspire us to change our way of thinking. This may be translated into our way of working as testers. Remember that staying only in the technical world, and being completely isolated from other disciplines, narrows your mind.

I recommend you to watch a very nice video on education [79]. It's a lecture from the 'Introduction to Economics' course given by Prof. Amos Witztum at London School of Economics. In this video Prof. Witztum splendidly explains the role of education, the way it works and the benefits you get from it. He refers to economics, but the things he says are universal and so valid for testers as well.

TQED Model

4

4.1   Introduction

Due to recurring and widespread problems with software quality and testing effec-tiveness, we suggest going back to the roots of the testing craft. A deep thought on the testing foundations should allow us to create a reasonable approach for deriving good tests. In this chapter we propose a simple fault model founded on the natural software characteristics. We call it 'TQED model'. These four letters come from the four basic elements used to describe the working software (or any other artifact existing in the SDLC): time, quantity, events and data. The acronym can also stand for 'Tested. Quod Erat Demonstrandum' ('Tested. What was to be demonstrated'). The wording 'q.e.d' is often used at the end of proofs of the math theorems.[1]

The model, as it will be shown later, is very generic, hence applicable to any type of tester's activity. The main goal for designing this model was to *support tester's thinking*. TQED, among others, allows us to:

- perform a systematic analysis of the test basis,
- conduct an effective review of this basis,
- understand better the different aspects of software behavior,
- catch the relationships between software components and documentation,
- perform a system-thinking approach to optimize the testing effort,
- design strong, effective test cases with high probability of bug detection,
- design our own test techniques, strategies and approaches,
- increase our creativity.

---

[1]In most cases it is impossible to prove that there are no bugs in the system. This problem in general is undecidable, because in particular we should test if the program will finish its computations for all inputs. We know that the halting problem is undecidable. 'Q.E.D.' phrase should be therefore treated facetiously.

© Springer International Publishing AG 2018   145
A. Roman, *Thinking-Driven Testing*, https://doi.org/10.1007/978-3-319-73195-7_4

In Sect. 4.2 we present the model's origin. The idea behind our model comes from physics. A physical description of the world we are living in is translated into a universal language that can be used to describe the way the software works.

The merits of the model, described in detail in Sect. 4.3, are: simplicity, understandability, flexibility and genericity. The model may be helpful in constructing the effective test cases by a careful analysis of how software under test (SUT) works and how it can fail. However, due to its genericity, it may be used practically everywhere, where there is a need to generate creative ideas, analyze complex structures or derive test cases. As TQED is derived from a very natural and intelligible software analysis regarding error-proneness, it has also an educational value. It may be a great tool used in the education process by guiding students or novice testers to discover formal test design techniques or even to construct their own techniques.

In Sect. 4.4 we formally describe the model, its structure, components and the relations between them. Next, in Sect. 4.5 we take a closer look at these components (data, events, time and quantity) and their interactions. We provide a wide list of possible interpretations of these entities in the real software. This list is definitely not exhaustive—it is just an example of how the model can be used by testers in practice.

Section 4.6 is devoted to the issue of applying the model in practice. It shows how the model can be utilized not only to follow a given test strategy, but also to build our own approach to testing. We show how the model can be a driver for developing the test strategy from the test problem analysis. In Sect. 4.7 we make an effort to justify the model's universality by comparing our model to other approaches. We show that these approaches can be easily derived from the TQED model.

Finally, in Sect. 4.8 we show some more concrete examples of applying the TQED model to the real testing problems. Section 4.9 concludes the whole chapter.

4.2   Origin of the Model

4.2.1   The Background

It is a well-known fact that any kind of software is being constantly tested by its users. But, as quality matters, it should be thoroughly tested by the development team in the first place. Surprisingly, performing well in this crucial software engineering activity is still hard to achieve. There are many reports clearly supporting this fact. For example, according to the Chaos Report [80] only 29% of all IT projects in 2015 were successful, that is, completed on time, within budget and delivered with the promised quality (see Fig. 4.1).

It is quite worrisome that not much has changed during the five consecutive years (2011–2015). Success rate seems to remain on a constant level of ca. 27–31%. Among other factors, the report specifies poor requirements, technical incompetence and lack of user involvement as major causes of project failures. Why it this so? On one hand, developers often have little or no background in testing. On the other hand, testers have little or no background in software development and requirements engineering. Some education here would not be a bad idea for improving the test process.

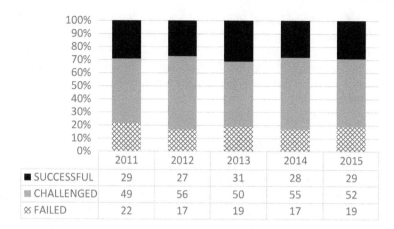

	2011	2012	2013	2014	2015
■ SUCCESSFUL	29	27	31	28	29
▨ CHALLENGED	49	56	50	55	52
⊠ FAILED	22	17	19	17	19

Fig. 4.1 Success rate of IT projects according to Chaos Report

But it seems to us that there is another reason for poor software quality. It is much more subtle and—in our opinion—much more fundamental. IT industry loves new technologies, tools, programming languages, etc. We think that new tools will automate everything (including testing), that new technologies will immediately solve our problems and that introducing a new programming language in the company will immediately improve the final quality of the software—just because. Having no real, rational arguments for that, we believe that all this stuff is a silver bullet or some other software quality snake oil. We love this illusion that the *high complexity of the modern technologies immediately implies their high robustness and applicability*. In all this madness of unceasing progress of technology we have somehow lost the ability to have deeper reflections about the foundations of our craft. And the ability of how to transform this reflection into a working solution, which in many cases can be much more effective than just relying on a new tool or some new, sophisticated method.

We would like to follow this approach, apparently neglected in the area of software testing, and return to the roots of the testing craft. Starting with a funda-mental principle—a reflection on how software works—we will identify the software's primary 'components' (hereinafter called software dimensions). These basic software elements will help us to build a software fault model which shows the ways in which software may fail. This method may as well be applied to any document and identify many defects in it. The model guides testing by being a handy tool for providing good, effective test cases. Using the analogy from physics: software's dimensions are like basic units in the SI system; the fault model is like the equations that use SI units and describe the laws of physics. After introducing the model, we propose a test strategy based on it and show how it can be applied to a real testing problem.

The introduced model has an additional 'side effect': it may be successfully used as a teaching tool in testing classes. By analyzing and applying the model, students will be able to discover many well-known formal test case design techniques, like combinatorial testing, state machine testing and so on. In Sect. 4.7 we give an example of a mapping between the model elements and some well-known test design techniques.

4.2.2 Inspiration from Physics

To test the software well, we need to know when something goes wrong and be able to distinguish between the failure from the correct action. Such an approach leads us to the so-called fault model. A fault model tells us in what ways the software being tested may fail. Bearing that in mind we can design, in a more or less systematic way, a set of tests that may reveal the failure modes described by our model. Many fault models were proposed in the literature. Some of them are very detailed and focused on one specific aspect of a SUT (a good example may be mutation testing [81], where the fault is modeled as a slight, but well-defined change in the original code). Other models are more general.

Probably the one that is best recognized is the Whittaker's model described in his excellent book 'How to Break Software'. Whittaker builds his model by understanding the software's environment first (OS kernel, API, user interface, file system). Next, by analyzing the connections between these components Whittaker derives many examples of software attacks which could 'expose faults and force the software to exhibit its functionality efficiently and effectively' [59].

It is worth noting that most of the fault models serve as the defect prediction tools used by the quality assurance engineers [82]. By using such models we are able to predict, for example, the number of field defects, that is defects present in the software released to a client. Our model (like Whittaker's one) is not meant for quality assurance purposes, but for software testers, as a simple and practical tool to boost creativity, develop interesting test ideas and design effective test cases. It cannot be used as a fault prediction model.

When we ask someone 'what does the computer program really do?', probably the most frequent answer would be 'it processes *data*'. This is perfectly fine: every program accepts some input data, transforms them and outputs other data. This process takes place in *time*: a program is not able to return the answer immediately—it needs to perform an algorithm, so it requires several steps. The actions that our program undertakes are a result of some *events* that either come from the inside of a software or are external, and come from the environment in which software operates. Data and events can be described *quantitatively*. For example, size of particular data can be large or small, events can occur frequently or rarely, etc.

We have just come up with the four basic software dimensions: data (D), events (E), time (T) and quantity (Q). These concepts are very general—notice that *any* software and its action can be reduced to, and expressed with *only* these four basic ideas. We may support this rather strong thesis in the following way: software and computation are part of the physical world. Everything that happens in this world can

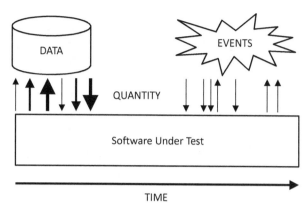

Fig. 4.2 Four basic software dimensions

be described by using several basic properties like mass, thermodynamic temperature, time or amount of substance. Consider the following analogies between the physical world and the working software:

- data is like matter—it is a substance that represents information,
- events are like thermodynamics, which describes the transformations of the physical objects,
- time is exactly the time that we know from physics,
- quantity is like the amount of substance.

Our model uses these four entities as a foundation. All other, more complicated ideas and relations will be built on this base. Figure 4.2 shows figuratively our concept of the basic software dimensions.

As TQED will be described in terms of these four dimensions, we have to explain why we decided to define a software in such a way. What are the benefits of this approach? The fundamental idea behind our model is as follows. If we are able to describe any aspect of any software with these four characteristics, we can also do this for failures and bugs present in the code and documentation. Hence, if we can describe the software detailed enough, theoretically we should be able to identify all the risks, bugs, threats, possible failures and unexpected behaviors that may happen. This is because every cause of a software problem can be expressed in terms of relationships between data, events, time and quantity. If we have a test that is able to catch these relationships, it should be able to identify the problem.

Figure 4.3 shows the analogy between physics and our model. In science we first observe some phenomenon, gather some data, build a theory and finally use it to both examine the phenomenon's nature and predict the phenomenon's future behavior. If the theory is valid, it gives good predictions. Physics can describe any phenomenon by equations that use objects measured in terms of basic SI units (mass, time, weight, temperature, etc.). In our approach, we observe and analyze the software, model its structure and behavior in terms of the TQED model, and using this description we design tests. If software is well modeled, our tests should reveal a bug.

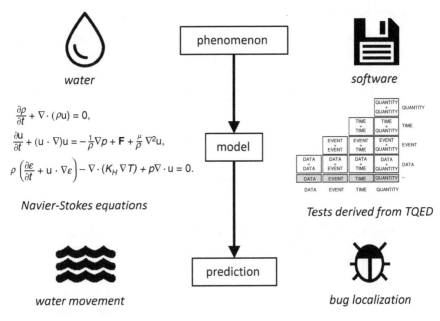

Fig. 4.3 Analogy between physics and TQED model

4.3 Model Features

Before we define the full TQED model, let us describe in detail its main characteristics, which are:

- simplicity,
- understandability,
- flexibility,
- genericity.

4.3.1 Simplicity

TQED uses very simple ideas and concepts. In fact, it consists only of four software dimensions (data, events, time, quantity) and their combinations. That's all—there's really no rocket science here. Also, the TQED metamodel,[2] presented in Fig. 4.4, is quite straightforward.

---

[2]Metamodel is a model of the model, i.e. the formal description of the given model structure, its elements and relationships between them. The example relation between model and metamodel may be a source code of a Java computer program and the formal grammar that generates all valid (syntactically correct) Java programs.

Fig. 4.4 Metamodel of
TQED model

The metamodel describes the TQED model structure. TQED consists of elements called 'software dimensions' and their combinations. Symbol '1..*' represents the relations between these two concepts. It means that one combination may be built of at least one software dimension, but there is no upper limit of the components. Also, any dimension can be a part of one or more combinations.

Simplicity implies all other important features: understandability, flexibility and genericity.

4.3.2   Understandability

Because the model is simple, it is intelligible. Anyone who studies it learns it very quickly. The model uses common ideas—everyone knows the notion of data, event, etc. By using comprehensible notions which most IT (and not-IT) people are familiar with, it is easy to remember and understand. However, be aware of the fact, that understandability does *not* imply *ease of use*. The level of sophistication of TQED-based tests may vary. Unexperienced testers may design simpler test cases, more experienced ones will probably construct more advanced test suites. Model effectiveness strongly depends on our experience, but to some extent the model itself allows testers to boost their creativity. We will show this in more detail in Sect. 4.5.5.

4.3.3   Flexibility

As TQED is simple and generic (see below), and in fact proposes a specific *way of thinking*, we may use it for any kind of tester's activity, because thinking is required in all actions taken by testing professionals. Hence, TQED can be applied:

* for both software- and hardware-related testing problems,
* for any software type (web, console-based, distributed, mobile, embedded, SaaS, etc.),
* at any test level (unit, integration, system, acceptance testing, etc.),
* at any stage of the SDLC (requirements elicitation, analysis and modeling, architecture design, low-level design, implementation phase, testing, debugging, maintenance, etc.),
* for any test type (functional, non-functional, black-box, white-box, experience-based, formal, informal, etc.),
* for any fault/failure type considered (logic, control flow, data-related, GUI, API, CLI, communication-related, etc.).

It can also serve well as a framework for constructing (or revealing) test design techniques. This makes it a handy tool when establishing the test strategy/test approach in a given project or situation.

4.3.4   Genericity

The TQED model can be narrowed down to a more detailed model. Genericity, together with flexibility, makes the model universal in the sense Barry Boehm described his spiral model, introduced in [83]. In the later paper [84] Boehm described the spiral model as 'a risk-driven process model generator'. This means that any software development model can be described in terms of a particular form of the spiral model. We could say the same about TQED: it can be viewed as a 'test approach generator'. In Sect. 4.7 we take a closer look on this topic. For example, we show how different fault models, like Whittaker's software attacks, can be described in terms of a strategy derived from the TQED model.

Genericity of the model creates an irremovable trade-off. The model's universality gives an extremely broad field of applications, but, on the other hand, it makes the model more difficult to use. This difficulty is unavoidable and cannot be eliminated completely. It's because—as we said earlier—the TQED model proposes a specific way of *thinking*. Any problem that a tester has to solve requires some kind of analysis. TQED may guide us in this analysis, but it cannot think for us. Because of its genericity it also requires a tester to choose the proper form of the model so that it fits the problem.

TQED can be also used on a higher level of abstraction. Namely, it can be applied on an organizational-level as a tool for test process improvement by identifying possible areas of improvement (see Sect. 4.8 for an example).

4.3.5   Educational Value

Apart from the four basic characteristics described above, the TQED model has also some educational value. If a novice tester uses the model in practice, she will be able to discover the well-known, established software test design techniques. Because the process of discovering things takes place by performing real work, from the educational point of view it has a big advantage over learning these techniques in a classroom.

The other advantage is that knowing only the method proposed by the TQED model, a novice tester will be able to use the techniques that she may even not be aware of. Using the same approach in other projects allows the tester to *generalize* this approach and inductively discover a design technique. See Sect. 4.7.2 for the details on the relationship between formal test design techniques and dimensions combinations generated from the TQED model.

4.4   Model Structure and Model Components

In the previous sections we said that the basic TQED elements are four so-called software dimensions: data, events, time and quantity. As we aim to build a fault model, we need to construct it in a way that could tell us what can go wrong. Having our four basic dimensions in place is not enough. Of course, there may be some error in a file (data), some input string may be too large (quantity), an unexpected exception may occur (event) and so on. But this is still too general—software is much more complicated than this. We should build a new layer upon our four basic dimensions. Consider the following situation: a failure may happen when we use a certain model of a printer together with a certain model of a web browser. Both printer and web browser can be considered as a Data dimension. But the error results by a combination of these two entities. Hence, we should consider different combinations of dimensions. Together with the basic dimensions they constitute our final model, presented in Fig. 4.5.

At the bottom part of the model we have our four basic dimensions (gray rectangles), which label the consecutive columns of the model. Each row is also labeled with the basic dimensions. Above the bottom layer we build the possible combinations of dimensions according to the labels of the rows and columns. For example, at the crossing of Event row and Time column we have a combination Event+Time.

While Data and Events may be considered as the real objects, Time and Quantity are abstract notions. Therefore, to create a meaningful combination, abstract notions may require to be combined with one or more real objects: data or event. If we want to use such a dimension or combination to identify some 'concrete' test conditions, we usually need to combine it with at least one 'real' dimension. However, it is perfectly OK to use only the abstract dimensions and still be able to define a natural test approach. For example, Time itself may represent the reliability testing, where

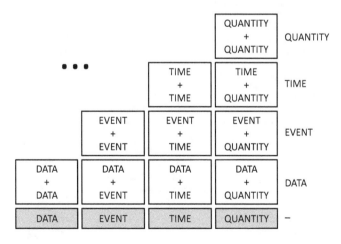

Fig. 4.5 TQED model

we operate the software normally and just observe if failures occur and how often they happen.

The dots in the upper left part of the model suggest that there may be more complicated combinations of dimensions. For example, Data+Event+Time denotes a combination of Data, Event and Time. A real equivalent of a situation described by this combination might be defining and using a variable in the source code. We have the following relations here (assume that the variable of interest is called x):

- variable x (its value) is represented by Data,
- defining the variable value (e.g., x:=5) and using it (e.g., y:=x+1) are represented by Events,
- the *sequence* of first defining and then using the variable is represented by Time.

The combinations may also contain two or more instances of the same dimension. For example, combination Data+Data (resp. Data+Data+Data) may represent the combination of two (resp. three) variables (as in pair-wise or triple-wise testing). Of course, the meaning, or physical interpretation of the combinations is up to the tester. For example, the single Data dimension, in a given context may be interpreted by one tester as something related to a single variable, and by another as the arbitrary combination of many variables. The model does not impose the meaning (semantics) of the structures it produces in terms of a concrete system, problem or situation. It always depends on the context and on the tester's interpretation.

The general meaning of the model components, abstracting from the concrete instances of the real systems, problems and situations, is shown in Table 4.1. The columns show respectively: dimension name, its formal meaning, the intuitive meaning and concrete examples of the dimension's instances. The third column

Table 4.1 The meaning of TQED model components

Dimension	What represents	Intuition	Examples
Data	'Static' variables, objects, elements or parts of the system or its environment, system's state	Information that is expanded in time	Variable's value, file name, a concrete server, document, etc.
Event	'Dynamic' phenomena within the system or its environment, that may cause changes	Incidents that have a very short, almost punctual duration in time	Using the variable, pressing the button, throwing an exception, hardware failure, etc.
Time	Progress of existence	Allows us to express the sequencing of different incidents; introduces ordering	The passage of time, the ordering of elements, etc.
Quantity	The magnitude or multitude of different objects present in a system or its environment	Quantity/volume of objects	File size, system load, very large or very small value, etc.

may be helpful during the identification of different dimensions in the system or its environment.

Hereinafter we will use the following convention. For the sake of simplicity, single dimensions will be represented by single capital letters: D, E, T, Q. The combinations will be denoted by the strings composed of these letters. For example, DQ means 'combination of Data+Quantity' and DDEEEQ represents the (rather complicated) combination of Data+Data+Event+Event+Event+Quantity. The realizations of dimensions (for example, a particular variable as an example of Data dimension, a particular API call as an example of Event dimension, etc.) hereinafter will be called phenomena, elements or objects. We do not use one, 'official' name, because of a huge diversity of these entities. We just use the most appropriate word in a given situation.

Before we move to the next sections describing and explaining the TQED model in detail, let us briefly explain the basic notions we use regarding the data and events. This is important, as we frequently refer to the terms used as a standard terminology in different computer science areas. However, we understand these terms in a different, more general way. For example, by 'object' we do not mean the instance of a class, like it is done in the object-oriented programming, but any material thing that may be perceived by the senses.

By 'Data', we understand any type of information that exists in time and space. The Data must carry some information and must be situated in some physical storage medium. The information may change (for example, a variable may change its value), but between the changes it is 'static', that is—does not change. The variable may be subject to different transformations being still *the same* variable. This concept is illustrated symbolically in Fig. 4.6, being also a rephrased idea of dimensions shown in Fig. 4.2. At some point, the data is created with its value stored in some physical storage medium (like memory). Then, after some time, its value may change. Finally, the information may be destroyed by removing the data from the memory. The moments of creation, value change and removing are the

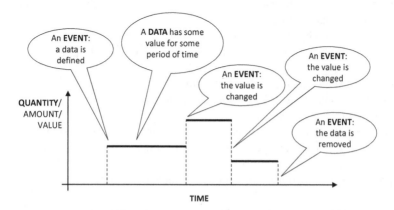

Fig. 4.6 The difference between the concepts of model's dimensions

events, because they are the phenomena that occur instantly, taking almost no time. Between the events the information is constant, 'expanded in time'. Notice, that any physical object (like the memory itself) may be also considered as a Data object.

4.5   Heuristics for Model Components

In the previous sections we were talking about the TQED model in a bit abstract way. To 'feel' the model, we now present the examples of real entities that can be represented by the model's dimensions and their combinations. Remember, however, that this list is definitely not exhaustive. Every project requires an individual approach in identifying different types of objects that can be further used to derive good test ideas. First we will focus on the four main dimensions. Then, we will investigate their combinations. In Chap. 5 we will give even more concrete examples and show how the TQED model can be applied in different testing techniques.

4.5.1   Data

It represents the value of qualitative or quantitative variable. The Data is probably the broadest dimension in terms of the TQED model. The examples of D objects are:

- input/internal/output data
- variable, its value, type, properties
- browser's cookie
- sent/received message
- file name, file content
- database record
- line of code
- web form field/its value
- attribute (for example, variable type, web form field attribute like color, size, position, validation rule, etc.)
- class/object (in object-oriented programming), the state of the object,
- type of software/hardware entity (for example, printer model, application version, etc.)
- state (for example, a particular application screen)
- configuration element (for example, its version, autor, etc.)
- piece of a hardware (switch, server, printer, etc.)
- document (for example, user manual, requirement, project design, but also a message for a user, a report, an instruction for a user, a hint in a form of a pop-up box, etc.)
- application-specific object (for example, a table or a figure in the document)
- model
- 'hidden' data, e.g., data representing a property of another data (for example, the number of characters in a string, the number of decimal places in case of a real number variable, etc.)

Data can be categorized according to many different criteria.

- **Complexity.** Data can be simple and complex. Simple data has no internal structure, while complex data has. This condition is somehow blurred. For example, we may consider a string as a simple data, as opposed to a record with several fields (a complex data). But we may as well claim that string is a complex structure composed of single characters. The criterion is always up to the tester. Complexity impacts testing—simple data is usually easier to handle, because there are no dependencies and combinations as in the case of the complex data. In practice, complex data may be represented as the DD (Data+Data) combination, described later. However, in some situations we may treat complex data as a simple data at the higher abstraction level. For example, web requests may be treated as simple data, when we analyze the network communication process on a system level and we are not interested in the detailed structure of each request, because they are indivisible on this test level.

Example

Suppose we have a complex variable user, which contains the following information:

```
record user
    int id
    string name
    string surname
    int yearOfBirth
    int monthOfBirth
    int dayOfBirth
end record
```

Notice that there are some relationships between variables monthOfBirth and dayOfBirth. What would happen, if we submit to the system a record, in which monthOfBirth=4 and dayOfBirth=31? Each of these variables treated separately is perfectly fine. However, their *combination* is not, because April has only 30 days. Another constraint is related to leap years and number of days in February. When testing complex structures, we have to take into account such constraints and internal relationships between variables.

- **Validity.** Data can be valid and invalid. Valid data is supposed to be accepted by a SUT, while invalid data shouldn't. Data can be invalid because of their syntax or their semantics. Invalid data is heavily used in so-called negative (or dirty) testing, where we want to check the program tolerance on the erroneous data. This type of testing is typical in API testing, where we can almost arbitrarily modify API requests and messages.

Example

Suppose that a variable `index` (representing the record number) has value 145, but there are only 144 records. When the application wants to read a record number `index`, something wrong may happen. The syntax is correct—the variable represents a valid number, but its meaning has no sense in this particular context. On the other hand, if `index` has a value 'abc', it is syntactically wrong, because its formal structure does not comply to the rules defining its valid format.

There are well-known, classic 'default' negative values for different types of variables. For example, for a numeric field, the typical 'negative'[3] values might be:

1. an empty field
2. NULL value
3. 0 (zero)
4. negative value
5. maximal possible value
6. maximal possible value + 1
7. minimal possible value
8. minimal possible value − 1
9. white character (for example, space, tab, etc.)
10. number with white character (for example 4.55_), where '_' denotes space
11. number split with white character (for example 97 23)
12. arithmetic expression (for example 56+44)
13. a number preceded by 0 (like 034)
14. a number preceded by + (like +72)
15. a number with decimal part, but equal to 0 (like 45.000)
16. a real number (like 5.42)
17. a real number with too high precision (like 1.00000000001 for an 8-digit precision)
18. a number in a scientific notation (like 2.0E+03)
19. a non-numerical string (like 'abc')
20. SQL injection
21. a string containing diacritic characters[4]

---

[3]We put 'negative' in quotes, because not always all these values are negative. The list rather presents some examples of interesting and worth checking test ideas.

[4]Diacritic character is a character with a glyph added. Different languages use different diacritics. The diacritics are important when testing data fields and the way these symbols are handled by the SUT.

- **Visibility.** Data can be visible outside the application or can be an internal variable. This criterion is very important, because internal data play an important role inside the application logic and can be easily missed in the analysis.

Example

Suppose the function under test has to compute the mean value for the set of numbers taken from standard input in a form of a table of integers. The (pseudo) code of this function looks as follows.

```
function ComputeMean(input x[])
begin
  define integer i
  define integer count:=0
  define sum
  loop for i from 1 to x.size() step by 1
    sum:=sum+x[i]
    count:=count+1
  end loop
  return sum/count
end
```

This program takes a table x[] from standard input, but in order to compute the mean value of the elements it uses several other variables:

- i, the loop iterator,
- count, the variable that counts the number of elements of the table x,
- sum, the sum of all elements analyzed so far.

Analysis of internal data may lead to several interesting, potentially error-prone situations. For example, the first loop iteration should start with the i value representing the number of the first index of x[]. If x[] is indexed from 0, and i (as in our code) starts with 1, this is a bug. We can detect this bug by providing a table for which $\frac{1}{n+1}\sum_{i=0}^{n}x[i] \neq \frac{1}{n}\sum_{i=1}^{n}x[i]$. Notice that a test with all values $x[i]$ being equal will *not* detect this bug, although it may be interesting for some completely other reason! This exemplary analysis is very important—it is a nice example of how the tester thinks in order to provide the effective set of tests, that are able to detect a bug of a given type.

Another problem is with the internal variable sum. After the loop termination it should return the sum of all elements. But sum was not initialized before the loop, so theoretically we don't know what is its value in the moment of its definition. Different programming languages have different rules here.

(continued)

For example, in C it is assumed that a number variable that is not initialized, has a default value 0. But in other languages this value may be undefined and may depend on what values were in the memory assigned to this variable. This type of problem is usually detected during static analyses, reviews and the compilation process.

Finally, we have an internal variable `count`, which is used in the formula in the last line. However, if `count` equals 0, the formula will divide by 0 which is not allowed. This bug may be detected by a test with an empty table (that is, table with no elements). By the way, `count` is redundant, as `x` has the method `size()`, which returns the number of its elements. This method can be used in place of `count`. This 'anomaly' (variable redundancy) is related to the code quality. Bad code quality won't throw any warning or error during the compilation, but will make the code harder to maintain.

Input and output data are usually easy to handle. The problem is that internal data is often not visible to the tester. In such a case the tester can only think of how the algorithm works and what type of internal structures, algorithmic constructions and data it can use. This model may not necessarily correspond ideally to the software, but still it is some starting point for the analysis. For example, take the above code. If we didn't have access to the internal program structure and we knew only that the program computes the mean value, we might have visualised the algorithm and discover some internal variables that might have played an important role. Identifying the internal variables (real or modeled) is very helpful in designing smart, strong tests.

- **Variability.** Some data values can be constant (fixed), which means that they should never (constants) or almost never (configuration values) change. Another type of stable data can be the version of the OS, printer type and so on. Other data values can be variable, which means that they change more or less frequently. The most natural test for a constant data is to try to change it (for example, change the OS, configuration, printer, etc.). For variable data we may try to prevent the changes (for example, we may try to lock a file in other applications to prevent the file name change in SUT).

4.5.2 Events

Events are incidents that have a very short, almost punctual duration in time. These are the phenomena about which we can say that they 'occur' or 'happen'. This feature distinguishes them from data, which 'are'. Events usually cause changes. They model the dynamics of a system. The sample phenomena that fall into the E category are:

- creating a variable, defining its value, using it in computations or removing it from the memory
- moving from one executed line of code to another
- invoking a method, function or procedure
- throwing an exception
- pressing a button by the user
- sending or receiving a message by the system
- performing some action by the user (closing the web browser, switching between applications, pressing a key on a keyboard, plugging/unplugging a device, turning off a computer, etc.)
- performing some action by the OS (assigning a memory area for a process, executing a process, halting/disposing the process, sending/receiving a message to/from an application, etc.)
- change of the environment (lack of memory, lack of disc space, higher CPU usage)
- performing some action by a hardware, database, network, etc.
- creating a file, changing its content, changing its attributes (read/write/append) or its name
- performing a transition between two states of a system
- performing an application-specific action (e.g., moving, selecting, resizing or removing an object in Power Point; inserting a coin into coffee machine; sending an e-mail;, etc.)
- performing an object transformation (for example, encoding/decoding the message, calculating an arithmetic expression, evaluating the logic expression, changing the user's access rights, etc.)
- creating a copy of an object
- invoking any type of a change
- fulfilling some property (for example, achieving a given level of code coverage, a given network transfer, etc.)

Notice that most of the events are operations on Data objects. Therefore, after identifying the Data objects, we can analyze each of them with respect to the possible transformations or changes that may be performed on them. This way we may identify many different events that may be worth to test. Some Events may be more abstract (like moving from one state to another or fulfilling some property).

Events may be caused by the user, system or environment. Understanding their origin may be also helpful during their identification. Figure 4.7 shows figuratively a universum of events together with their relations, which may be quite complicated. This model identifies seven types of events. We call them E0, E1, . . ., E6. The types are put in an increasing order of difficulty of handling them. Let's review them in detail.

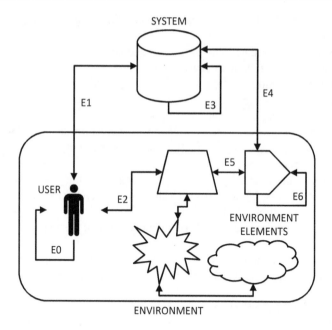

Fig. 4.7 Universum of events

E0. **Pure user events**. These events do not impact directly a system or environment.
They are restricted only to user behavior. An example may be a wrong understanding of a user manual. Such events may simulate user's mistakes and
omissions. They are the easiest events to invoke, because they depend only on
us. We don't need to interact with or instrument any other entities, like system,
environment components and so on.

E1. **Events between user and system**. These events are caused by users (for
example, pressing a button, filling a form, etc.). From the tester's point of
view these events are the most controllable. They can be directly invoked by
a user (tester). However, they may be problematic if we want to perform some
action that is not expected by the system. It may be impossible—if the system
has some validating mechanisms (for example, transition between two system
states under specific conditions is prohibited)—or difficult—when it requires
some more complicated test harness to induce the event (for example,
performing two actions in parallel or in a very short period of time, like pressing
two buttons at the same time, quickly clicking 'Send' button more than once and
so on).

E2. **Events between user and environment**. These events do not impact the system
directly, but may affect its behavior. For example, when a user creates in another
application a very large file that takes all the available disk space, this may
influence the way the SUT works. From the tester's perspective, E2 type events
are typical during the environment instrumentation for performing a test scenario. They also often represent situations that are rare, unexpectable or far from

obvious, but may reveal/lead to many deeply hidden bugs. As these events do not involve the system directly, usually they are not able to detect any problems straightaway. They play a role of a set-up step in a test scenario—they represent the initial conditions that have to be fulfilled to perform the appropriate test.

E3. **Events within a system**. They take place inside a system, without any user or environment involvement; the example may be changing the value of a variable, changing the system's state, etc.; from the tester's point of view these events may be hard to invoke, force or produce, because usually we are not able to control the system's internal state; usually, to invoke an internal event, we have to prepare a particular set of data, or invoke a sequence of events of other type (like E2) to bring the system to a state in which a desirable event may happen. If a system consists of some subsystems, the events can be distinguished between these components. They will have the same nature as E4 or E5 type events. They are useful in integration testing, when we want to test the communication between entities.

E4. **Events between system and environment**. These are usually invisible for the user. An example of such an event may be an API call between the application and operation system. Controlling these events may be difficult and usually requires not only the instrumented environment (that is, an environment in which we may simulate different actions), but also—as in case of E1 type events—preparing first some data to initiate a process of a proper communication between SUT and environment.

E5. **Events between the environment entities**. They have the nature similar to E3 type events, however they usually are much more difficult to handle. This is because SUT can be often controlled by a tester. We may instrument the code or prepare the environment in a way that will force a certain system behavior. It is much harder to control the events between environmental events, like communication between an operating system and database or between a network interface and COTS software (with no access to the source code) that collaborates with our SUT.

E6. **Events within the environment entities**. Similar to E1 type events, because each environment entity can be treated as a proper system, like the SUT. They are even much harder than E5 events to control, because in case of the former we may at least instrument the communication channel between environment objects. Here, it is much harder, because environment elements are often third-party entities over which we have no control (like an external web service). For example, we are usually not able to control things like network load or failure.

As the System Under Test is a *system*, it is natural that events do not occur in isolation. Every event has one or more logical consequences. Events may cause other events, or change data, its properties, etc. When designing test scenarios, the tester has to take it into account. Hence, a single test may be composed of a sequence of events. If such relations between events are difficult to spot immediately, the tester can use the TQED model and analyze dimension combinations like EE, ET, EQ, etc. (see the next section) to identify these high-level scenarios.

When designing tests or even just thinking about test ideas, it is important to analyze all types of possible events. The tester should not restrict to the most obvious events, like E1. The more varied types of events identified, the more thorough the testing will be. This, in result, will minimize the residual risk in the system.

Example

Suppose we test a text field in a GUI. We think about any types of events associated with this text field. A list of GUI element properties may give us some hints. For example, a text field has the 'width' and 'height' properties. This suggests that we may try to resize the window. We may try to make the text field as big as possible, even try to exceed the application window boundaries. After that we may minimize the application, then return to the application and see if the text field size returned to a default value or holds the resized values. Or we may put into a field a lot of text so that a vertical and/or horizontal scroll bar appears. If a text field accepts only a limited amount of text, we may try to copy and paste to the field a higher volume of text.

4.5.3 Quantity

Quantity expresses the amount of something. As a dimension, it is of an abstract nature. Data and events are 'real', 'material' things or actions. In contrast, quantity is a property, not a phenomenon. Therefore, during the analysis it makes much more sense to consider it in combination with other dimensions.

Quantity is a magnitude or multitude of entities present in a system or environment. It may also be related to the boundaries of different objects. The example interpretations of Quantity are:

- empty set/zero elements (nothing)
- value below the minimal possible value
- minimal possible value
- low value
- average, typical value
- high value
- maximal possible value
- value over the maximal possible value
- value within/outside the area denoted by some statistical properties of a variable distribution; the examples of these properties can be: mean value, median, standard deviation, quartile, quantile, etc.
- value on a domain boundary
- value just below/just above the boundary

The Quantity may be related to the variables themselves, but also to their 'numerical' properties. The following example explains it more in detail.

Example

Suppose we test an interest calculation system. It takes as the input the value of the loan (or deposit), interest rate and compounding frequency (e.g., the number of times the accumulated interest is paid out or capitalized). The system calculates the total repayment value based on this data. The pseudo-code of the algorithm looks like this (we assume that InterestRate is a value between 0 and 1):

```
function CalculateTotalValue(unsigned double InitialValue,
                             unsigned double InterestRate,
                             unsigned int NumberOfRates)
begin
1   int i
2   int FinalValue := InitialValue
3   loop for i from 1 to NumberOfRates step by 1
4     FinalValue := FinalValue * (1 + InterestRate)
5   end loop
6   return FinalValue
end
```

The Q dimension regarding the variable FinalValue may be viewed in at least two ways. First, we can analyze the FinalValue 'quantity' as its magnitude, that is—its value. For example, we may analyze what happens if FinalValue is 0, or what happens if it is a very large number (exceeding the double type maximal possible value). But we may also apply the analysis to the FinalValue precision. The algorithm is a financial system, and the FinalValue is given in a currency unit, so the natural question is about the 'quantity of precision'. The quantity of most interest here is 2, because currencies have precision to two decimal places, but we may also analyze quantities like 'the biggest possible value', which means here 'the greatest possible precision'. The FinalValue in line 4 is multiplied by a real value, so the result will be a real number. How are the numbers rounded? If the result is 23.445, will it become 23.44 or 23.45? The analysis of dimension Q regarding the number of decimal places allows us to ask questions like this. Notice that in fact the Q analysis was done in combination of D dimension (we analyzed the quantity of a variable or the quantity of the number of decimal digits).

We mentioned earlier that Q may be related to a 'statistical property of a quantity'. The following example illustrates this case.

Example

Suppose we conduct performance testing and we measure the response time of some function. We execute the function 1000 times under the typical load and obtain 1000 measurements. They form the distribution shown in Fig. 4.8.

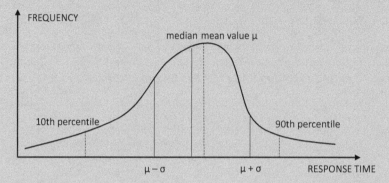

Fig. 4.8 Response time distribution

The analysis of dimension Q may indicate several interesting quantities that may be helpful in the further analysis. First, we have the mean value, which represents the average response time. In fact, mean value does not say much about the performance and it is not enough to detect the performance issues by analyzing only the mean value. The median splits the sample into two equal parts. In our case it will be the value such that half of the measurements fall below this value, and the other half over this value. Symbol σ denotes the standard deviation, which is the measure of dispersion. The bigger it is, the bigger are the deviations of the observations from the mean value. 10th and 90th percentiles are the values that cut resp. 10% and 90% of the sample values.

Having these values identified we may, for example, assume that everything that falls below 10th percentile and over 90th percentile (or below mean minus three standard deviations and over the mean plus three standard deviations) are the values that occur rarely, which may indicate that they may be burdened with measurement error. We may eliminate these values from our analysis. But, if this is the case, we may take a closer look at these test executions and find out why they gave us the results that deviate from the mean value so much. In other words—what was the reason for such fast (resp. slow) response?

The maximal, minimal, typical values, as well as different types of borders of variables' domains can be usually found in the requirements specification document. Therefore, a careful documentation analysis is a must. However, a tester needs to remember that there are many other entities falling under Q dimension analysis, but they are not visible at first glance.

4.5.4   Time

Time is the progress of existence. Similar to Quantity, it is also an abstract dimension, so it is usually analyzed in combination with other, 'real' dimensions like Data and Events. However, we can imagine a test that falls into the pure Time dimension: a reliability testing, where we just run the program and observe if/when it fails. In such a test we do not analyze any data or events. We just wait and observe the application.

Time may be discrete or continuous. It may be also measured in different units, for example:

- normal, real (clock) time,
- time represented as the number of actions (if we're focused on actions rather than on the real passage of time),
- time represented as CPU cycles (this is important when we want to attribute the right portion of time to a tested application in an environment with many other processes being run; we count then only the CPU cycles in which our SUT was processed by the operating system, so we eliminate the measurement error caused, for example, by another process run in the background and causing a longer response time of our application).

Here are some (test) ideas that can be utilized when considering dimension T:

- measuring or enforcing a given speed (or rate) of something: fast, slow, typical,
- measuring or enforcing a given amount of time between events,
- waiting (doing nothing) for a given amount of time,
- analyzing the time relationships between events,
- setting a time threshold for a given action,
- modeling something as event-driven, cyclic or anything in between,
- analyzing synchronous and asynchronous behavior of events
- analyzing possible deadlocks in a system.

The T dimension is also related to the ordering of elements/events that are sent or received. We may analyze different types of time relations, which is quite handy when designing time-related test scenarios. Five possible time relationships between two objects are presented in Fig. 4.9.

- Finish-to-start relation between tasks A and B means that B can start after A is finished. This is the most natural type of relation, presenting the typical sequence of actions.
- Finish-to-finish relation between tasks A and B means that B can be finished only after A is finished. It is not important when these both tasks started and which has started earlier.

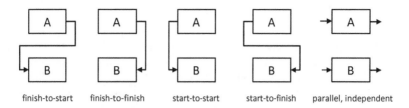

Fig. 4.9 Time relationships between tasks

- Start-to-start relation between tasks A and B means that B can start only after A has started. We are not interested when and in what ordering these tasks are finished.
- Start-to-finish relation between tasks A and B means that B can be finished only when A has already started. This type of relation is the most 'weird' one and is not encountered often.
- Parallel, or independent, relation between tasks A and B means that the tasks are not related in time.

Example

Here we show a test idea that verifies how the disturbance in a time relationship impacts the SUT. Suppose we test the functionality of opening a software work product from a file. The file can also be renamed. The natural sequence of events in this case might be: opening a file, closing the file after the work is done, renaming the file. The relation between these events is of 'finish-to-start' type. We can start our work on a project only when it is correctly opened, and we can rename the file only when the work is done and file is closed. However, we may check the disturbed sequencing of these actions. The test scenario looks like this:

1. Open the dialog 'Open File' in the application. The list of files should be shown in the dialog box.
2. Make sure you see the 'abc.txt' file.
3. Switch to OS console and rename 'abc.txt' to 'def.txt'
4. Return to the application and select 'abc.txt' file. See what happens.

This test checks in fact, if the 'Open File' dialog reacts on-line when the file names change. Another version of such a test would be to open some file in the application, switching to OS console and trying to rename the file. It is expected that OS should not allow us to change this name, because the file should be locked by the application.

(continued)

A more practical version of this test would be for a web form with the possibility of submitting a file:

1. Select a file to be sent and put its name into the web form.
2. Change the file name.
3. Try to submit the form.

4.5.5 Combinations of Dimensions

As in the case of basic dimensions, let us think now how the combinations of them may be related to a SUT. Note that this is just an inspirational example—such an analysis should be done for each SUT individually, as each application is different, operates in the different environment, has different testing goals, risks identified, and so on. Also, a test strategy being in force may forbid testing some aspects of a SUT. Table 4.2 presents the sample dimension combinations together with concrete examples of their application.

4.6 Using the TQED Model for Building an Effective Test Approach

The idea behind applying the TQED model in practice is very simple. Each identified element should be analyzed with respect to all dimensions and different dimension combinations. This analysis should be helpful not only in identifying fault models for these elements, but also other elements. Therefore, the application of the TQED approach is iterative. Elements can be both real (like concrete variables, events, configuration elements, user actions, etc.) and 'virtual' (like imaginable internal variables or even abstract objects, like quantity, duration or frequency of entities).

It must be noted that the TQED approach is just a proposition. It is *not* a universal solver of testing problems. The process involves a creative and rationally thinking tester. The most creative part is the identification of the elements. Once we do that, we try to develop new elements from the possible interpretation of different dimensions and their combinations for particular, previously identified objects. TQED is a simple 'creativity boosting framework', but the most important part of it is a substantive work of a thinking tester. Remember that the model will not guide you through the test analysis and design process. It will not design test cases for you. It is just a tool which you can use for designing and developing *your* test ideas.

The model will allow a tester to gain more advantages, when he possesses the skills described in Figs. 1.12 and 1.13. Probably the most important skills are: system, analytical and logical thinking. Of course, the effectiveness of the TQED model utilization depends heavily on the technical and business knowledge the tester possesses. The more he knows about the business and technology, the better.

Table 4.2 Sample dimension combinations

Type	Possible interpretations and ideas	Examples
DD	Combination or interaction of data, high-dimensional domains, relation between input and output, data comparing	Testing the form on the web page, where several fields together take a combination of values; testing if there are proper relationships between data, for example if arrival date is later or equal the departure date
DE	Data-driven interaction, focusing on the content/parameters of events (for example messages between two systems), performing operations on objects	Attempting to create a file with a 'weird' name containing special or language-specific characters
DT	Data durability (both logical and physical), data validity	Testing if an archived data imported from an old version of the system is correct; testing if correct data is available at a given moment of time
DQ	Amount/volume of data, boundaries of data domains, quantities of data parameters	Testing computing precision, testing minimal and maximal possible values, testing if a SUT can handle very large file
EE	Combination of events, realization of a business logic, IF-THEN rules, comparing two events	Testing an income call while a mobile app is running, testing if a SUT takes correct actions when a combination of conditions holds, testing the logical value of a formula in the code for different logical values of its parts
ET	Sequence of actions in time, duration of an event (too long, too short), achieving the same goal in different ways	Testing, in the auto-correction mode in Word, if we obtain a different effect when we delete a character and then write another one and when we select a character and then write another one; filling a form and then waiting for a long time and doing nothing
EQ	Extreme values for events, very small/very large number of events	Testing the SUT behavior when there's a lack of disk space, lack of memory, high CPU usage
TT	Time relations, concurrency, time comparing	Race condition testing, concurrency testing, comparing the run-time of two similar applications
TQ	Frequency, intensity, very short/very long periods of time	Stress testing
QQ	Different quantities of different objects at the same time, comparing two or more quantities	Testing the processing of a high volume of data under low-space and low-memory conditions; testing a very long number with a very small decimal precision
DET	Sequences of operations on data	Testing if data life cycle is correct, that is, for example, if first the data is defined, then used and then killed
DETQ	Sequences of events on data of different magnitude	Sending a lot of large size messages in a short period of time

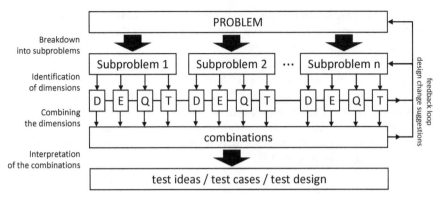

Fig. 4.10   Using the TQED model

Before we apply our model for supporting test cases design, we need to understand the conditions under which the SUT operates, the environment in which it works, project-related factors (like risks, time available, etc.) and testing goals. In short, we need to know what should be tested and at what level of detail. Answering these questions helps us to focus on the appropriate entities that are the realizations of the model dimensions. For example, when performing low-level unit tests, we will probably focus on variables, function calls and so on. But for a high-level test of a business process, the objects identified will probably be also high-level (processes, users, business-related events and so on).

The general procedure for creating an effective test strategy is shown in Fig. 4.10 and may look as follows.

4.6.1   Formulate the Test Problem

A test problem needs to be clearly stated, because it guides us in the next steps of the procedure. Test problem definition allows us to understand what types of 'subproblems' our main test problem consists of, what should be the proper level of abstraction when defining Dimension objects and—if possible—what kinds of bugs we are looking for.

4.6.2   Identify Subproblems

Subproblems represent the object types. A subproblem may be:

- Structural (for example, if problem = 'test system X', subproblems may represent something like 'test subsystem X-1', 'test subsystem X-2' and so on). Structural subproblems represent the object types related to structural or functional areas of a SUT.

- Related to a certain abstraction level (for example, if problem = 'test process X', subproblems may be like 'test the data flow in X', 'test the usability of X', 'test the interfaces of X/interactions between X-1 and X-2' and so on). This allows us to provide the Dimension objects on a proper abstraction level.
- User-focused. We may try to understand what aspects of a SUT are the most important for an end user. We can do this during the meetings, by conducting interviews, surveys or participant observations. Keeping in mind the well-defined business goal that justifies the system development allows us to understand the type of a business problem we solve for a client, so we can better understand the quality factors affecting the SUT.

4.6.3   Identify Objects

Having identified the subproblems, we go through four basic Dimensions (Data, Events, Quantity, Time) and identify objects falling into these categories within a given subproblem. We may utilize here the heuristics from Sect. 4.5. Remember that we should identify not only the obvious, visible, 'physical' objects, but also these latent ones.

4.6.4   Identify Combinations

Once we have identified all basic objects, we try to interpret their combinations. If a given combination of dimensions makes sense, we may include it to our set of test ideas. During this phase we may also discover other basic objects, not identified in the previous phase. When it happens, we add them to the basic Dimensions and repeat the 'Identify combinations' step for the augmented set of entities.

4.6.5   Identify Test Ideas

Each identified object or combination of object is analyzed subject to the test conditions. In other words, for a given entity we think what it suggests to us to test and how this test should be performed. The result of this phase may be just the set of high-level test ideas, as well as a very detailed set of concrete test cases or test scenarios.

4.7   Model's Universality

4.7.1   TQED as Generator of Test Approaches

Notice that our model is conceptual. It provides us with some basic notions that can be mapped to some real entities in our test project. Analysis of these notions and their combinations allows us to perceive very concrete risk areas or defect-prone places in a SUT. For example, when testing a ticket machine, we can map the 'Data' dimension to the real entity of this system, for example the number of normal or reduced tickets. Next, by analyzing the DDQ combination we may derive some worthwhile test conditions, for example the one in which the total number of chosen normal and reduced tickets is a boundary (maximal) value. By combining different dimensions related to the specific attributes of a SUT we are able to derive many test conditions, some of which may be quite non-trivial.

This approach is universal: dimensions themselves are only abstractions, hence they may be used in any kind of test type on any level of abstraction. The method fits in with the unit testing of a single class as well as with the system testing of a piece of hardware. Also, the model can be applied to any kind of a SW/HW test project, as all components of a SUT can be expressed in terms of the four basic software dimensions. We mentioned earlier that the model is generic and can be narrowed down to any other fault model. For example, each of Whittaker's software attacks [59] can be assigned to a dimension or to the combination of them: attack 3 'explore allowable character sets and data types' and attack 7 'force different outputs to be generated for each input' fall under D category; attack 4 'overflow input buffers' fits into DQ; attack 15 'force a function to call recursively' is an example of ET category; etc.

It may be advisable to perform the conceptual mapping for more than two dimensions. For example, one may consider combinations like DETQ or DDEQQT. Considering a specific number of combinations should reflect the optimal trade-off between the risk, quality of tests, time and model simplicity. Exploratory testers may use the model as well. It can serve as a practical tester's roadmap when performing the exploratory testing session. It can also help the tester in inventing valuable ad-hoc tests and in organizing the session in a systematic way.

The above-mentioned examples show that TQED may play a role of a 'test models generator' in the same way as Boehm's spiral model is a 'SDLC model generator'. In the following subsection we show the relations between TQED dimensions and well-known formal test design techniques.

4.7.2   TQED as Generator of Formal Test Design Techniques

There is plethora of literature on test design techniques. We recommend books [10, 85, 86] on functional testing techniques and [87–89] on non-functional ones. Each technique can be expressed in terms of our four basic dimensions and/or their combinations, as shown in Table 4.3. Again—this is just an example that comes from a particular interpretation of the TQED dimensions. Each tester can interpret it

Table 4.3 TQED dimensions and test design techniques

Dimension(s)	Example test design techniques
D	Techniques related to simple domain or data analysis, or data quality issues, such as: Equivalence Partitioning, dirty testing, SQL injection attack, API testing, happy path testing, data completeness testing, data validity testing, data accuracy testing; also Each Choice technique—the simplest form of the combinatorial testing
E	Event-related techniques, such as: GUI testing, requirements validation, statement coverage, decision coverage
Q	Techniques focused around magnitude or multitude, such as: Boundary Value Analysis, performance testing, stress testing
T	Techniques in which time plays a primary role, for example reliability testing or any type of a performance testing, where the expected test result is expressed in time-related condition (for example 'system response should be in less than 10 ms')
DD	Techniques related to combination/interaction of data, more advanced domain analysis and some types of combination-driven data quality testing, such as: all types of combinatorial testing (pair-wise testing, triple-wise testing, full combinatorial testing), classification tree method, data consistency testing
DE	Techniques related to performing single actions on data (not involving time) or data-driven interaction with user, system or environment, such as: some types of usability testing, event-related dirty testing (for example attempting to create a file with a nonacceptable name)
DQ	Techniques related to the amount of data, such as: Boundary Value Analysis, load testing, dirty testing applied to data syntax (for example, testing too long/ too short strings, rounding and digit precision testing, tests involving large datasets and so on)
DT	Techniques for checking data properties in time (not involving events), such as durability testing or timeliness testing
EE	Techniques driven by combinations of events, such as: decision tables, cause-effect graphs, condition coverage, Condition/Decision coverage, MC/DC coverage
EQ	Techniques describing extreme types of events, such as spike testing or stress testing (together with simulating extreme environmental conditions like lack of disk space or memory); also white-box techniques in which the number of model elements covered is important, for example loop testing (loop coverage)
ET	Techniques that focus on sequences of actions in time, such as: state machine testing, reliability testing, use case testing, different types of path testing (happy path testing, full path coverage, linearly independent paths coverage and so on); also some 'negative' form of testing, for example doing nothing for a long time
QQ	Techniques that combine quantities of events or data, such as spike testing or combinatorial performance testing (for example, testing in the presence of low disk space and high CPU usage)
QT	Techniques related to frequency or intensity, such as: soak testing, performance testing, stress testing
TT	Techniques focusing on time relations and concurrency, such as: race condition testing, concurrency testing, data flow testing
DDE	Techniques involving actions on combination of data; a typical example is integration testing and its different forms, like API testing, interface testing and so on

(continued)

Table 4.3 (continued)

Dimension(s)	Example test design techniques
DET	Techniques imposing actions on objects in time; a typical example is data flow testing or CRUD testing
EET	Techniques that consider time-related combination of events, such as concurrency testing with verification of different relations between events in time (for example, testing an incoming call while another application is used on a mobile phone)
DEQT	Techniques that involve all types of objects and activities, for example error guessing or exploratory testing.

in her own way, so she may classify the techniques differently (for example, a given technique may be even matched with one or more dimensions).

4.8   TQED in Practice: A Ticket Machine Example

We will now show how the TQED model can be applied in practice. Assume that we have to perform a system testing of a ticket machine. Although it is a piece of hardware, we may disregard all the physical parts and treat the machine as it would be a software. As we need to perform system testing, we will use a black-box approach. The only documentation we have is the machine itself and the instruction written on it (see Fig. 4.11).

By pressing two upper buttons a user can change the number of normal and reduced tickets to buy. Pressing 'Cancel' zeroes the values. After pressing a 'Buy' button a user inserts the coins and/or banknotes to pay for the tickets. The machine gives change. After a payment the tickets are printed and passed over to the dispenser. Let us apply the TQED approach for this SUT. We will not perform the full analysis, as it would take too much space. Instead, to show how one can benefit from the model, we will focus on some non-trivial test cases that can be derived using the TQED approach.

Following the TQED process, we first need to formulate the test problem. It is quite simple: our task is to test the ticket machine, which is a piece of hardware. This implies several important things: first, we have no access to the underlying software. Second, we will test the physical object, so we will have to pay attention to 'physical' actions that a user can perform when operating the machine.

Second step is to identify the subproblems. Here are some ideas of subproblems that will allow us to possibly identify more instances of different TQED dimensions:

- the machine is a hardware with a mechanical interface, so we will have to test this interface (buttons, coin/ticket dispenser, coin/banknote slots);
- the machine has some non-trivial business logic: there are some rules about the maximal number of tickets to buy in one session, and also some rules about the types of notes that can be used depending on the total amount;

Fig. 4.11 Ticket vending
machine

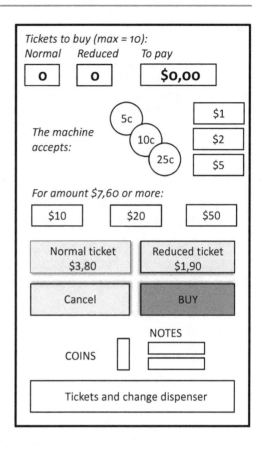

- the machine is a real-time physical system with the UI being accessible all the time, so probably it will be possible to enforce some non-allowed actions.

In third step we should identify objects—that is, the real entities related to basic dimensions. This is shown in Table 4.4.

Next, we should identify combinations and provide the test ideas. Let us provide some examples of the non-trivial test cases by analyzing several compositions of dimensions. They are shown in Table 4.5. The first column shows the abstract combinations of dimensions. The second one describes the mapping to the real entities of a SUT. The last one contains the test conditions related to the given combinations. We just give a sample of some non-trivial test ideas.

Theoretically, one can analyze all combinations for all mapped entities up to a given number of basic dimensions and therefore derive in a simple, almost mechanical way a very strong test suite. The number and types of combinations and tests are of course a matter of many factors, like risk analysis, available resources, test strategy and so on.

Table 4.4 Real entities for a ticket machine mapped to the basic software dimensions

Dimension	Real entity mapped to this dimension
D	Coin/banknote denomination, # of normal/reduced tickets to buy, # of ticket cards in the machine, # of coins/banknotes of different denominations in the machine, # of inserted coins/banknotes of different denominations, total price; valid and invalid coins/banknotes
E	Pressing a button, giving a change, inserting a coin/banknote, printing a ticket, power on/off; 'negative' events: waiting a long time, inserting a banknote into a slot but holding it back so that it cannot be accepted by a machine, inserting not valid objects into coin/banknote slots, hitting a machine, turning off the power
T	Long/short/typical period of time between actions
Q	Low or high value, boundary or close to the boundary, maximal possible value, minimal possible value

Table 4.5 Tracing the test cases/test scenarios to the TQED elements and mapped real entities

Combination	Mapping to the real entities	Test idea
D	Denominations	Use all kind of coins and banknotes; also use invalid denominations, non-US banknotes and things that are not coins/banknotes
EEE	Inserting a coin + Power off + Power on	Insert a coin; turn the power off; turn the power on; will the machine return the coin or remember that it was inserted before switching the machine off?
DDQ	Coin denomination + Total price + Boundary value (max)	Insert only the coins with the minimal denomination (5c) for the highest possible price ($38)—will the machine accept such a large number of coins?
ET	Inserting a coin + Slow time	After inserting the coin wait for a long time. Will the machine return your cash after some period of time, or will it be waiting for a user to perform the next action?
EET	Printing a ticket + Pushing 'Cancel' button + Short time between events	After pushing 'OK', which tells the machine to print the tickets, immediately push the 'Cancel' button. Will the machine cancel the action and return the money, or will it ignore the latter action?
DEQ	Price + Inserting a banknote + Value below [$7.60, $38]	Select tickets for less than $7.60, but try to pay with a $10 banknote—will the machine accept it or reject, according to the instruction?

(continued)

Table 4.5 (continued)

Combination	Mapping to the real entities	Test idea
EET	Pushing 'Normal ticket' button + Pushing 'Reduced ticket' button + The same time	Push two buttons at the same time. Will the machine add increase the number of both normal and reduced tickets by 1, the number of only one ticket type or do nothing?
EQTQ	Pushing 'Normal ticket' button + Pushing 'Normal ticket' button + Fast time + Large value	Push quickly (TQ) 'Normal ticket' button 10 times (EQ). Will the machine handle all these events properly and increase the number of normal tickets by 10 or by a smaller number?
EETT	Pushing 'Normal ticket' button + Pushing 'Reduced ticket' button + Long time + Normal time	Push the 'Normal ticket' button, hold it and while pressing it, push 'Reduced ticket' button. Will both events be handled properly, just one of them or none?
DDQQ	Number of normal tickets + Number of ticket cards in the machine + Large amount + Small amount	Select more tickets to buy than the number of ticket cards in the machine. Will the machine accept your order, return the money or print only as many tickets as possible and give you change for the non-printed tickets?
DDQQET	Total price + Number of 5c coins in the machine + Boundary value for price + Boundary value for number of 5c coins in the machine + Inserting a coin + Specific sequence of events	Prepare the test environment by placing no 5c coins in the machine (DQ). Order one reduced ticket for $1.90 (DQ) and insert coins and banknotes (E) in the following order (T): 10c, 20c, 20c, 20c, 25c, $1. How will the machine react? Will it print the ticket and give no change or return your money?

Note that when analyzing some combinations a beginner tester may discover some well-known test design techniques. For example, when analyzing a single dimension related to a given entity (for example, E for pressing a button) a tester may derive the tests that cover each kind of this event, which is an example of applying the equivalence partition technique; when analyzing DDQ for normal/reduced tickets and low/high values, she may discover the combinatorial testing, and so on. The TQED model may be a good tool to use in testing classes. It may help to develop some crucial tester skills, like creativity, analytical thinking, understanding the connections and relationships between the SUT elements, how they influence the residual risk, etc.

4.9 Conclusions

In this section we presented TQED—a simple model for supporting the tester's thinking. The model can be mainly used for test case design, but also in all other software development areas, like requirements engineering, risk analysis or code reviews. The model decomposes the SUT into the basic dimensions of four types: data, events, time, and quantity. Mapping them to the real entities of a given software and analyzing their combinations allows the tester to derive many interesting, non-trivial test cases or test scenarios. The model is simple, understandable, flexible and generic. It may be used within any test type or test level. The model was built from scratch: we started from a simple reflection on how software works by considering the software as a physical object existing in a space-time. This allowed us to derive the basic software dimensions, their combinations, and—finally—to construct a coherent approach to test case design.

It may seem that the TQED model is nothing new and does not bring any value into testing. It's true that the model utilizes well-known concepts that have been used by testers since the very beginning of the software testing. The original idea is to introduce a very simple framework that combines these ideas and therefore gives a new, novel look to testing.

It must be remembered, though, that the TQED model is just a proposition of an organized test approach. It is by all means *no silver bullet for testing*. It supports the tester in a testing process, imposes an organized, engineering approach, but does not excuse a tester from thinking. Software decomposition, choosing the right level of abstraction, prioritizing the tests according to the risk analysis and mapping the dimensions and their combinations to the real entities—all of them are the creative parts and cannot be automated.

Testing Techniques

5

5.1 Introduction

In Chap. 2 we described several testing strategies. Here we will go through some testing techniques, so first we need to explain the difference between strategy and tactics. Strategy is a long-term plan designed for achieving major goals for the organization, team or project. Strategy defines an approach that is a general guidance. Tactics, on the other hand, utilize specific resources, tools and techniques, in order to achieve sub-goals that support the overall mission. In terms of testing, strategy is usually defined in a test plan or other high-level document like this. Tactics are related to the specific testing actions and activities conducted by a tester.

The tester's toolbox is full of different tactics. Figure 5.1 symbolically presents their sources. Let's analyze them (in the following part of this paragraph they are written in italics). The final product of a development project is of course the working software, represented by a *source code*. As software has to solve a particular business problem, the goals we need to achieve are written in a *requirement document* or in a more formal requirements specification. Requirements, as well as some low-level software architecture details can be formally represented by *software models* and the non-functional characteristics by *quality models*. Software is used by *users* who have their *experience and intuition* that allow them to think of different ways the software can be used (or tested). Software always contains bugs, which can be represented by *error models*. These models represent the possible ways the software can fail.

When we start a testing project, we need to select the right tactics. The rational approach is to rely not only on one tactic, but to take advantage of all of them. Usually different tactics can be used most effectively in certain moments of time. Before and after that time a given tactic may be weak or even useless or harmful. It is crucial to know when to apply which of them to be the most effective. In the next subsections we will discuss this issue in more detail.

© Springer International Publishing AG 2018   181
A. Roman, *Thinking-Driven Testing*, https://doi.org/10.1007/978-3-319-73195-7_5

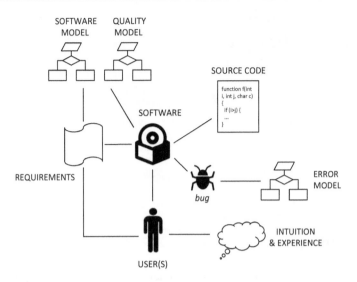

Fig. 5.1 Sources of tactics in software testing

Before we select and apply a given tactic, we need to answer the following questions:

- what are the available approaches?
- what information do we have about the software under test?
- what is the goal of testing?

The answers to these questions may, but do not have to be put in an official, well-structured document. The most important thing is to be aware of them and keep them in mind while designing the right tactics. Let's say it once again: in a tester's work it is the effectiveness which counts, not aesthetic.

The following sections do not describe a testing approach in an organizational sense. Rather they present the ideas that may be used in all possible testing problems, requiring both a very formal and sophisticated approach and completely informal ones.

In Sect. 5.2 we start our considerations with an important notion of oracle and relate to it the so-called 'oracle problem'. We discuss when it really occurs and how can we deal with it. The subsequent sections are devoted to different testing tactics: based on document analysis (Sect. 5.3), software models (Sect. 5.4), source code (Sect. 5.5), error model (Sect. 5.6), quality model (Sect. 5.7), statistics (Sect. 5.8), intuition and experience (Sect. 5.9) and other people (Sect. 5.10).

In the majority of these techniques the TQED model can be effectively used. We give examples of how to apply it when following a given tactic. When working with the TQED model, a feedback loop between TQED and tactics usually occurs: the TQED model impacts the method, and developing the method frequently brings some new ideas that can be used in the model.

No matter which tactic we choose, it is important to remember that it is not a machine for mindless test cases generation. Testing is not mechanical. Of course, we can automate tests, but every single tester's activity needs to involve thinking and analysis. In Sect. 3.3.4 we said that a professional tester can always reasonably justify the thing he does at a given moment of time. This is what thinking's about. If at any moment of time we have a feeling that we follow some rules, techniques or methods *just because*, we need to stop and analyze this situation. We have to ask ourselves: why are we doing this? What benefit do we expect from this action? No model or technique, even the best one, can be an excuse for performing mindless actions.

TQED can be used to boost our creativity, but some ideas emerging from the model may be useless, have no sense or a very low added value. The model just arouses the tester's creativity, but the rest of the work is solely the tester's responsibility. There is no one correct theoretical answer to any testing problem. The answer depends on the assumptions, chosen techniques and judgement calls which the test planner makes.

5.2 Test Oracle Problem

5.2.1 Test Oracle Problem from the Theoretical Point of View

An oracle[1] is an entity that is able to predict the future or give us the correct answer for our question. In software testing an oracle is a machine that is able to tell us whether the test passes or fails. From the theoretical point of view the oracle problem is a very important issue. Testing, technically, is a form of quality *control*. In order to control we need to be able to compare the real outcome against the expected one. That's why in many formal documents or standards describing the test case document one of its most important parts is an 'expected result' field. If we cannot say whether the test failed or passed, we do not bring much added value to the testing process.

Some techniques for test design include some form of an oracle by definition. For example, decision tables model the behavior of a system in terms of the business rules. Each column of a decision table consists of two parts: conditions and actions. Depending on the combination of logical values of the conditions (that is, whether they hold or not) the actions are defined. These logical values of actions describe the expected test case output (that is, the expected system's behavior). In a so-called model-based testing the models *by definition* are able to give us a correct answer and we just have to compare it with the actual one.

---

[1]This ancient name comes after the person able to provide wise and insightful counsel or prophecies about the future. The most famous oracle was seated in the Sanctuary of Apollo in Delphi (Δελφοί), in the upper-central part of the ancient Greece, near Mount Parnassus.

However, not all techniques give us this opportunity. For example, Equivalence Class Partitioning method splits a given domain into disjoint classes and it is expected that for any two elements lying in the same class the system's behavior should be 'the same'. In particular, it means that if for one of those elements the program fails, it should fail for the other. And if for one of them the system works fine, it should work fine as well for the other. However, the method doesn't tell us what we should understand by 'a correct behavior'.

This may be problematic, because—as testers—we need to know what we should expect. Another issue is test automation or automatic test data generation. There are many methods for a quick generation of test data or test cases fulfilling a given type of coverage. But these methods usually cannot tell us what should be the expected output.

Hence, from the theoretical point of view, the oracle problem is an important issue. Luckily, as we will see later, in practice we can live with it without (almost) any troubles.

5.2.2   Test Oracle Problem from the Practical Point of View

The good news is that in practice the oracle problem isn't usually very important. Sounds weird, but it really isn't. In most cases the tester is able to evaluate the system's behavior. In fact, the more the tester knows the system/business/etc., and the more experienced she is, the less important is the oracle problem. An intuition plays an important role here. However, we need to be careful, because intuition is not always right. Therefore, the tester's criticism, precision and attention cannot be overestimated.

There are many cases where the oracle problem just doesn't exist. Probably the most obvious example is a situation in which we test some SUT and the only thing we are interested in is if the program fails. The system failure can be easily detected and we do not need any sophisticated oracle here. Here are some other, maybe less obvious examples:

- evidently wrong answer that can be detected even by a non-specialist,
- time issues (for example, an action, like generating the report, done suspiciously too fast or too slow),
- impossibility of performing the subsequent action in the system (system hangs up).

Of course, the reality is not so simple. There are many cases in which we cannot really tell what should be the expected answer. For example, when we run a test that validates a high-level business process, or when we perform exploratory testing, and someone asks us: 'what is the expected result of your test', the only thing we can tell is that 'the system works just fine'. Which means: nothing wrong happened. This of course implies that everything that happened was correct, but it may be very difficult to formally describe what do we mean by saying 'correct' in this case.

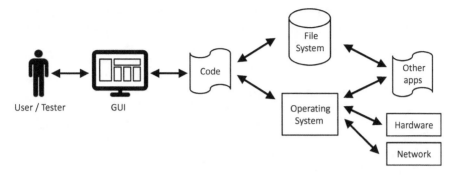

Fig. 5.2 When the test really passes?

Another issue is this: OK, the program did what it should, but how can we be *sure* that a test has passed? Look at the Fig. 5.2. It represents the typical situation in testing: a tester has access to a SUT via some kind of an interface (like API, GUI or CLI). This is usually the only touchpoint with a system understood as SUT together with all other entities in the environment. So, to say that we are *sure* that a test has passed, we would've had to prove that the state of the *whole system* is as expected. Hence, apart from the right answer/right behavior visible on the screen, we would have to demonstrate, among others, that:

- the code run-time was correct, the lines of code were executed exactly in the order in which they should be executed, with a proper number of times, and the program's internal state is correct,
- the operating system behaved as it should (for example, it assigned the expected amount of memory),
- the file system was not corrupted and that all the files contain the proper (expected) data,
- the internal states of other applications co-existing with our application are correct,
- the hardware worked as expected,
- there were no network/communication errors,
- and so on.

As we see, it is practically impossible to define the expected result even for the most simple test case! But again, from the practical point of view this is not a big problem. Usually all problems hidden behind the GUI propagate to the application and emanate as failures. Performing the root cause analysis we may localize these problems deep in the system's architecture. But what about problems that really occurred, but were not visible through the user interface? We might say that as long as a user doesn't see a failure, everything is fine, even if deep inside the environment something is wrong.

Sometimes it works, but a professional tester obviously cannot ignore this. One of the advantages of system thinking combined with analytical thinking is that being aware of such issues, a tester can plan in advance the test scenarios that are able to detect this kind of latent problem. There are several tactics that can be used here:

- during the verification of a test result we simply check the state of the different parts of the system (for example, we may directly verify that after some operation in the SUT the database is consistent),
- designing and performing the test scenarios in a way that can reveal the latent bugs (for example, invoking a certain sequence of test steps that results in a visible failure),
- performing some type of a static analysis of the SUT architecture taking into account the SUT interactions with the environment,
- using the 'built-in testing' approach (see the next subsection).

All the above methods work fine. The only problem is the effort needed to apply them. A tester needs to know how to find a good trade-off between the cost/effort needed to create some form of a test oracle and the benefits of using it. The answer may come from the detailed risk analysis, which, in turn, may be supported by a TQED model. For example, we may identify different TQED dimensions within the whole environment and analyze them with respect to the risk related to them and to their combinations.

We've already said that an oracle is easy to build when we are interested only in the fact whether a SUT crashes. At the end of this subsection let us give two other situations in which creating the oracle is very easy:

- when it is easy to verify the results computed by SUT (in this case an oracle does not necessarily give us the correct answer, but rather plays a role of a smart comparator),
- when the computation is reversible.

Here are the two examples for both these situations:

Example
Suppose that our SUT implements a new, fast sorting algorithm. We would like to test it with millions of random test cases. The system accepts an array of numbers as input and returns the same sequence, but in an ascending order. The pseudo-code shown below implements a simple oracle for verifying if the output is correct (the notation O[i] means the i-th element of the array O):

```
function oracle
input: I (input array of size m), O (output array of size n)
1. if (m≠n) return 'wrong result - test failed';
2. for (i in 1...n-1) do
```

(continued)

```
3.    if O[i+1] < O[i] return 'wrong result – test failed';
4. for (i in 1...m) do
5.    if I[i] is not in O return 'wrong result – test failed';
6.    remove I[i] from O
7. return 'test passed'
```

In the above example the algorithm checks three things: first, if O and I have the same number of elements. Second, if O array is sorted (lines 2–3). Third, if I and O contain exactly the same set of elements (lines 4–6). If any of these conditions is not fulfilled, the oracle says that the actual result is wrong. The result is correct if and only if all these three conditions are fulfilled. Notice, that in this case the oracle doesn't compute the expected result itself, but derives it from the input and the actual result.

Example
Suppose that we test a new function root(x) for computing the square root of a given number. The oracle can easily verify the correctness of the computations by checking, if $x = root(x) \cdot root(x)$, assuming there are no rounding errors (if we are not sure about how the rounding works, we can always check the equality with root squares that are the integer values). Another, more practical example, is this: suppose we want to check the correctness of the procedure Add that adds a new user in a system. If D is a state of the database before adding this user, and D.X denotes the state of D after performing X, an oracle can check if D = D.Add(x).Del(x), where Del is a procedure of removing a user from the database. Notice that this won't work if Del won't report any problem when, for example, we want to remove an account that does not exist.

No matter how difficult it is to create an oracle for a given problem, the developer's team should make this task as easy as possible by instrumenting the code that allows an exhaustive logging and controlling the run-time. The analysis of such logs may allow us to look beyond the user interface (see Fig. 5.2) and see what's going on inside the application and its interfaces with other elements in the system's environment.

The logging mechanism enables us to verify the test passing more thoroughly. The extent to which the system's actions are logged should be defined by a tester, together with a developer, as it is the latter who debugs code. Logging may be useful also when a product is released to the customer, as the logs may be helpful in analyzing the field bugs. However, some clients may be reluctant to use such mechanisms, for example because of the fear of losing their privacy. Code instrumentation and logging also affects the system's performance.

Last but not least, we need to discuss the problem of the 'apparent test passing'. In many cases, from the formal point of view, the SUT returns the correct answer and such a test is usually classified as 'passed'. However, the answer may be returned in a wrong way. For example, the layout of the returned report makes it hard to read. These 'informal fails' are usually very subtle and related to the usability issues. For a good tester simply checking the result is not enough. She should also check if the way it was returned was also correct. It may require some communication with business analytics or the client, so it definitely takes the tester's time. But in return we obtain much higher built-in quality.

5.3   Testing Based on Document Analysis

Documentation, apart from the direct communication with a client, is a standard source of information about the software, hence it constitutes a natural 'knowledge database' of a SUT. Before we describe in detail the document-based testing approach, let us distinguish between two ways in which we can look at the documentation:

- as a basis for deriving tests,
- as an artifact that itself can be subject to test.

The latter is very important because of quite a paradoxical phenomenon: the documentation usually tells us how the software should be built (it reflects the architectural design), but as itself it is not a working software. From the psychological point of view, people tend to diminish its role and treat it as a 'necessary evil'. They have a feeling of losing their precious time for performing a pointless—according to them—paperwork, creating documents that no one will ever read.

Therefore, no one likes to create documentation. When people do it, it is frequent that someone told them to do this and they just carry out the command. Often the documentation is written after the software is created (!), just because there is a formal requirement that the system has to be documented. This of course results in a low documentation quality. So, the documentation becomes a normal test object.

However, we will not discuss here the documentation testing issues. Throughout this section we assume that the documentation is just a basis for deriving tests. We focus on methods that may be useful in analyzing the documentation from this point of view. Also, we only focus here on a textual documentation. The documents in a form of models are discussed later, in Sects. 5.4, 5.6 and 5.7.

As this book is primarily on *thinking* in testing, let us now make a deeper thought on the documentation. What kind of information can we, as testers, reveal from analyzing the documentation? Of course, the most obvious information is the document's content. It is natural: a document was written for a certain purpose of informing its reader about something. And this 'something' just makes its contents.

However, we may infer more interesting information by analyzing (or interpreting) the document structure and the *reasons* behind this structure. Such analysis is usually neglected, probably because the premises behind a certain document structure are not seen at first glance. However, they may carry quite a lot of valuable information.

Let's analyze one of the most popular documents used in the agile processes, namely user stories. A user story is a short, simple description of a feature written from the perspective of someone who needs it from the system. They are usually structured as shown in the left part of Fig. 5.3.

The document consists of three parts:

- **as a [user type]**—this part of a user story gives information about the type of a user that needs some functionality. The user type shows the business context of the problem, because different types of users may have completely different expectations from the same functionality.
- **I want [goal]**—this part of a user story describes directly the goal a given user type wants to achieve. Usually the goal implies a functionality to implement.
- **so that [reason/effect]**—this part of a user story gives the justification for the document. Namely, it explains what kind of a *business* problem the user wants to solve.

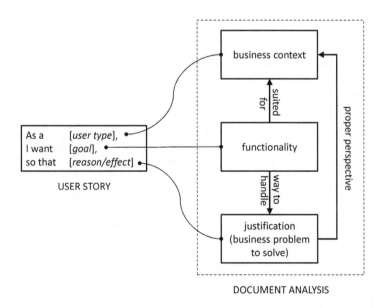

Fig. 5.3 User story and the analysis of its structure

The third part of a user story (so that [reason/effect]) is frequently omitted or diminished, but from the tester's point of view it is of huge value, because it directly relates the functionality (I want [goal]) with the business need. In Sect. 1.2.4 we discussed the importance of understanding that testing should be done from the business perspective, if we want to achieve a high product quality.

The first part of a user story (as a [user type]) gives us the business context: we are informed *who* wants to solve the business problem. This information impacts things like usability testing, because different types of users may have different expectations about the solution and the way it will be used by them.

Let us now give an example of the analysis of a user story from the tester's perspective.

Example

The following user story comes from https://www.mountaingoatsoftware.com/agile/user-stories.

- As a *vice president of marketing*,
- I want *to select a holiday season to be used when reviewing the performance of past advertising campaigns*
- so that *I can identify profitable ones.*

Additional conditions of satisfaction (acceptance criteria):

- Make sure it works with major retail holidays: Christmas, Easter, President's Day, Mother's Day, Father's Day, Labor Day, New Year's Day.
- Support holidays that span two calendar years (none span three).
- Holiday seasons can be set from one holiday to the next (such as Thanksgiving to Christmas).
- Holiday seasons can be set to be a number of days prior to the holiday.

Let us analyze this document. From the direct content analysis we see that a high-level manager needs some functionality in the reporting module of an application that would allow her to select a particular period of time when reviewing a performance report. The reason for that is that she wants to identify the most profitable one. The user story is extended by so-called additional conditions of satisfaction, which describe the requirement in more detail by, for example, making sure the developer won't forget about several important retail holidays.

We will now use the TQED model to perform a high-level analysis of this requirement, assuming that we are interested in the acceptance tests only. The analysis will only result in a set of test ideas, not the concrete test cases. This more detailed work can of course be done subsequently.

(continued)

The test problem (which in our case equals the subproblem) is directly related to the user story description: we need to test a certain functionality from the VP's point of view, bearing in mind the business problem she has. In Table 5.1 we present the main objects identified during the analysis of the user story.

Table 5.1 High-level TQED analysis of the user story

Dimension	Objects
Data	VP of marketing, performance report, holiday season, campaign, holiday types
Event	Selecting a season, reviewing the performance
Quantity	Number of days prior to the holiday, number of calendar years
Time	Holidays dates

Dimension combinations and test ideas derived from them are presented in Fig. 5.4, in a form of a mind map. Each textual element of the map was created by analyzing its predecessing element(s) using the ideas related to proper dimensions.

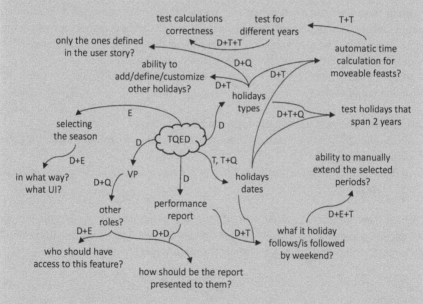

Fig. 5.4 Mind map for analyzing a user story

(continued)

The analysis allowed us to indicate several important issues, for example:

- Will the desired feature be used only by a VP, or also by some other users?
- Should we implement a mechanism that allows to define new holidays, or should we just restrict to the ones defined in a user story? How is the information about the holidays stored? Can a user have a direct access to it (security issues)? Can he change this information? If so, how will the software react?
- Will the profit calculations be correct in case of a 'weird' report configuration (for example, involving a holiday that falls on a leap year, spans 2 years, etc.?

By performing this analysis we do not only generate many interesting test ideas, but also, at the same time, we perform a review of the user story. This approach allows us to communicate with the client, review, correct and detail the document.

Apart from user stories there are also many other document types. In particular, documents containing a lot of textual information, like requirements specification. These artifacts can be also subject to the TQED analysis, in this case, similar to the model creation in the case of the object-oriented analysis.

We can easily identify TQED elements occurring *explicitly* in the text using the following simple rules:

- data-related objects are usually represented by nouns,
- event-related objects are usually represented by verbs or by nouns describing the events,
- quantity- and time-related objects are usually represented by adjectives, adverbs and numerals.

Once these objects are identified, during the combinations generation it may happen that some new, previously hidden objects emerge. Let's see how this method works in practice. This time, we will analyze a low-level example.

Example
Our team is asked to provide a functionality for counting the score in a bowling game. The rules that describe how the score is calculated play the role of a requirement and are shown in Fig. 5.5 (the document was taken from [90]). For the sake of simplicity, we do not consider UI issues—we focus only on the rules. The testers are expected to provide a set of test cases for validating the score calculating subsystem.

(continued)

Rule 2 – The Game
2a. Definition
A game of American tenpins consists of ten (10) frames. A player delivers two balls in each of the first nine frames unless a strike is scored. In the 10th frame, a player delivers three balls if a strike or spare is scored. Every frame must be completed by each player bowling in regular order.
2b. How Scored
Except when a strike is scored, the number of pins knocked down by the player's first delivery is to be marked next to the small square in the upper right-hand corner of that frame, and the number of pins knocked down by the player's second delivery is to be marked inside the small square. If none of the standing pins are knocked down by the second delivery in a frame, the score sheet shall be marked with a (-). The count for the two deliveries in the frame shall be recorded immediately. A frame-by-frame account on scoring and calculating can be found on the Rules page of BOWL.com.
2c. Strike
A strike is made when the full setup of 10 pins is knocked down with the first delivery in a frame. It is marked by an (x) in the small square in the upper right-hand corner of the frame where it was made. The count for one strike is 10 plus the number of pins knocked down on the player's next two deliveries.
2d. Double
Two consecutive strikes is a double. The count for the first strike is 20 plus the number of pins knocked down with the first delivery following the second strike.
2e. Triple or Turkey
Three successive strikes is a triple or turkey. The count for the first strike is 30. To bowl the maximum score of 300, the player must bowl 12 strikes in succession.
2f. Spare
A spare is scored when pins left standing after the first delivery are knocked down with the second delivery in that frame. It is marked by a (/) in the small square in the upper right-hand corner of the frame. The count for a spare is 10 plus the number of pins knocked down by the player's next delivery.

Fig. 5.5 Bowling game rules

Let us perform a TQED analysis and try to find some interesting test ideas. The obvious data objects are: points, pins, frame and delivery. The events objects are: knocking down the pins, strike, spare, calculating the score. The quantities come directly from the text—the explicitly given values are: 9, 10 [rounds] (rule 2a), 2, 3 [balls] (rule 2a), 2 [delivery #] (rule 2b), 10 [pins] (rule 2c), 10 [points] (rule 2c), 2 [deliveries] (rule 2c), 2 [consecutive strikes] (rule 2d), 20 [points] (rule 2d), 1 [delivery #] (rule 2d), 3 [strikes] (rule 2c), 30 [points] (rule 2e), 1 [strike #] (rule 2e), 300 [points] (rule 2e), 12 [strikes] (rule 2e), 1 [delivery #] (rule 2f), 2 [delivery #] (rule 2f), 10 [points] (rule 2f). Time-related entities are, for example: 'regular order' (rule 2a), count recorded immediately (rule 2b), two consecutive strikes (rule 2d), 12 strikes in succession (rule 2e), 'next delivery' (rule 2f), etc.

The most straightforward idea would be to test the correctness of score computation for 'significantly' different situations, which would require the software to utilize all the rules from the analyzed document. Let us analyze the events corresponding to these rules, together with the constraints between them:

(continued)

- a score for a given frame depends: (1) only on the present frame, (2) on this and subsequent frame, (3) on this and two subsequent frames
- within each frame there may be (4) one or (5) two deliveries
- in 10th frame a player delivers (6) two or (7) three frames
- in the second delivery (8) none of the standing pins are knocked down or (9) at least one

Notice that (1) happens only when a player gets less than 10 points in a given frame, (2)—when he gets exactly 10 points in exactly two deliveries, (3)—when there's a strike in this frame. Situation (4) happens if and only if there's a strike, and (7)—if and only if there's a strike or spare in the 10th round.

The simplest test set would validate the score computation for each of the above test conditions, enumerated by (1)–(9). Notice that because (6) and (7) cannot be tested together, we need at least three tests. In case we would like to combine the events, as (7) can happen in one of the two mutually exclusive situations, we would have to prepare at least four tests. Each test is represented by a 10 frame scoring table for a player. The sample two tests for independent testing of (1)–(9) are shown in Table 5.2. Test conditions are denoted only the first time they are tested.

Table 5.2 Tests for score calculation in bowling

Frame	1	2	3	4	5	6	7	8	9	10
Pins knocked down	3+4	5+5	10	10	10	3+0	0+0	3+4	1+9	4+5
Frame score	7	20	30	23	13	3	0	7	19	9
Test condition tested	(1), (5), (9)	(2)	(3), (4)			(8)				(6)

Frame	1	2	3	4	5	6	7	8	9	10
Pins knocked down	10	3+6	3+7	6+0	8+2	8+1	8+1	3+4	2+6	10+5+3
Frame score	19	9	16	6	18	9	9	7	8	18
Test condition tested										(7)

Using dimension combinations we can design some more thorough tests, for example:

- E+T: sequence of events, for example: three consecutive strikes, strike +spare+strike, etc.,
- E+E: two deliveries after a spare in a given frame to check, if only the result from the first delivery will be added to the given frame's score,

(continued)

- D+Q: boundary values for score: a game with the minimal (0) and maximal (300) points,
- E+Q: 'boundary events': three strikes in the 10th round vs. spare+strike in the third delivery (to see if a system allows for a fourth delivery).

From the tester's point of view it is reasonable to *define the requirement as a software property that can be verified in testing*. When analyzing any document that describes or specifies requirements, a good practice is to assume that *each* sentence in this document describes some property, and therefore is equally important. This means that for each statement we should be able to provide at least one test condition, that is, something that can be tested or verified. If we are unable to relate any test condition to a given sentence, two situations are possible:

- the sentence is redundant/unnecessary, thus should be removed from the document, or
- the sentence should be analyzed more deeply, because it may contain some latent requirements that we are unable to spot at the time.

5.4 Testing Based on Software Model

Some documentations use formal descriptions of software or its parts by presenting this content in form of a formal software model. A formal model uses a well-defined, precise language so that it is unequivocal. Theoretically, every person who reads such a model, should understand it in exactly the same way. Practice is, unfortunately, slightly different, even in the case of a very formal modeling language like UML, but this topic goes beyond the scope of this book.

From the tester's point of view, we may divide the software models into two groups: the first one gathers models that describe directly the software architecture. The examples may be UML models, like: class diagram, activity diagram, communication diagram, use case diagram and so on. To the second group belong models related to formal test design techniques. These are models like: domain model, decision table, state machine, classification tree, cause-effect graphs and so on.

Models from the first group are usually the basis for software development and are derived from the 'technical' requirements, usually irrelevant from the user's point of view. They describe the software architecture, its desired internal structure, etc. These models are used by developers to *create* the software. For the purpose of this section we will refer to these models as 'technical documentation' or 'technical models'. Models from the second group are usually derived directly from the (business) requirements specification. They are used by testers to *validate* the software. We will refer to them as 'business documentation' or 'business models'.

The reason why we differentiate these two groups is extremely important from the tester's perspective. Notice that—at least from the theoretical point of view—technical models should never be used as a basis for the testing activities. This is because the software is built according to them, so if a model is wrong, and hence is the software, our tests will not discover that, because the software will perfectly conform to the wrong model. Tests created upon technical models will of course also be wrong—if such a test passes, it means that it gives a false positive answer. The only thing we could detect is the inconsistency between the model and the software. But if the model is wrong, such tests may be a waste of time, because even when we detect this, probably the software will be 'corrected' so that it conforms to the (wrong) model.

Business documentation, on the other hand, may serve well as a test basis. These documents represent the user's point of view. So the chance that they will be wrong is minimal. However, formal software models that represent the user's perspective don't really help much in generating test ideas. Usually, these models are related to the formal test design techniques. These techniques generate tests from the models almost automatically. Finally, as in the case of the technical documentation, business models can also be reviewed or analyzed in order to detect inconsistencies, redundancy, contradictions or other problems with the model itself.

The moral from this story is this: in contrast to business documentation, the technical one should not be a base for tests. If so, a natural question arises immediately: can it be then of any use for a tester? If we cannot test on the faith of the technical model, we could step back and test the model itself. But how can we provide the expected answer? Obviously, we cannot derive it from the technical documentation, as it is the test subject.[2] We could do it with the requirements as a test base, however business-related statements may not be a good source of truth about the technical documents. Sometimes it may work, sometimes it may be very difficult or even impossible to perform. Hence, there are at least two possible things we can do with technical documentation:

- if it is possible to use the business documentation, use it as a test basis for testing the technical documentation (it is something like 'backward' or 'reverse' validation, where we validate the architecture using the business requirements),
- use technical documentation as an additional source of test ideas (for example, by using a TQED model) to increase the strength of the test suites related to business requirements.

In the following part of this section, we will see how we can realize the above ideas in practice. Table 5.3 summarizes the benefits and potential problems (opportunities and risks) when working with different document types.

---

[2]See the example with the Polish constitutional crisis described in Sect. 3.2.4 to recall why explaining a theory by itself is logical nonsense.

Table 5.3 Opportunities and risks for different documentation types

Documentation type	Opportunities	Risks
Business	May serve well as a test basis or as an oracle	Doesn't support creativity—they offer a limited view on a system
Technical	May increase creativity as an additional source of test ideas	Cannot really serve as a test basis or as a test oracle

5.4.1 Business Software Models

There are many test design techniques which use software models in support of testing. We will not describe them in detail, because there are a lot of resources available—see for example books [15–18, 24, 40, 62, 85, 86]. We will just shortly characterize some of these techniques and discuss the general issues related to them.

The main characteristic of a business software model is that the tests are derived from it in a way that covers this model's components. The well-defined rules of building the model and then successively deriving test cases from it allows us to be systematic and also to not forget about any important test. These formal test design techniques are not only a good way of testing certain aspects of a SUT, but are also an excellent tool for a static form of requirements testing. They may be very helpful in an early detection of contradictions, ambiguities and other problems in the requirement documents.

Example

Calculation of points for the FIFA World Ranking is given by a formula $P = M \cdot I \cdot T \cdot C \cdot 100$, where, in particular, M stands for the points related to the result of a match. The official FIFA document [91] gives the following rule for calculating M: 'Points for a victory (3 points), a draw (1 point) or a defeat (0 points). In a penalty shoot-out the winning team gains 2 points, the losing team 1 point'. Suppose we have to implement a function that calculates M. Since the requirement given above obviously describes a business rule for this purpose, we may use a decision table to model it. The table may look like the one shown in Fig. 5.6.

Rule # →	1	2	3	4	5	6
CONDITIONS						
Match result	WIN	WIN	DRAW	DRAW	LOSS	LOSS
Penalties?	YES	NO	YES	NO	YES	NO
ACTION						
Points assigned	2	3	???	1	1	0

Fig. 5.6 Decision table for the FIFA points calculation rules

(continued)

We have two conditions: the match result (a given team may win, draw or lose) and the penalties (they are at the end of a match or not). Depending on the six possible combinations of these two conditions a given number of points is assigned. Each table's column represents a coverage element, so we should provide six tests for covering all of them, therefore validating the FIFA rules. But before we start to design, implement and execute our tests, let us define the expected output (action) for each of the six combinations. Notice that when we try to do this in case of the draw with penalties (column 3) the result cannot be determined from the requirement. A tester familiar with the FIFA rules may know that penalties must end with a conclusive result—one team must win and the other lose. However, formally, the requirement doesn't say anything about this situation. A tester should immediately sort this out by, for example, consulting with a client, business analyst or another competent person.

The above example shows how effective a sole test design is—without any test implementation and execution—in finding different requirements issues. In this case it was possible, because a decision table forces us to analyze all condition combinations, while a requirement misses one of them. In a normal, textual form of a requirement, it is very easy to skip some of them when describing business rules. Formal models may restrict our creativity in generating valuable test ideas, but on the other hand they force the tester to be very systematic and accurate in checking all possible situations the model is able to provide.

The characterization of the most common model-based test design techniques is given in Table 5.4. Each technique is described by its name, the underlying model it uses, the software feature that is described by the model and the way of deriving tests from these models. Some techniques provide only one way of coverage, some others offer the whole family of the coverage criteria.

5.4.2   Model as a Form of Idealization

Models don't necessarily need to be given in advance. They may be created in the tester's mind, as the idea of a representation of the SUT. They don't need to reflect the exact structure of the original problem, but may be a very helpful tool in generating test ideas. A tester can create several models, one being the refinement of another.

Table 5.4 Characterization of the most common model-based formal test design techniques

Technique	Model	What it represents?	Way of deriving tests
Equivalence partitioning	Domain model	Model (structure) of the input, output or any other domain	Covering equivalence classes
Boundary value analysis	Domain model	Boundaries of the domain	Testing boundary values
Domain testing	Domain model	Multidimensional version of the above techniques	Many coverage types that use ON, OFF, IN and OUT points
Classification tree	Domain model	Combinations of elements from different domains	Many coverage criteria related to different types of combinations
Decision table	Business rules	Business logic realized by SUT	Covering each column of the table
Cause-effect graphs	Cause-effect graph	Business logic realized by SUT	Covering different combinations of causes/effects
State transition testing	Finite state machine	Dynamic behavior of a SUT	Covering different elements of a machine (states, transitions, etc.)
Syntax testing	Formal grammar	Valid structure of the object (for example string variable)	Many coverage types related to the way we generate strings from the grammar

Example

We need to perform high-level tests for a system supporting the publication workflow in an editorial office of some journal. The client described the workflow in the following way: when an author finishes writing a publication, he can send it to the editorial office. The editor-in-chief appoints the lead editor who then takes care about all further processing actions. He sends the paper to the appropriate reviewers who review the paper. The reviewers may take one of the following actions:

- accept the paper for publication,
- accept the paper for publication but recommend a minor review,
- recommend a major review and the second reviewing round,
- reject the paper.

The decision is sent to the editor, who communicates it to the author. Apart from rejecting, for all other decisions the paper is either published without any further actions, or the author corrects the paper according to the reviewers' remarks and resubmits the paper again.

(continued)

The software is built and we need to perform some tests for the business scenarios of this system. A tester may think first of how the developer could implement this application and come up with the model presented in Fig. 5.7.

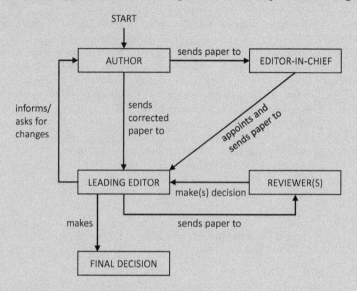

Fig. 5.7 The first idealization of the SUT

Let's apply the TQED approach to generate some ideas that will allow us to validate the model and—if it's correct—help us in generating test ideas. The most obvious Data objects are: paper, author, leading editor, editor-in-chief, reviewer. The possible Events are: sending the paper to the editor-in-chief, passing the paper to the leading editor, sending the paper by a leading editor to the reviewer, making the decision by a reviewer, informing the author about the decision, sending the corrected version of the paper to the leading editor and making the final decision by the leading editor.

Let's validate the model by generating some initial bunch of test ideas that result from the combination of dimensions. Here are some examples:

- E+E (combination of events): analyze the sequences of events described by the model
- E+T (sequences of events, concurrency): analyze if the model allows concurrent events and if they are allowed
- D+Q (quantity of data): is it possible to have more than one object of a given type within a single process?

(continued)

As for the E+E combination, we see that the model allows, for example, for the following sequences: Author $\rightarrow$ sends corrected paper to $\rightarrow$ Leading editor $\rightarrow$ makes $\rightarrow$ Final decision. It is probably unlikely that such a process is allowed by the system: a paper first needs to be sent to the editor-in-chief, and only after he sends the paper to the leading editor, the communication is between author and the leading editor. Notice that the model allows many other strange sequences, for example:

- when the leading editor asks the author to correct the paper, the author can send the corrected version to the editor-in-chief,
- a reviewer can decide to publish the paper, but the leading editor rejects the publication or a reviewer rejects and leading editor publishes it (both these situations may be acceptable, but a tester should know under what conditions this can happen),
- the leading editor receives the paper from the editor-in-chief and makes a decision (for example, publishes the paper) without sending it to the reviewer.

As we see, the model seems to be quite wrong. It does not take into account different conditions which result in a certain process flow.

As for the E+T combination, we can consider the following situations regarding the paper processed:

- after submitting the first version of the paper, can the author send the next version while the first one is being processed at the 'leading editor' or 'reviewer' state?
- can the author, reviewer and leading editor undertake their actions concurrently? For example, the author sends the corrected version of the paper, at the same time the reviewer sends another review, and the leading editor sends some other information to the author?

The simplest way to overcome these kinds of problems is to say that the model is always in one state and the only action that can be made is one of the actions going from this state. However, when testing if system conforms to the model, we can of course try to force the occurrence of the parallel actions.

As for the D+Q combination, we may combine 'reviewer' with 'quantity', which immediately results in the following question: what happens if there is more than one reviewer? Each of them can review the article independently, but what if they don't reach a consensus with their decisions? What is the business rule for such a situation? There may be several possibilities:

(continued)

- reviewers must reach a consensus—the system allows them to compare their reviews and collectively make up the decision;
- the final decision is up to the leading editor, who analyzes all the reviewers he receives and decides about the final decision.

By analyzing the combination D+D+E for 'reviewer's decision' + 'reviewer's decision' + 'making decision by the leading editor' we may come up to the following problem: if all the reviewers decide about the acceptance of the paper, does the leading editor have the possibility to make another decision, or the system won't allow for this?

The analysis described above may induce us to refine our model. We should include the different workflows for different statuses of the paper (new one, corrected one). We should also take into account that there may be more than one reviewer. The improved model is shown in Fig. 5.8.

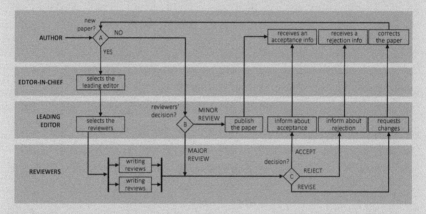

Fig. 5.8 An improved idealization of the SUT

Notice that now it is not allowed that the editor changes the reviewer's decision: if the reviewers decided upon minor review, the revised paper can be published directly by the leading editor. If the reviewers wanted a major review to be done, the editor must resend the corrected paper to the reviewers for the second review round.

In the improved model each 'swim line' represents one actor in the system. Rhombuses denote decision points and the vertical lines before and after 'writing reviews' states represent the concurrency. Analyzing now the T+T combination for this we may come up with the next question: the reviewers usually have some time for writing a review. What happens if some of them send their review within the allowed time and the others don't? Will the final decision be based only on the reviews done in time? Or will the reviewers be

(continued)

warned by the system that the time has exceeded (or that the deadline is approaching)? Such time-related events are definitely worth testing.

Having an improved model, we may also think of applying some formal coverage criteria to our model. For example, treating this workflow as a control flow graph, we may need to design tests such that:

- each edge (process flow) will be traversed at least once,
- each decision point will be evaluated at least once for true and at least once for false,
- each pair of decisions will be evaluated in every possible combination (true-true, true-false, false-true, false-false; this is sometimes called decision to decision coverage or DD-paths coverage),
- each loop will be executed exactly 0 times, exactly once, and more than once,
- and so on.

The example test scenarios for covering the DD-paths coverage are given in Table 5.5. The decision points in Fig. 5.8 are denoted by A, B, C.

Table 5.5 Test scenarios for covering the DD-paths

		Covering decisions in DD-paths (showing only first occurrence)			
#	Scenario	A→B	A→C	B→C	C→A
1	New paper (A), accept (C)		YES/ ACC		
2	New paper (A), reject (C)		YES/ REJ		
3	New paper (A), revise (minor) (C), corrected paper (A), minor review (B)	NO/ MIN	YES/ REV		REV/ NO
4	New paper (A), revise (major) (C), corrected paper (A), major review (B), revise (C), corrected paper (A), major review (B), accept (C)	NO/ MAJ		MAJ/ REV MAJ/ ACC	
5	New paper (A), revise (major) (C), corrected paper (A), major review (B), reject (C)			MAJ/ REJ	

Notice that not all DD-paths are feasible: the model forbids us to execute YES/MIN or YES/MAJ for the DD-path A→B; MIN/ACC, MIN/REV and MIN/REJ for the DD-path B→C; NO/ACC, NO/REV and NO/REJ for the DD-path A→C; and REV/YES, REJ/NO, ACC/NO, REJ/YES and ACC/YES for the DD-path C→A. But this does not mean that we cannot check if the SUT conforms to the model, that is, if it also forbids that. Notice that the refined, corrected model also allows us to find some 'negative' test cases.

The above example showed also an interesting thing regarding the coupling between the TQED model and the idealized software model. Applying the TQED approach to the first version of the idealized model allowed us to notice some drawbacks of the latter. This forced us to refine the model and the refinement allowed us, in turn, to notice some other interesting TQED dimension combinations which we missed earlier. This is an excellent illustration of the benefits from the iterative application of the TQED model in conjunction with some other entity to which the TQED model is applied.

5.4.3   Technical Software Models

We mentioned earlier, that we may use a business documentation as a test basis for testing the technical documentation. Such a 'backward' validation allows us to check the architectural design against business requirements. This may seem to be weird, as the 'normal' sequence of events is this: first we gather requirements, then design something that fulfills them, and then we build the solution and test it against the requirements. Here we do something different: We gather the requirements, design something, think in advance about high-level tests for a proposed solution and use these ideas to verify the design. If everything is OK, we build the solution. If not, we correct the design.

Such an approach is very effective in terms of the ROI, because it detects design defects very early. Design defects are the worst kind of defects: they are hard to spot during the design and implementation phases, because it is hard to 'see' the whole design and its usefulness during low-level design, implementation and test activities, like developing a single module, integration testing and so on. The design defects usually appear when the application is fully integrated and when we are able to perform full, end-to-end business scenarios. Correcting a design defect usually requires a lot of work that costs a lot of money.

In order for a tester to be effective in this process, she needs to be familiar with the models that are used during the business analysis and architectural design. The examples of these models are:

- UML structure diagrams, which describe the static, structural properties of the software and its design; these are[3]: class diagram, object diagram, package diagram, composite structure diagram, component diagram, deployment diagram and profile diagram,
- UML behavior diagrams, which model the dynamics of the designed software; these are: use case diagram, activity diagram, state machine diagram, interaction diagram.

Some of these models may be perfectly viewed as the business models, for example use case diagram or high-level activity or state machine diagrams. However, in the

---

[3]We refer here to the UML standard in version 2.5.

following we focus on the technical aspects of the discussed models. The following, simple example shows how testing can reveal some faults in the architectural models.

Example
The e-library project allows the librarians to manage their library resources through a web-based system. The system, in particular, should allow us to create different types of catalogues for the readers (for example, catalogue for humanities, for science and so on). Each catalogue contains a set of book cards. A single book card represents a single, physical copy of a book owned by the library.

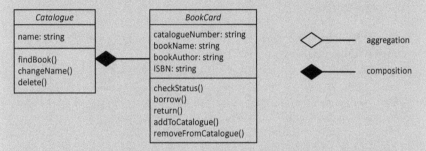

Fig. 5.9 Fragment of the class diagram and two types of relations between classes

The system is designed using the object-oriented approach. Figure 5.9 shows a fragment of the class diagram for the system (on the left). The fragment describes two classes representing two main entities: catalogue and book card, together with a relation between them. In the object-oriented approach the classes may be related in several ways, for example:

- **dependency**—class A depends on class B if A needs to call B to perform some operation; a change in B may result in a need of change of A; this is the weakest relation between classes;
- **association**—represents a temporary relation between the objects of two classes, but the lifetimes of these objects are independent: removing one object does not necessarily mean that the other one needs to be also destroyed;
- **aggregation**—represents a 'whole-to-part' relationship, where 'part' can belong to many 'wholes', and 'whole' does not manage the existence of the 'part'; this relation is stronger than an association, because the 'whole' in some sense owns the 'part', but is not the only owner[4];

(continued)

---

[4]Aggregations are discouraged in UML 2.1, since they do not have a clear semantics.

- **composition**—represents a 'whole-to-part' relationship, where 'whole' is the only owner of a 'part'; this is the strongest relationship between classes: neither 'whole', nor 'part' can exist without each other and their lifetimes are strongly correlated: destroying the 'whole' results in destroying the 'part'.

Our diagram shows a composition between the catalogue and book cards, which means that the book card is a part of the catalogue. Let's imagine that the system is implemented and we can perform the acceptance tests. We may apply now the TQED model to generate some test ideas. Let us consider the following dimensions:

- data: catalogue, book card
- event: add to catalogue, delete catalogue
- quantity: relation 'many-to-many' between catalogues and book cards

By analyzing the combination DDEEQ to the above-mentioned dimensions, we may come up to the following test scenario:

1. create catalogue X, create catalogue Y
2. add book Z to catalogue X
3. add book Z to catalogue Y
4. delete catalogue X

In this scenario, we created two catalogues and added the same book to both of them. This is perfectly correct, because the requirements don't restrict the number of catalogues which may contain a given book. The following question arises: what should happen after step 4. in our scenario? When we delete catalogue X, we should also remove all the books from this catalogue, in particular the book Z. But this book belongs also to the catalogue Y. We see that there is a problem with the relation between classes 'catalogue' and 'book card'. It should not be the composition, but aggregation. We discovered a flaw in the software design. If this is done early in the software development process, the cost of fixing it is zero, because we just have to erase the composition and substitute it with aggregation.

Another test might realize the DQ combination for Data=book author and Quantity=more than one. What happens if a book has more than one author? Is it possible to add such a book to the catalogue? Obviously, the model does not allow this. Probably, the 'author' field should be a list of strings, not a single string.

Another way of using the technical documentation is to analyze it as a source for test ideas. In fact, this is exactly the same activity as described in the above-mentioned example. Using this class diagram we may easily identify data and events: data entities are the classes' fields: catalogue name, catalogue number, book name, book author, book ISBN number. Events may be related to the methods in the classes: finding a book, changing the name of a catalogue, deleting the catalogue, checking the book status, borrowing and returning a book, adding a book to and removing it from the catalogue. We may also consider events like creating a catalogue, creating a book card, removing the book card. Some example test ideas resulting from the TQED analysis are given below:

- borrow a book, try to borrow it again;
- borrow a book, delete the book card, try to return a book;
- create two catalogues and try to name them with the same name;
- create a book card with a very long title;
- create a book card with a very long list of authors;
- create a book with empty 'book name' field;
- borrow a book that does not belong to any catalogue.

Technical models are not necessarily very formal, like the class model described above. The typical example of a less formal model is a use case diagram. It has a very well defined structure, so there is some formalism, but the content of the diagram does not follow any formal rules. If we want to generate the test ideas from a use case, we may use a technique that analyzes the scenario described in the use case and incrementally 'expands' the scenario. The scenario enlargement may follow the 'local' version of the TQED analysis.

In this version of the method we analyze every single step of a use case and we try to answer the following questions:

- is there any alternative path that begins in this step?
- can we complicate the data processed in this step?
- can something unexpected happen in this step?
- what would happen in this step if a given use case precondition does not hold?

Example
Let us consider the example of the editorial system described in Sect. 5.4.2 and the use case that represents the typical submission process:
    USE CASE: Typical submission process
    Preconditions: author is logged in the system and has an article in place

1. The author sends the article to the editor-in-chief.
2. The editor-in-chief chooses the leading editor and sends him the article.
3. The leading editor initially accepts the article and sends it to two reviewers.
4. Both reviewers write positive reviews and send them back to the leading editor.

(continued)

5. The leading editor accepts the paper, informs the author and publishes the article.

Here are some examples of the unexpected situations that may hold within this process:

- in step 1, the article may be already reviewed—can it be sent to the editor-in-chief?
- in step 2, the editor-in-chief may do nothing—is it possible? Will the author be informed about it?
- in step 3, the leading editor may send the article to only one reviewer or may not send it to the reviewers at all—is this possible? And if so, what should happen then?
- in step 4, the reviews may contradict each other—who makes the final decision?
- in step 4, the reviewers may not perform their reviews—will the leading editor be alerted about it? Will the reviewers receive an automatic reminder?
- in step 5, the leading editor may make the decision that contradicts to the decision of the reviewers—is it possible? If so, what should happen?

This method is a useful trick for discovering the so-called exceptions, or alternating paths in the use case.

5.5   Testing Based on Code

As in case of the technical documentation, the source code cannot be the test oracle. How can we then use the source code in testing? There are two typical approaches:

- treat code as a test object, that is—test it directly; the most frequent type of testing is code review
- treat source code as a means to compute black-box tests thoroughness using different types of coverage metrics

5.5.1   Code Review

When performing code review a tester should look at the source code from at least two perspectives:

- 'big picture'—what does the reviewed code do as a whole? View the code as an algorithm, investigate its correctness, complexity, halting property,
- 'detailed review'—inspect every single instruction, separately from the other instructions.

When performing a detailed review, the following (or similar) checklist may be used. The checklist items should be applied to every analyzed instruction, one by one:

- is a given computation done at the right time (not too early and not too late)?
- is it possible for an arithmetic error to occur (like division by zero, using negative numbers when only non-negative values are expected, wrong precision, wrong constant values)?
- are all the variables involved in the computation initialized and defined? do they have the correct values?
- is the type of the returned value defined correctly?
- when invoking a function, can it return some unexpected value?
- how are the unexpected situations (exceptions) handled? can we catch all possible exceptions and handle them properly?
- are the function parameters given in the right order?
- can we invoke a function with the incorrect input values?
- if short-circuiting[5] takes place, can it lead to some unexpected behavior because of not executing some part of the decision being checked?
- can we exceed the boundaries of the variable's value?
- how fast will the invoked function finish its computations?

The effectiveness of this method relies strongly on the expert knowledge of a programming language used, its syntax, semantics, good practices on code writing, etc. The code review should be conducted together with the experienced developers. However, it may be a good idea to involve also some inexperienced programmers or even people outside the project and without any technical knowledge. This is because such people can ask 'weird' questions allowing the experts to overcome the rut thinking and pay attention to issues that they would never have thought of if they would have to conduct the review on their own.

---

[5]Short-circuiting is a mechanism that allows us to calculate the value of only a part of the logical expression to infer about the value of the whole expression, thus saving time. For example, if we know that in the expression "E = A OR B" A is true, there is no need to calculate the value of B, because no matter what it is, E is true.

Example
The following code comes from the Linux kernel repository [92].

```
 1 int next_pidmap(struct pid_namespace *pid_ns, unsigned int
   last)
 2 {
 3     int offset;
 4     struct pidmap *map, *end;
 5
 6     if (last >= PID_MAX_LIMIT)
 7         return -1;
 8
 9     offset = (last + 1) & BITS_PER_PAGE_MASK;
10     map = &pid_ns->pidmap[(last + 1)/BITS_PER_PAGE];
11     end = &pid_ns->pidmap[PIDMAP_ENTRIES];
12     for (; map < end; map++, offset = 0) {
13         if (unlikely(!map->page))
14             continue;
15         offset = find_next_bit((map)->page, BITS_PER_PAGE,
           offset);
16         if (offset < BITS_PER_PAGE)
17             return mk_pid(pid_ns, map, offset);
18     }
19     return -1;
20 }
```

Here are some example issues that might be checked during the code
review:

- line 6: can the constant `PID_MAX_LIMIT` be negative? where does it
  come from?
- line 10: does the calculation of the array element (the number between the [
  ] brackets) always return an integer? what if `last+1` is not divided by
  `BITS_PER_PAGE`?
- line 13: can the function `unlikely()` return an unexpected value? how
  fast will it return the result?

5.5.2   Code as a Means for Coverage Metrics

The most typical use of source code in testing is to provide the different type of code
coverage measures for black-box tests, as follows. First, we execute the black-box
test suite, designed without any prior knowledge about the internal structure of the

software. Next, we measure the code coverage achieved by these tests, but in terms of the white-box[6] coverage metrics. This measure may be helpful in evaluating how strong our test suite is (but we need to be very careful with that—see Sect. 6.2).

Each coverage metric is related to some error hypothesis. For example, when we try to achieve statement coverage (that is, we want every line of code to be executed at least once during the tests), we assume that the failure will occur when we execute a faulty line. However, execution of a faulty line does not necessarily lead to the failure. We may of course use some stronger coverage criteria, like decision coverage, MC/DC coverage, loop coverage, path coverage and so on (see [10, 81] for more information on white-box testing). The stronger the method we use, the more detailed the error hypothesis is verified.

Of course, covering all possible white-box criteria does not guarantee that we tested the software well. In particular, the tests derived directly and solely from the code analysis are of little value from the tester's perspective: it is difficult to use them at the system or acceptance test levels.[7] A much better idea is to test the software with black-box methods, and *then* use the white-box coverage metrics to assess the thoroughness of these tests. White-box metrics should be used as a post mortem analysis, not as the goal of itself. This is because the latter does not take into account the business view of the system. If our tests are designed upon some specification (or even our intuition, common sense, guessing, etc.) *and* at the same time the white-box coverage metrics are high for these tests, we may consider them as strong. The coverage analysis may of course allow us to define some additional tests that will increase the coverage.

Nevertheless, one must be very careful when using these metrics. A professional tester knows that they are just a pale reflection of the test thoroughness, because they are indirect metrics. Coverage of different code structures does not translate directly into the ability of a test suite to detect errors. In Sect. 6.2 we discuss this problem in more detail.

White-box testing is often used in unit testing performed by developers. They write their unit tests so that the test suite ideally achieves 100% statement coverage and 100% decision coverage. The main problem with these techniques is that very often it is hard or even impossible to find the input parameters (the only thing we control in unit tests) for which we force the software to behave in a precisely defined way. Of course there are tools that support us in providing test data for covering certain parts of the code, but in general this is a very difficult task (see the code example in Sect. 6.2). For example, we may require that a control flow reaches some inner loop, executes it a given number of times, so that some variable will exceed a certain value, which will result in evaluating some decision outcome to false, etc.

In system tests the straightforward use of white-box methods makes no sense when applied to the source code. As we mentioned earlier, it can be used to evaluate

---

[6]In fact, a white box is as transparent as black box. To emphasize the knowledge of the *internal* structure of the object under test, some authors prefer to use the term 'glass-box' instead.

[7]Of course, they are still useful at the unit and integration test levels.

the strength of the black-box test suite. However, we can use white-box techniques directly on higher test levels. For example, we may apply them to the models describing business process workflows, to a given set of requirements, to the elements of the menu and so on. An example of this application was presented in the example from Sect. 5.4.2, where we applied a DD coverage technique to the business process. In such cases the white-box methods are used to derive the high-level black-box tests.

5.6   Testing Based on Error Model

Testing may be driven by error models. In this approach, the starting point is the defect or failure we want to discover. After it is set, we perform the test activities in order to reveal this bug. In fact, every rational testing is based on an error model, even when this model is not given explicitly. We wrote earlier that a professional tester is always able to justify the actions she undertakes. This is because she knows exactly what she wants to achieve, and she knows that because she has in her mind an error model that drives her actions. She just knows what she wants to validate at a given moment.

We can distinguish between two main types of error models:

- error models embedded into formal test design techniques,
- explicit error models.

The first type of model occurs in the formal test design techniques. Each test design technique has the ability to discover a certain type of defect. Table 5.6 shows some examples of techniques together with their corresponding error models.

Explicit error models describe the concrete types of faults, for example:

- an undefined value for a variable,
- a buffer overflow for a variable,
- software is unable to handle a file whose name contains special characters.

A good example of the approach that uses this kind of error model is so-called software attacks. For more information on this topic, see [59–61].

Table 5.6 Formal test design techniques and corresponding error models

Technique	What the corresponding error model represents?
Domain analysis, BVA	Wrong handling of data
Decision coverage	Wrong handling of business logic
State machine testing	Wrong handling of sequence of actions
Decision tables, cause-effect graphs	Wrong handling of business rules
Data flow testing, CRUD testing	Wrong handling of data operations (definitions, uses)
Random testing	Data causing errors form a hidden pattern in the domain

Before a tester starts testing, she should be very clear on what is she going to validate. This does not only increase the chances of revealing an error, but also allows us to use the proper, most effective method. For example, when we test an algorithm for granting a loan, there will be probably much of business logic testing, as well as issues with roundings, boundary values and so on.

When a tester is not sure about the significance of a given error model, she may use some well-known software and design metrics to reveal the most important risk areas. For example:

- high cyclomatic complexity may indicate that there is a rich business logic in the module under test, so probably we should focus on business logic testing,
- low cohesion means that a class performs more than one function, which—from the architectural point of view—is not a good idea; a class should be refactored and split to two or more cohesive classes; classes with high cohesion are robust, reliable and reusable; therefore, a good strategy for low cohesion may be maintainability and negative testing,
- high coupling means that there is a high dependency between two classes or modules, which is undesirable; classes with high coupling should be subject to integration and data-oriented testing, because communication overhead likely increases the occurrence of integration and data-related errors.

Error models may emerge from different risk management activities. For example, different error models can be derived from the risk analysis. The TQED method can be efficiently used here, because it supports testers in creativity, which is crucial during brainstorming sessions or other risk analysis techniques.

5.7   Testing Based on Quality Model

Quality models are a good basis for defining non-functional testing. This is because they usually focus on so-called quality characteristics of the software, which are the non-functional aspects of the software. Historically the earliest software quality models—by McCabe and by Boehm—did not consider functionality as a quality characteristic. The newer ones, like ISO/IEC 25000, include it as one of the quality features.

When we look at the quality models (especially in sources that refer to the original publications), they all look very similar: they just enumerate the quality characteristics and sub-characteristics. However, they also offer us a certain view, or idea, about software quality. Hence, we may utilize quality models in at least two effective ways:

- treat the quality model just as a checklist that enumerates software features or characteristics that should be tested,

- use the quality view that a model offers to organize testing, define the testing strategy and align the testing process with all other development activities within a SDLC to provide (or assure) the adequate level of quality in the final product.

The original publications that describe the quality models, usually offer much more information than the simple diagrams or lists of characteristics. Therefore, in case a professional tester wants to use such a model, she should always read the original source, not the publications that refer to it. These usually simplify the models. Let us now review the most important quality models. For each of them we will investigate what the model offers, and in what way it explains the quality. In case of the first model, McCall's one, we will describe it in more detail, to show how much useful information the original papers on these models[8] contain.

5.7.1   McCall's Model

McCall's model [93] is probably the first formally defined software quality model. It was developed in 1977 for the US Air Force. The model is shown in Fig. 5.10. It aims towards the software development process and attempts to bridge the gap between users and developers by focusing on a number of quality factors reflecting both users' and developers' views and priorities. These characteristics come from an extensive literature research done by McCall and co-authors.

The model consists of:

- 3 software product activities,
- 11 factors,
- 23 quality criteria,
- metrics.

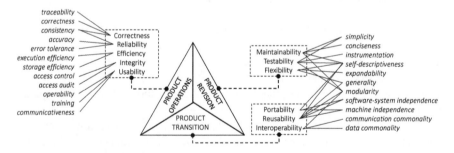

Fig. 5.10 McCall's Quality model

---

[8]For example, McCall's Model is written in a three-volume report. The first volume has 168 pages, the second one 155, and the third one 42. Altogether, the whole quality model is defined on over 360 pages!

McCall's model recognizes three different orientations that one could take in looking at a delivered software product. These orientations correspond to three software product activities representing different product life cycle phases: operation, revision and transition. Factors describe the external view of the software, as viewed by the users (so-called external quality). Quality criteria describe the internal view of the software, as seen by the developer (so-called internal quality). Metrics are defined to provide a scale and method for measurement of the quality criteria.

Relations between product activities, factors and quality criteria are shown in Fig. 5.10. For example, when looking at product operation, users pay attention to such things as correctness (does it do what I want?), reliability (does it do it accurately all of the time?), efficiency (will it run on my hardware as well as it can?), integrity (is it secure?) and usability (can I run it and use it?). During the development process, to provide the proper level of the reliability, the developers should focus on things like consistency, accuracy and error tolerance.

The establishment of criteria for each factor has a fourfold purpose [93]:

1. The set of criteria for each factor further defines the factor.
2. Criteria which affect more than one factor help describe the relationships between factors.
3. Criteria allow a one-to-one relationship to be established between metrics and criteria.
4. Criteria establish the working hierarchical nature of the framework for factors in software quality.

The original model of McCall gives much more information about factors and criteria, like the trade-offs between the different factors. For example, there is a natural trade-off between efficiency and factors like integrity, usability, maintainability, testability, flexibility, portability, reusability and interoperability. It means that achieving a high quality level of efficiency usually results in a low quality level of the latter factors. The other trade-offs are between integrity and flexibility, reliability and usability, integrity and reusability, and between integrity and interoperability.

This observation is very important from both the tester and managerial point of view. Many managers aim to achieve the highest possible quality in every software aspect. This is impossible because of the above-mentioned trade-offs. A good idea is to analyze which factors are crucial from the users' point of view and focus on achieving the highest possible quality for them, consciously sacrificing the quality level of less important factors. Each project may have completely different factor importance prioritization, which depends on things like: software type, user type, time and budget available, user's requirements, business problem to solve and so on. Each quality criterion should be measured. McCall's model provides a large number of metrics for all the criteria defined.

The idea behind McCall's model is that the quality factors, when viewed together, should give us the 'big picture' of the software quality.

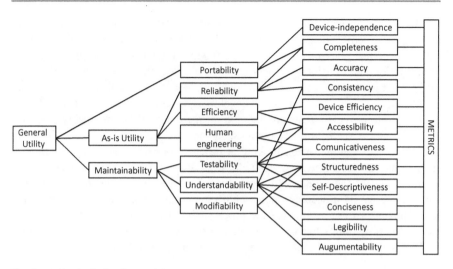

Fig. 5.11 Boehm's Quality model

5.7.2   Boehm's Quality Model

Boehm's Quality model was described in 1978 in [94]. It is similar to McCall's Quality model: it shows the hierarchical dependencies between high-, medium- and low-level characteristics. The model is presented in Fig. 5.11.

High-level characteristics represent the three main client's points of view on the software:

- **as-is utility**: how well can I use the software?
- **maintainability**: how easy it is to understand, modify and test the software?
- **portability**: is it possible to use the software after changing its environment?

The medium layer is composed of the seven quality factors that together describe the software quality. The low-level layer contains so-called primitive characteristics, which provide the foundation for deriving the low-level metrics. These metrics may then be related to the quality factors, therefore measuring the high-level characteristics of the system.

Boehm's model puts emphasis on the maintainability, which is one of the three main quality factors. From the tester's perspective it is quite reasonable, because the biggest software costs usually occur after the release and are related to different maintainability activities. It is important to test the maintainability in advance, before the release. Good maintainability may substantially reduce the after-release costs.

5.7.3   ISO 9126 and ISO 25000 Quality Models

The ISO 9126 Quality Model is similar to McCall's and Boehm's models, because in fact it was based on them. It also presents a hierarchical structure of quality factors, but contrary to the two earlier models, the sub-characteristics are disjoint, that is, one quality subcharacteristic belongs to exactly one characteristic. Moreover, the ISO model introduced the 'functionality' characteristic, which was missing from both McCall's and Boehm's models. ISO 25000 is much more extensive compared to the replaced ISO 9126 and describes more quality subcharacteristics.

The ISO model defines indicators to measure quality subcharacteristics and data elements to construct the indicators. It may be of practical use for testers who want to quantitatively measure the software quality characteristics. Subcharacteristics in ISO 9126 and ISO 25000 are related more to the user-centric quality aspects, in contrast to the previous models, which emphasize the internal quality. Hence, ISO models reflect more the user point of view, while McCall's and Boehm's models reflect more of a product view.

This user-centric approach makes the ISO models very interesting from the tester's point of view. We said earlier, that the main goal of the development team is not to write the software, but to solve the client's business problem. As it is the client, who is our real boss, all the testing activities have to be subordinated to the client's needs. ISO models may help us understand which quality characteristics may be important from the user's point of view and how to measure them.

5.7.4   Problems with Quality Models

The quality models, as any other models, are not perfect. They may help us in understanding different quality points of view and different relations between quality characteristics, but they also have some drawbacks and there are some caveats that a professional tester needs to be aware of. Here is the list of the problems discussed in the literature (cf. [95, 96]):

- quality models do not conform to an explicit meta-model, hence the semantics of the model elements is not precisely defined and may be subjectively interpreted by the reader,
- quality models are generally not integrated into the various tasks connected to quality, although they should act as a central repository of quality information; for example, specification of quality requirements and the evaluation of software quality are usually not based on the same model,
- quality models do not address different views on quality; for example, in terms of the Garvin views on quality, contemporary models usually focus on the user or product perspective, but the value-based view, very important in the IT manufacturing, is largely missing in them,
- current quality models are not customizable in terms of the variety of software systems; the same model serves for a huge business information system and for a tiny embedded controller, but it is rational to take a slightly different perspective for these completely different types of systems,
- most quality models follow a hierarchical and taxonomic decomposition of quality factors, but they do not follow any defined guidelines and may be

arbitrary; this ambiguous decomposition may also result in overlapping between different quality factors (for example, code quality is an important factor for maintainability, but at the same time it is related to the security),

- the models lack a rationale for determining which quality factors should be included in the quality definition—this is probably an unsolvable problem, as the notion of quality is multidimensional and very subjective: the definition of high quality depends on who evaluates the quality,
- the models lack a rationale for deciding which criteria relate to a particular factor (for example, it is not clear why portability is a top-level characteristic of ISO 9126),
- most quality model frameworks do not provide ways for using the quality models for constructive quality assurance (for example, it is unknown how and when the quality models should be communicated to different stakeholders),
- the models don't provide any method for transforming the low-level metrics measurements into the top-level quality factors, which makes it impossible to verify that the chosen metrics really affect the observed behavior of a factor—this makes the models untestable.

From the rational tester's point of view we should follow the advice of Ed Yourdon, who pointed out that 'sometimes less-than-perfect is good enough' [97]. This means that only business goals and priorities can determine how much 'less than perfect' we are willing to accept. As for the quality, the tester should focus on things that are important from the user's perspective. The most efficient ways of discovering which factors are important for the users and why are the following:

- discussions with users and other stakeholders,
- iterative approaches to software development, so that there's a frequent feedback from the user who is able to see the subsequent versions of the system,
- tester's *common sense*, which allows us to prioritize things and decide when a 'good enough' quality is achieved.

5.8   Testing Based on Randomness and Statistics

When speaking about application of statistics to software testing, we need to distinguish between two things:

- using statistics to *analyze data* from software tests,
- using statistics to *generate* tests.

The first activity is useful when we want to evaluate the software reliability growth. This can be done in terms of things like: number of defects, defect density, mean time between failures and so on. Data on defects and failures may be collected and used as input to prediction models, like the software reliability growth model. Such models may predict what is the expected number of latent defects in the software, what is the expected time to next failure and so on. This requires from a tester a very good understanding of statistics and mathematical modeling.

Another activity that uses statistics as the method of analyzing data is more of qualitative nature. We may analyze what types of defects occur and when. If we classify each defect into different categories, we may use this data to provide many different reports that can be used in the quality improvement, for example by supporting root cause analyses. An example of such a method is Orthogonal Defect Classification [98], a concept that enables in-process feedback to software developers by extracting signatures on the development process from defects.

The second way of using statistics allows us to automatically generate tests. The statistical methods may help us, for example, in generating test data that covers evenly the input domain. Such an approach is useful in detecting errors represented by domain points that form different patterns. Unfortunately, random testing often is not the best idea for generating test data—this is usually the least efficient method for detecting errors. However, there are some situations, where random testing may be a really powerful tool.

Example

In pair-wise testing we try to test all the possible combinations of values of any two input parameters. For example, if a test is executed for a given browser (IE or Firefox), operating system (Windows or Linux) and file type (pdf, xls or txt), we have three parameters, two of which have two possible values and one has three possible values. For each pair of values of any two factors we want to have at least one test in which this pair will be present. In our problem six tests are enough:

Test	Browser	OS	File type
1	IE	Windows	pdf
2	Firefox	Linux	pdf
3	Firefox	Windows	xls
4	IE	Linux	xls
5	IE	Windows	txt
6	Firefox	Linux	txt

For example, the pair (browser=IE, file type=xls) is contained in test 4; (OS=Windows, file type=txt) is present in test 5; and so on. Unfortunately, the problem of computing the *minimal* number of tests that achieve the full pair-wise coverage, in general is a hard problem.[9] Probably there does not exist a fast algorithm for computing it for an arbitrary configuration of

(continued)

---

[9]In theoretical computer science terminology we can say that the decision version of this problem (that is, deciding, for an input number n whether n tests is enough to achieve the coverage) is NP-complete.

parameters and their values. There exist some sophisticated, heuristic algorithms that try to produce the smallest number of test cases, however they don't guarantee the optimal solution.

From the practical point of view, we do not need the smallest possible number of test cases. A sub-optimal solution is usually also accepted. Surprisingly, generating combinations randomly allows us not only to quickly achieve a high coverage, but also to make such a random test suite as effective as the one that gives 100% pair-wise coverage. Moreover, constructing an algorithm that randomly generates the combinations is very easy. In the literature there exist conflicting results: some papers show that there is no difference between pair-wise and random technique regarding test effectiveness [99], others claim that pair-wise or combinatorial approaches in general provide only a small improvement over the random approach [100]. Nevertheless, the simple, random approach may be considered here as quite effective.

The second example uses a probabilistic model for simulating the user behavior.

Example
An operational profile is a statistical description of actions made by users in the system. For example, Fig. 5.12 shows a probabilistic model, called a Markov chain, that models the behavior of the ATM user. Such models can be created upon the historical data on the ATM machines use.

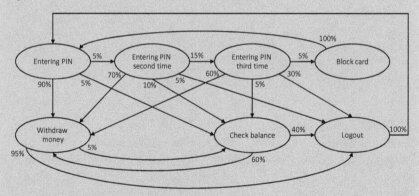

Fig. 5.12 Markov chain for the ATM user behavior

Suppose that we analyzed historical data and it shows that after entering the card into the ATM and entering the PIN, 90% of users wanted to withdraw money, 5% checked their account balance and 5% entered an incorrect PIN. After withdrawing the money 95% of users logged out, and 5% wanted to

(continued)

check their balance. And so on. For each user action we have a probabilistic distribution of the following actions. Having such a model we can use it to *simulate* the true user behavior in terms of the sequence of actions they undertake. Being in a given state, we generate a random number which gives us the next action. For example, being in 'Entering PIN' state we may generate a natural number between 1 and 100. If the result is between 1 and 90, we move to the 'Withdraw money' state and simulate the money withdraw. If it is between 91 and 95—we simulate that a user entered an incorrect PIN and we move to the 'Entering PIN second time' state. If it is between 96 and 100—we simulate that a user checks the account balance and we move to 'Check balance state'. Then, we repeat the whole procedure.

The approach shown in the last example allows us to model the *real* user behavior, so we can simulate the software as it would operate in a *real* environment. Similar statistical models (like probability distributions) can be used to model the typical system load, arrival of requests to the system and many other phenomena that occur in the real world. Changing model parameters we can easily simulate some atypical situations, for example heavy load, extremely high arrival rate and so on.

Table 5.7 summarizes the advantages and disadvantages of the random testing.

5.9 Testing Based on Intuition and Experience

Testing based on intuition and experience should never be underestimated. An experienced tester who knows very well not only the SUT, but also the organization and the development team, is able to predict quite accurately what types of defects will be inserted into the software and which parts of the source code are error-prone. Such a tester knows developers, architects and analytics very well. She knows when they make mistakes, which software aspects are hard for them to design or develop and so on. She knows the client and she can tell very precisely why the client won't be pleased with the current version of the software.

However, there is a very thin boundary between rational and irrational testing based on intuition and experience. The first one is done by a professional who knows

Table 5.7 Advantages and disadvantages of the random testing

Advantages	Disadvantages
• an economic technique—we don't need to waste time for a careful test design and test data selection • unbiased—the tests are generated by a machine and are independent of each other • quick—the test data generation is usually fast	• able to find only some basic bugs (e.g., wrong arithmetic operator) • only as precise as the specification is • may miss boundary-related bugs, even if they are very basic and easy to detect in manual testing

what she's doing. It is usually well planned, and takes form of the exploratory testing, session-based testing or error guessing [14, 15]. The second one is just a so-called 'ad-hoc' testing: unplanned, random, and hence, completely ineffective. A tester needs to be sure that she is able to perform this type of testing effectively. In Fig. 1.13 we presented the model of tester's development. One of the features that characterize a professional tester being at the highest level ('art') of her development, is 'continuous development'. This implies that a professional tester is conscious and rational about her abilities and experience. She can precisely perform a self assessment about her knowledge about the system, team and her skills and decide whether she's able to effectively perform the experience-based testing.

To achieve this level of professionalism a tester needs time. It is impossible to get familiar with a never seen system in a moment. Therefore, a professional tester needs patience. It is very difficult, because people like to see the results of their work immediately. Many people fret when they do not achieve quickly the desired level of experience and are often discouraged. A wise tester knows that 'no pain, no gain'.

The above-mentioned considerations concern experience rather than intuition. The intuition comes with both experience and self development and the main driver that allows us to train our intuition is *curiosity*. A curious tester will be always more effective than the one that is not interested in his profession, nor in other areas of knowledge. Sections 2.2 and 3.8 give you some hints on how to manage your professional development.

5.10 Testing Based on Other People

5.10.1 Who?

The last of the testing techniques described in this chapter directly involves other people in the testing process. The involvement may take many different forms. The fact that we rely on other people does not mean that this technique is weaker or worse than any other techniques. Like other approaches, it has its pros and cons. In some situations it may not fit at all, but in some others it may be the best available option. Table 5.8 shows the example groups of people that can be involved in the testing, and in what way their involvement may be beneficial to the quality level.

5.10.2 What?

It is important to understand that different groups of people have different experience levels in testing, different motivations to do testing, and different attitudes towards negative testing. Some of them will work fine at the unit or integration testing level, some others may be effective at higher levels, like system or acceptance testing. Involvement of a given group of people should be done in the most effective way. For example, it makes no sense to involve end users to perform unit testing, but it makes a lot of sense to engage them in the acceptance tests of the early UI prototype.

Table 5.8 Pros and cons of involving different groups of people in testing

Group	Advantages	Disadvantages
(Known) clients	Direct software validation against real business needs, source of business information	Due to lack of testing knowledge, usually focus on positive testing; reluctance to cooperate
(Unknown) users	Wide range of different types of users allows us to validate the system in many different ways	High costs; difficult to choose the representative sample
Team members, testers	Working together boosts creativity, makes problems easier to solve	Bias due to sharing the common tester's point of view
Team members, not testers	Allows us to perform wide range of test types (for example unit tests)	Usually difficult to involve them due to time constraints (they have other duties)
Outsourced specialists	Can conduct tests that require expert knowledge or special tools	High costs; outsourced testing is often a team members' excuse of taking responsibility for quality
Crowd testing	Quick way to perform a wide system and acceptance testing	Very expensive; hard to uniform the way of reporting issues; tendency to raise trivial bugs if done in the pay-per-bug model

To make the best use of other people in testing, we should consider different testing activities. Apart from 'typical' testing based on test cases or test scenarios, we may propose other forms of testing, such as:

- testing by filling up **surveys** or **questionnaires**—this type of testing is useful when it is hard to quantify quality characteristics which are subjective by their nature; the classic example is usability,
- **crowd testing**—testing tasks are delegated to a group of people, usually experts on testing outsourced by our company; testing is typically performed through some online platform,
- **observations**—we observe how well users are able to use the software.

Table 5.9 presents pros and cons for different techniques used in the approach of testing based on other people.

5.10.3 When?

When we plan to rely on other people in testing our product, we need to involve them in the right moment. Each group of users should be involved at the right time, with the use of a proper technique, so that their testing is as effective as it is possible.

Efficiency of the activities performed by non-testers highly depends on the moment of the execution of these activities. For example, consider the usability testing done with the use of the surveys or questionnaires. When a final version of the GUI design is done, it may be much easier for us to construct the questionnaire

Table 5.9 Pros and cons for different techniques related to testing by other people

Technique	Advantages	Disadvantages
Surveys	Uniform approach to all users, we may use statistical methods to compare results and draw statistically confirmed conclusions	Time consuming (survey/ questionnaire preparation, interviews with users when using surveys), things that we check form a closed list that must be defined in advance
Crowd testing	High availability of testers, crowdsourced services are usually available on short notice, natural wide coverage of different platform and environment configurations	Very expensive, testers may tend to raise trivial bugs, when 'paid-by-bug' model is used, redundancy in findings may happen (many testers may raise the same bug thus wasting their time)
Observations	Ability to observe users in their real environments when they work with the real software	Expensive, take much time, measurement process not uniform, results usually of qualitative nature

with the adequate and appropriate questions for the precise GUI evaluation. However, in the earlier phases, when a GUI design evolves in the consecutive prototypes, users may give us their constant, up-to-date feedback that allows the UX designers to improve the design.

Some companies have this 'testing done by a client' policy. In this approach, during the development, testing is usually restricted only to some form of a unit testing performed by the developers and also some smoke tests before the release. When a product is released, the company gathers information about the problems from the client. Such an approach has one inevitable advantage: it is easy to introduce and cheap, at least in the initial project phases. However, it has also several disadvantages:

- responsibility for quality is de facto transferred to the client, who—if not aware about this model—may just resign from our services because of the frequent, recurring problems with software quality,
- field defects may be hard to reproduce, localize and correct, thus making the development process more expensive in later phases, like maintainability.

Testing Pitfalls and How to Avoid Them

6

6.1 Introduction

Testing is mainly about different types of thinking: analytical thinking, creative thinking, system thinking, critical thinking and so on. Hence, a professional tester has many occasions to make mistakes during this intellectual process. In this chapter we discuss some of the common testing pitfalls or bad practices. We also discuss how to avoid them or—at least—how to reduce the consequences of their impact on the process, if they occur.

6.2 Deceptive Coverage Metrics

In Sect. 1.2.8 we quoted Lord Kelvin who said that 'to measure is to *know*' and that 'if you can't measure, you can't improve it'. It is obvious that a quantitative approach is necessary if we want to measure the effectiveness of our tests, testing process and our improving actions. To do this, we need measures. Measurements are common in software engineering, yet many people tend to use them credulously, like they were the sole source of truth. Metrics *do* say important things about the things they measure, but the measurement quality and thus good metrics applicability depend on many things, such as:

- **alignment with business**—metrics should explain the phenomena directly related with the business,
- **intelligibility**—we should understand what the metric really says, what is its meaning; the metric should also have a clear operational definition, that is—the description of *how* to measure it,
- **actionability**—metrics should trigger appropriate actions, they shouldn't be used to measure just for the sake of measuring,
- **consistency**—two measurements of a given metric should give exactly the same results (except when the measured characteristic changes in time).

© Springer International Publishing AG 2018
A. Roman, *Thinking-Driven Testing*, https://doi.org/10.1007/978-3-319-73195-7_6

Testing is complicated, so it is impossible to report, let's say, the current state of the testing process, with only one metric. One number will not describe the multi-dimensional, complicated and dynamic situation in the project. Hence, a set of metrics should be used. This set needs to be carefully chosen. It shouldn't be too small, so that we won't capture any important information. It shouldn't also be too big, so that we don't compute redundant metrics and don't complicate the overall description of the process.

Nowadays, in the era of automation and sophisticated tools for metrics monitoring, collecting and reporting, we can easily measure a lot of things. It is tempting to measure everything, but we should remember that measurement is not an end in itself: it does not exist for its own sake. The metrics are *used to describe and understand phenomena*. It is wise and reasonable to select a *right* set of metrics to measure. There are some techniques for supporting this process, for example the Goal-Question-Metric technique [101]. This technique allows us to select the set of metrics in a three-step process of defining a measurement model:

- defining the overall goal we want to achieve (conceptual level),
- providing a set of questions we need to answer in order to reach the goal (operational level),
- associating a set of metrics with every question, to answer it in a measurable way (quantitative level).

Once when we select the right metrics and start collecting the measurements, we need to know how to interpret them. In testing one of the most popular types of metrics is coverage. In general, a coverage metric can be defined as follows:

$$Coverage = \frac{Number\ of\ elements\ covered\ by\ tests}{Total\ number\ of\ elements}.$$

Elements to cover are often called test conditions. Some sources, like the ISO 29119 norm, distinguish between 'test conditions' and 'coverage elements', but we won't go into the details—it's not important for our considerations. The important thing is that the coverage metrics serve as a measure of test thoroughness. Testers and managers use it to check 'how much' of a certain structure was covered by tests.

For the most formal black-box test design techniques it is relatively easy to achieve 100% coverage. The test conditions are model elements and usually the model gives us clear instruction how to design tests to cover these elements. For example, in a decision table test conditions are represented by their columns. To achieve the 100% coverage, for each column we have to provide one test in which we force certain conditions to be hold, as defined in this column. In a finite state machine model we may define different types of coverage, like: cover every state, every transition between states, every two consecutive transitions, and so on.

The situation gets more complicated in case of a white-box coverage metrics. This is because they are defined at the very low level—code level. At this level we are not able to control the system behavior like we can do in the case of the high-level black-box models. To understand this, consider the following piece of code:

```
 1 function f(int x, int y, int z)
 2 if (x+y+z>11)
 3    return x+y-z
 4 int p = f(x, 2*y^z, x*z-y*y+7)
 5 int q = round(x/y+z/x)
 6 int r = 0
 7 while (p>0) do
 8    q = q*f(p,p,p)
 9    p = p-7
10    if (q>5)
11       r = r+1
12 if (r>17)
13    return g(r)
14 else
15    return 0
16 end
```

Suppose we want to achieve the simplest white-box coverage—a statement coverage. This criterion requires that every statement needs to be executed at least once in at least one of our tests. So, in particular, we need to execute the line number 13. It will be executed if $r > 17$ in line 12, so only if the while in line 11 will be executed at least 17 times. This, in turn, depends on the value of q, which is computed in line 8 by recursive execution of the analyzed function, and also on the value of p. . . .. We should immediately see that it is hard (if at all possible) to give the input values x, y, z such that the algorithm reaches line 13.

This simple analysis should give you the concept of how complicated it is to force a certain control flow, when the only thing we can do is to define the input values. But low controllability of the flow is not the only reason why achieving 100% code-related coverage is difficult. Another one is this: if there are try-catch code fragments, which handle different types of exceptions (unexpected situations), it may turn out that some exceptions are very hard to be induced. This means that we won't be able to execute the 'catch' part of the code for these exceptions. This results in less than 100% coverage.

The moral from this story is that achieving 100% coverage—even for the simplest code coverage metrics—in many cases is impossible, so it definitely shouldn't be the main goal of testing. In some testing teams we may observe this 'coverage culture'—testers and developers are forced to achieve the highest code coverage, whereas the goal should be defined in a completely different way. As our main goal is to solve the client's business problem, we should just test if the software is able to solve it correctly. Coverage metrics are secondary measures, not so important in the overall analysis. Of course, it is reasonable to execute every statement at least once, to see if the executed lines do not cause errors. However, a good test suite, based on the high-level business objectives, gives a rational coverage. It may not be effective, from the economic point of view, to spend much time trying to increase the code coverage for another 1 or 2%. If the tests reflect the real use of the application, our test suite should be 'just enough' to validate the software.

Testers like to think about the coverage metrics as the objective measures of the goodness of their tests, but in most cases it is wishful thinking—coverage metrics *do not* give any decisive conclusions about the test suite thoroughness. They *may* say something about the level of reduced risk, but testers should be extremely careful while analyzing these metrics. The following example shows how partial information may lead us to completely wrong conclusions.

Example

Suppose we have the report on code coverage for four modules: A, B, C, D, presented in Table 6.1. The report gives information on the number of tests written for each module, time spent on designing them, and two types of coverage achieved for these tests: statement coverage (number of executed statements divided by the number of all statements in the code) and decision coverage (number of different outcomes in the decisions divided by the total number of all decision outcomes).

Table 6.1 Coverage report for some test project

Module	# of tests	Time spent	Statement coverage	Decision coverage
A	85	95	100%	100%
B	77	82	7%	11%
C	1	1	1%	50%
D	3	88	100%	95%

Tests for module A give a perfect coverage, in terms of both statements and branches covered. This was achieved by providing many tests for which it took a lot of time to design. But, as we achieved full statement and branch coverage—we may deduce that it was worth it. For module B we have the similar situation in terms of the test suite size and the effort, yet the coverage metrics are not very hopeful: we barely covered some small percentage of both statements and branches. Probably the test suite is not effective and we lost a lot of time designing it. Module C was tested only with one test, which covered half of the branches, but didn't cover almost any instruction. But, as we didn't lose much time on designing this test, we should probably have some time left to add some more tests. Probably we need much more tests to increase the statement coverage to a reasonable value. Module D is tested only with three tests, which required a very high effort—88 h, which gives more than 29 h per one test! We obtain high coverage metrics, but maybe we could do this in some shorter time?

(continued)

Now let's add some more information to the report: number of lines of code and number of branches in the individual modules. The extended report is presented in Table 6.2. Additional information is given in two columns with bolded data.

Table 6.2 Extended coverage report

Module	# of tests	Time spent	Statement coverage	Branch coverage	**LOC**	**# of decisions**
A	85	95	100%	100%	**45**	**0**
B	77	82	7%	11%	**156,666**	**3086**
C	1	1	1%	50%	**96,443**	**1**
D	3	88	100%	95%	**66,345**	**1085**

Now, the situation looks completely different. Module A has no branches—it consists of one so-called basic block. This means that all instructions will be executed one by one, no matter what are the input values.[1] Writing 85 tests (and spending 95 h for this!) for testing such a simple module is definitely a waste of time. Module B seemed to be poorly tested, but look how complex the module is. Maybe the tests are not so bad? Module C also seemed to require much more tests to increase the coverage. But notice that this code has only one decision, which means that to achieve 100% decision coverage (and hence, 100% statement coverage) we need to add only one more test, which probably will take us also around 1 h. So this situation isn't also as bad as we thought earlier. Finally, for module D we achieved almost full coverage with only three tests, but it required a lot of effort. But look at the module complexity: it is very large and also has a very complicated logical structure (over 1000 decision points). Yet, we were able to cover all these complex structures with only three tests—a tester who designed them is probably a genius![2]

As we saw in the example above, it is very important to have the full information about the examined phenomenon. In our case it was not only the *ratio* measures, but also the absolute measures of the software volume (number of lines and number of decisions).

Another aspect of the coverage is the *code importance*. Coverage measures assume that every line is equally important, which of course is not true. Some parts of a code are crucial for the system quality, reliability, etc., and some are not. Therefore, the impact of failure occurrence due to execution of part of the code varies and depends on

---

[1]It is in no way an artificial example—this may be a configuration module which assigns some initial values to the variables.

[2]The example refers to the coverage metrics issues only. In practice it is often better to have a few more simpler and easy to maintain tests than a few very complicated and hard to understand.

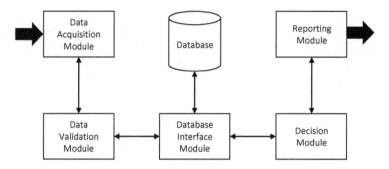

Fig. 6.1 Architecture of the loan granting system

the importance of this code. Suppose we test the loan granting system. Its architecture is depicted in Fig. 6.1. The system is composed of five modules:

- Data Acquisition Module—responsible for gathering the data from the user through a User Interface,
- Data Validation Module—responsible for formal data verification,
- Database Interface Module—responsible for communication with database, reading/writing from/to the database,
- Decision Module—responsible for assessing the risk related to granting the loan,
- Reporting Module—responsible for output for the system operator and client.

The most important business logic in this system lies in the Decision Module. This module contains the algorithm for the risk assessment. It is natural that this algorithm is crucial for the business and so it must be tested very thoroughly. Using code coverage metrics for the Decision Module makes therefore more sense, than doing the same for, let's say, the Data Acquisition Module. For the latter it may be perfectly enough to perform some black-box tests that verify the high-level rules and constraints related to the input data.

How to decide whether a given part of a code is important? It depends on many factors, such as risk, business expectations and so on. In general, we have at least four ways to support this decision process in a more technical way. These are:

- **Structural analysis**—knowing which parts of the code are complex from the structural point of view may identify the areas more exposed to the risk, just because of code complexity. The examples of the complexity indicators are measures like cyclomatic complexity (McCabe's Cyclomatic Complexity,[3] Essential Cyclomatic Complexity, predicate complexity and so on).

---

[3]Cyclomatic complexity is a measure of the structural complexity of the code. The simplest way to calculate it is to count the decision points and add 1. When computing it for a Control Flow Graph, we can equivalently calculate it as the number of edges minus number of nodes plus 2.

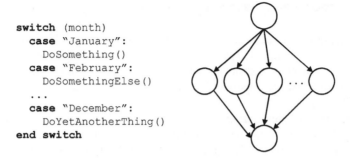

```
switch (month)
  case "January":
    DoSomething()
  case "February":
    DoSomethingElse()
  ...
  case "December":
    DoYetAnotherThing()
end switch
```

Fig. 6.2 An example of a simple code with large cyclomatic complexity

- **Algorithmic analysis**—by the direct analysis of the algorithms and the data structures they use we may identify the parts of the code which are the most complicated from the algorithmic point of view. The more complex the algorithm is, the more thoroughness in testing it requires.
- **Requirements and risk analysis**—this is the most straigtforward way to identify the important parts of a code. By analyzing the requirements or risks identified prior to development, we may decide which functionalities are crucial and therefore require more attention.
- **Code profiling**—this is the empirical way of examining which parts of the code are executed more often than others, and which functions are called more frequently than the others. There are many tools for performing code profiling (like gprof tool in Linux). After the analysis, we are able to detect the code parts in which the control flow spends the majority of time, therefore recognizing them as more important than the others.

No matter which methods we use to evaluate the code importance, we have to do it rationally. We cannot follow blindly the above-mentioned methods. For example, some code may have a very large cyclomatic complexity, but it may have a very simple structure, like the code in Fig. 6.2.

This code is a simple realization of a switch-case instruction, which selects 1 of the 12 code parts to be executed, depending on the month variable value. The cyclomatic complexity for this code is 12, which is considered to be a large value.[4] However, the code is simple and understandable—there is no 'spaghetti code' with many loops, logic decisions and so on.

---

[4]There's an engineering rule of thumb saying that code with cyclomatic complexity greater than 10 should be subject to a revision and possibly refactored due to its high structural complexity.

6.3   Reports and Data Presentation

One of the most important tester's responsibilities is reporting. This comes from the very nature of testing as quality *control*. This control is realized through reporting to management and other decision makers. When creating a report, the tester must remember the following important issues:

- **report's level of abstraction**—if the report is needed for some technical reasons, during the development phase, it will probably be very detailed and technical; if this is the final report from testing, it will be probably very general, as it has to describe the whole process in a short, concise form,
- **data correctness**—reports are the basis for decision making, so they have to contain accurate data; wrong data reported may imply making wrong business decisions,
- **intelligibility**—all metrics, methods and ways of presenting data should be explained, for example the reader should be clear about the definition of 'blocking test case', or should know precisely what it means that the bug severity equals 1,
- **data presentation**—reports need to be understandable and easy to interpret.

In this section we focus on the last issue—data presentation. We go through several bad practices which shouldn't be applied when creating a report. Most of them are related to the graphical form of the presented data, because—as a well-known English idiom says—a picture is worth a thousand words. Looking at a picture, graph or table allows us to digest the data faster and easier. Such data is also easier to interpret.

Figure 6.3 presents the map by Charles Joseph Minard (1781–1870), a French civil engineer recognized for his significant contribution in the field of information graphics in statistics. The map shows the course of the Napoleon's campaign of 1812

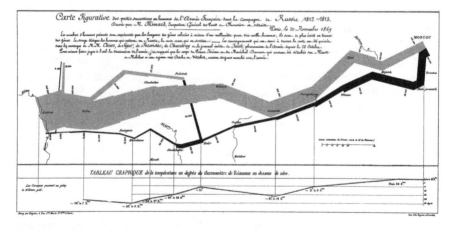

Fig. 6.3 Minard's map—probably the best statistical graph ever drawn

in Russia. Edward Tufte, a famous expert in data visualization, says that this map may be 'the best statistical graphic ever drawn' [102].

Why is it so? Let us investigate what exactly the graph represents. The brighter belt shows Napoleon's army's road to Moscow, the darker—the way back. The belts' loci show the geographic position of the army in time. Their width denotes the size of the army. For the way back, there is additional information about the temperature in the given moments of time (lower part of the chart). Why does Tufte say this is the perfect statistical chart? Notice that it does not contain any random or redundant information. Every characteristic of this graph has a well-defined purpose. Minard used every possible feature of the graph to present some relevant information: coordinates, colors, belt widths.

This is how the perfect graph—or report—should look like: minimum redundancy and maximal amount of information using different presentation techniques. Now we will go through some examples of bad practices in creating reports or other types of documents whose purpose is to present some data or some information.

Bad scaling   Bad scaling takes place when the zero of the scale is not visible on the chart. Diagrams with bad scaling may suggest existence of significant trends which in fact do not exist or are not as important as they seem to be. Look at Fig. 6.4a. This chart suggests that the measured value has a significantly increasing trend across the last four quarters. However, when we present the data correctly, with values on axis Y starting from 0, not from 1480 (Fig. 6.4b), we see that the four values are almost identical, the changes are practically irrelevant and there is no significant trend!

Wrong chart type selected   The chart type should fit the purpose of presenting the data. For example, the intention of the author of the charts (a) and (b) in Fig. 6.4 was to present the trend of some metric in time. But a histogram is not a good tool to present trends—it is used for representing the distribution of data. For presenting the time trend, the more proper chart is a control chart, like the one shown in Fig. 6.4c.

Using superfluous ornaments   The chart in Fig. 6.5a is a classical example of using superfluous ornaments that only make the chart less readable. The 3D form and weird projection make the chart completely illegible. One layer is hidden behind the other—if the value for module B in the black layer were much bigger, it would cover the gray layer behind it. The 3D projection makes it difficult to read the exact values

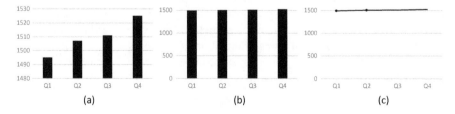

Fig. 6.4 Example of bad scaling and bad chart type selection

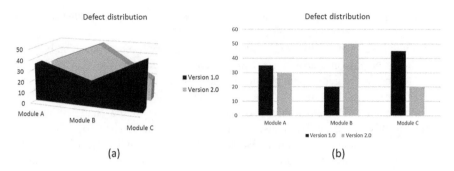

(a)   (b)

Fig. 6.5 Chart with weird ornaments and its corrected version

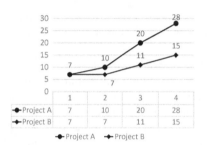

Phase	Project			
	A	B	C	D
Reqs	45%	35%	50%	30%
Design	35%	25%	35%	30%
Code	10%	25%	10%	20%
Tests	10%	15%	5%	20%
Total	**100%**	**100%**	**100%**	**100%**

Fig. 6.6 Bad and good redundancy

for the data. The 'area' type of the chart is completely unnecessary and suggests some (time?) relation between three modules. The intention was to present the distribution of the number of defects across three modules in two releases. The most convenient way to present this data, so that it may be easily compared between versions, is the histogram. Figure 6.5b shows much better representation of the same data.

Redundant information In the left chart of Fig. 6.6 every data point is described threefold: by the height on the graph, by the number next to the point and by the corresponding number in the table below the chart. Too much is not healthy. Such a redundance does not help in anything, but only obfuscates the data. However, there are situations in which redundancy is highly advisable. Look at the right part of Fig. 6.6. It presents the distributions of some measures for different projects across phases. We know that it is this way, not the other (that is, not for different phases across projects), because each column sums up to 100%. We can read it from the last row of the table. Theoretically, this information is not necessary, but it makes life easier for the report recipient. One look at the table and she will immediately know across which categories the distributions are defined.

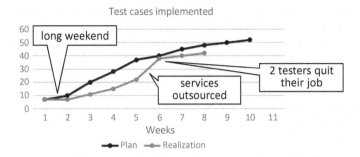

Fig. 6.7 Chart with additional information

Lack of contextual information It is a good practice to comment the graphs and charts, so that their interpretation will be easier and will not mislead the reader during the analysis. Consider the chart from Fig. 6.7.

It shows the information on the cumulative planned vs. realized test cases implementation. In week 2 no additional tests were implemented, but thanks to the additional information we know that this was a long weekend and people did not work then. The rapid increase in week 6 is due to additional workforce utilized. It brings back the situation from week 4, where the management made the decision about outsourcing the task because of an increasing delay against the plan. The slow growth in weeks 7 and 8 was due to the fact that two testers have quit their job, so the team effectiveness decreased.

As we see, every 'suspicious' place in the chart is commented, so the analysis of the overall situation is easier. This good practice also does not leave much room for arbitrary interpretations or for wasting time on analysis that are wrong in advance.

Accumulation of data on a single chart Every graph, chart or report should be legible and should contain only the essential information. Presenting 40 different control charts on one graph is not a good idea—such information will be completely unreadable.

6.4   In Models We Trust. Or Do We?

During her work, the tester works with many different models and uses them in many different areas. Some examples are:

- **software development life cycle models**—these are the models that organize the work within the project (waterfall, V-model, Scrum, Boehm spiral model, Rational Unified Process, Rapid Application Development and so on),

- **test process models**—they organize testing process within SDLC (TMap Fundamental Test Process, V-model and so on),
- **software models**—they describe software from different points of view and are used to provide the test cases using formal test design techniques (state machine, domain model, decision table, control flow graph, call graph, data flow graph, business process model and so on),
- **test improvement models**—they help to improve the testing process (TMMi [103], TPI Next [104], [5], and many others).

The main role the models play is to represent some structure or activity in an abstract form. This means that the model skips irrelevant characteristics of this structure or activity and focuses only on the most important, from its point of view, things. For example, the waterfall model is a sequential representation of software development phases—nothing more. The model does not say anything about how to develop the software or which techniques should be used in software testing. Hence, the models are good, generic frameworks for our everyday work.

Still, we need to be very careful with that. Credibility of the models varies. Some models (for example the ones used in formal test design techniques) are practical and work quite well. Some others, however, are still not examined well and they lack scientific evidence that they really work well. The classical examples are reliability models: in the literature there are hundreds of reliability models proposed, but the vast majority of them has never been used in practice—they are only theoretical constructs.

We will now discuss some typical problems with the models in IT.

Quality A typical problem with the models is their quality. For example, the so-called 'Agile Testing Quadrants' model [105] describes the test process for an agile methodology.

The model is presented in Fig. 6.8. It was designed for testers to make sure they covered all needed categories of testing. The quadrants categorize tests in two dimensions: business vs. technology activities and team support vs. product critique activities. However, there are at least two problems with this model:

- In fact, this model is a taxonomy of test techniques, grouped according to two factors: business/technology facing and validation/verification testing. However, there are some missing techniques, like integration testing[5]—if we want to strictly follow this model, we may not perform the integration tests at all.

---

[5]The model mentions 'component tests', but these are not integration tests, because, according to the definition by Fowler (https://martinfowler.com/bliki/ComponentTest.html), component tests are tests that 'limit the scope of the exercised software to a portion of the system under test'. This definition does not take into account verifying the interaction, communication or interfaces between different software components, which is the essence of integration testing.

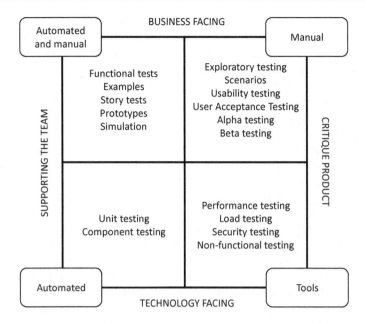

Fig. 6.8 Agile Testing Quadrants model

- The model's name suggests that it is devoted to agile development, but there is nothing in this model that would determine it *only* for agile projects—this is just the taxonomy of test techniques which is valid in *every* project; in fact, a taxonomy has nothing to do with any particular methodology. Therefore, using an agile approach, we won't find this model helpful more than using it in any other methodology. This is a methodological error: if we call this the 'agile' quadrant model, one expects that it refers to the agile characteristics in testing.

Inconsistency and lack of supporting evidences Some models are inconsistent and even contradictory. Probably the most interesting example is Scrum, because of its popularity. It is widely used despite the lack of scientific evidence of its efficiency. For example, Scrum says that the event called 'Daily Scrum' lasts 15 min. It is not known why it should be *exactly* 15 min. It also says that, for example, Sprint Planning is 'time-boxed to a maximum of 8 h for a 1-month Sprint'. We don't know the reasons for which it cannot be, for example, 9 h.

In the Scrum Guide the authors of Scrum call it 'framework', while it is evidently a software development method. What's more, it is a very prescriptive method. It is full of very strong claims like: sprint duration 'cannot be shortened', sprint lasts a 'month or less' (why not 5 weeks?), the Product Owner 'is one person, not a committee', there are no sub-teams in the Development Team and 'there are no exceptions to this rule' and so on. It is ironic that the Scrum Guide describes the agile approach and the method itself is absolutely not agile, leaving almost no room to manoeuvre for people that use this approach. Following the spirit of the method, such prescriptive parts should be reformulated and given as recommendations or good practices, not as absolute warrants and prohibitions.

The Scrum Guide is also contradictory in several places. For example, it says that the Scrum Master 'ensures the Product Owner knows how to arrange the Product Backlog', while few pages earlier it is said that the Product Owner 'is the sole person responsible for managing the Product Backlog'.

There are also some other methodological problems in this methodology. For example, the Scrum Guide claims that 'sprints limit risks to one calendar month of cost'. The intention was to say that using the sprints we increase predictability, but the risks do not follow the sprint horizons defined by the team—otherwise they wouldn't be risks.

In the end note, the Scrum Guide says that 'Scrum exists only in its entirety and functions well as a container for other techniques, methodologies and practices'. This is a very strong claim, which is obviously not true—Scrum practices have never been verified, for example it is not known if, let's say, 20 instead of the 15-min Daily Scrum would work better. It is not known if the method works less efficiently if applied only to some extent. Also, it is impossible to fully implement all Scrum postulates, because every model is just an idealization (see the end of this section).

From the tester's point of view, models such as Scrum don't bring much value. They may help the tester to find out the way the agile team works, but they won't help in providing better tests or in better work organization.

Models too prescriptive A good IT model describing the development cycle, software or process should be generic, if designed for a wide use. It is even more important, if the model serves as a creativity-boosting tool. The TQED model introduced in Chap. 4 has this property: it is independent of the software life cycle implemented, project type, team organization, particular testing technique applied, particular tool used and so on. It focuses only on the abstract idea of combining different entities called 'dimensions'. Some models, however, are too prescriptive. A good example may be the 'test pyramid' discussed in Sect. 2.5: it imposes a strict proportion of tests of a given type, regardless of the fact that the test organization must depend on many things, like project type.

Knowing how to use models is a crucial skill. They may be very helpful, but using them incorrectly or following them blindly may be very harmful. As statistician George Box said, 'all models are wrong but some are useful'. He wrote [106]:

> Now it would be very remarkable if any system existing in the real world could be exactly represented by any simple model. However, cunningly chosen parsimonious models often do provide remarkably useful approximations. For example, the law $PV = RT$ relating pressure P, volume V and temperature T of an 'ideal' gas via a constant R is not exactly true for any real gas, but it frequently provides a useful approximation and furthermore its structure is informative since it springs from a physical view of the behavior of gas molecules.

For such a model there is no need to ask the question 'Is the model true?'. If 'truth' is to be the 'whole truth' the answer must be 'No'. The only question of interest is 'Is the model illuminating and useful?'

6.5   Selecting the Technique

To be as effective as possible, the tester needs to be able to select the right technique for a given problem. Notice that the effectiveness is not only related to the number of defects found, but also to many other, equally important factors, like:

- **defect types**—some kinds of defects will be crucial in one project and completely irrelevant in others (for example, arithmetic rounding issues are extremely important in space rocket modules or accounting software, but have lower priority in mobile games when calculating a final score),
- **project type**—so-called safety critical systems should be tested more thoroughly than other systems and the budget for testing and quality assurance will be usually several times larger than the budget for the development,
- **optimality**—which means that we should find the most important bugs as early as possible; this is important especially in the context of such prosaic things as project constraints: time, budget and human resources.

Choosing the wrong approach to testing results in effectiveness decrease, because:

- choosing the approach not aligned with the business goals makes it harder to notice that we are building wrong software, that is, a software which does not solve the client's problem,
- not taking the project constraints into account may result in the lack of time for executing some important tests,
- choosing wrong/ineffective test techniques implies low defect detection and low software reliability after the release,
- poor reliability means higher maintenance costs.

Figure 6.9 shows a simple model that may be helpful in choosing the optimal test strategy. We need to take into account three important factors:

- what are we expected to do (business perspective)—this comes from all sorts of documentation, discussions with client, requirements specifications, plans and so on,
- what do we expect to find (product perspective)—this comes from the 'technical' analysis of the software resulting in so-called error hypotheses that should be validated by testing,
- what are the constraints (project perspective)—this comes from the project constraints like time, budget, resources and tools; to mitigate this kind of

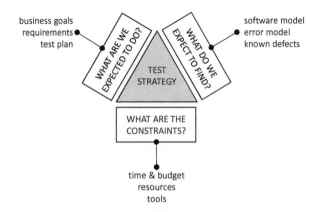

Fig. 6.9 Model for choosing the right test strategy

project-related risk a professional tester should prioritize her work in advance; it is more than certain that we won't have enough time or money to finish the whole testing project.

In some cases we may come to a conclusion, that the best way to test something is to perform a document analysis or code review. Such static techniques are perfectly fine and equally useful as the dynamic techniques (that is, testing by executing the software). What's more, static and dynamic techniques are complementary, because they are able to detect different types of problems. Static techniques are perfect to apply in the early development phases to find the design errors. This type of problem is very insidious, because if a design defect is not detected in the design phase, it will usually occur after the release or shortly before the release. This implies much higher removal costs. If such a defect is detected in the design phase, the removal cost is. . . zero—the error should be just rubbed out from the design and that's all!

6.6   Variance and Its Interpretation

Variance is the measure of dispersion. It shows how far a set of random numbers are spread out from their mean. Variance plays a central role in statistics and a professional tester must understand its meaning to interpret the results of different measurements. The formal definition of variance is as follows: let $X = (x_1, x_2, \ldots, x_N)$ be a sequence of numbers. Assuming that each x_i is equally likely to occur, the variance of this sequence is $\sigma^2 = \frac{1}{N} \sum_{i=1}^{N} (x_i - \mu)^2$, where $\mu = \frac{1}{N} \sum_{i=1}^{N} x_i$ is the mean value of X. If the x_i values have other probability distribution, $P(x_i) = p_i$, the variance can be calculated as $\sigma^2 = \sum_{i=1}^{N} p_i (x_i - \mu)^2$.

Notice that the variance is expressed in square units of the original units of x_i. For example, if x_i represents the number of field defects, the variance of this variable is given in (number of defects)^2. Such a value has no physical interpretation. Therefore, instead of the variance we often use its square root $\sigma = \sqrt{\sigma^2}$, which is called the standard deviation. It is expressed in original units, therefore it has a physical interpretation. If a variable follows the normal distribution, over 99.7% of the values are no further than 3 standard deviations from the mean value.

Describing a sample of measurements only by its mean does not tell us much. The variance gives us much more information—it shows what is the variability of the measurement and therefore it is a good measure of uncertainty. It is also a measure of the estimation error. Here is an example.

Example

A crucial requirement for a certain module of a safety-critical system is that its response time must be less than 1 s. We have two independent implementations of this module and need to choose which of them will be included in the system. To verify that the requirement is fulfilled, we run the performance tests for both implementations by measuring the module's response time. A test for each implementation runs the module 100 times and measures response times. Next, the response times are averaged. After the tests execution we achieved the following results:

- mean response time for version A of the module = 0.895 s,
- mean response time for version B of the module = 0.826 s.

Does it mean that module B is better than A and should be implemented in the system? Let's look at the full data, that is, histograms that represent the distributions of response times for both tests. The results are shown in Fig. 6.10.

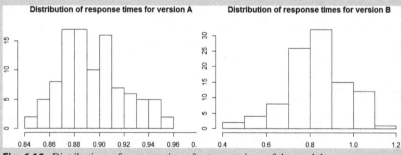

Fig. 6.10 Distributions of response times for two versions of the module

(continued)

The summary statistics for both experiments are given in Table 6.3. Notice that although both the mean response time and minimal response time are lower for version B, the maximal value for B exceeds the threshold of 1 s, while no response time for version A is greater than 1 s. This means that version A is better than B, despite its mean response time being slightly higher than in the case of B. A is better than B due to a much bigger standard deviation for version B.

Table 6.3 Summary statistics for both experiments

Module version	Minimum value	Mean value	Maximum value	Standard deviation
A	0.8435	0.8950	0.9532	0.025
B	0.4024	0.8261	1.1210	0.138

As standard deviation for A is much smaller, we can say that *version A of the module is more stable than version B*. Hence, it is more reliable in terms of the response time. In case of version B some run-times can be very fast (even around 0.4 s), but some of them may be greater than 1 s. Notice that if we analyze these tests only in terms of the mean values, we would choose version B and therefore make a serious mistake.

Here is another example that shows even better the role of variation as an error measure.

Example

Suppose we have two independent methods of predicting the number of field defects in the system's modules. Both methods give, on average, quite good prediction: the difference between true and predicted value is close to 0 in case of both methods. However, the standard deviation in case of the first method is 2.5, while in case of the second one is 16.0. What does it mean in practice?

Suppose we have a new release and we apply our models to predict the number of field defects. Let's say that the predictions from both methods are 168 and 142 resp. Which result is more reliable? The answer is: the more reliable is the first method. It is because it has a lower standard deviation. Assuming that the number of field defects follows the normal distribution and knowing the standard deviations of both methods we know that there is a 99.7% probability that 168 is somewhere between $x - 7.5$ and $x + 7.5$, where x is the true number of field defects and 7.5 is tripled standard deviation for the first method.

Similarly, we know that with 99.7% probability 142 is somewhere between $x - 48$ and $x + 48$. It is obvious that the first method is more credible, as the interval $x \pm 7.5$ is narrower than $x \pm 48$. Roughly speaking, we can predict that the true number x of field defects is somewhere between $168 - 7.5$ and

(continued)

168 + 7.5, so it lies somewhere between 160 and 176. Notice that in case of the second method, the resulting interval would be $[142 - 48, 142 + 48] = [94, 190]$. This prediction is much more inaccurate than the one from the first method!

The standard deviation of the estimator is called the *estimator's error*. The lower this standard deviation is, the more accurate are the results provided by this estimator.

6.7 Bad Planning

In Sect. 2.7 we discussed the role of the planning in the testing project, so we won't repeat here those arguments. In turn, in this section we will try to find out why people often make very basic mistakes regarding the planning activity. These basic mistakes are:

- shortening the time devoted to planning,
- underestimating the role of planning,
- planning only once at the beginning of the project,
- resignation from planning.

There are a few fundamental psychological reasons for all these problems with planning:

Conviction of understanding the problem The key moment that is the cause of all these troubles is the initial phase of the project, when the project vision becomes clear to everyone. When people finally have this vision in their minds, they feel they understand completely what they are supposed to do and that they can do it immediately. Everything is so clear and obvious, that team members do not feel any need for thinking and planning in advance any activities—everyone *knows* what should be done and when. Unfortunately, defining the goal and the vision is not enough to ensure the success. Projects usually do not run smoothly. During the development many different, weird and unexpected things occur. If we are not ready for this, we are asking for problems. Chaos, bad decisions, delays, conflicts—these are just a few of the whole bunch of results related to poor planning.

Risk aversion Because of the above-mentioned issues, planning should involve risk analysis. By its nature, risk is a negative event that, when materialized, negatively impacts the project. People (especially managers!) do not like to talk about 'bad things'. They love success stories and want to talk only about good things, about the project that perfectly follows the plan and so on. They project this view on the real project, but this is wishful thinking. Thinking positive about the project does not imply that it will indeed go well. A professional tester is a pessimist—during the test planning and risk analysis she should think of as many bad things that may happen, as possible. Only then the team will be able to think about how to mitigate these risks and when they materialize, everyone will be prepared and know what to do. This way the risk impact will be reduced.

Planning considered only as the initial activity The word 'planning' suggests that first we plan and then we carry out the plan. However, planning is not only the initial activity. It is a continuous activity. Plans should be updated on a regular basis, due to unexpected events that will happen earlier or later. Such an unexpected event may force us to change our plans. Also, the longer the project lasts, the more data we have, so we may update the plans by doing more accurate predictions. A good example here is the COCOMO II model, which has two phases: Early Design and Post-Architecture. In the first phase the uncertainty about many project parameters is bigger than in the second phase. The Post-Architecture model gives therefore better cost/effort predictions than the Early Design one.

6.8   Hastiness

In such an intellectually demanding activity as testing, hastiness is *always* bad. There are many English proverbs about the negative role of hastiness: 'hastily and well never meet'; 'always in a hurry, always behind'; 'haste trips over its own heels'; and so on. In the contemporary 'ASAP'[6] work environment we constantly experience situations that require hurried acting, which is almost always hasty.

A professional tester knows that her fundamental work tool is her intellect, and the fundamental activity is thinking. This cannot be done in a rush. We benefit from taking our time to think prior to acting, which is symbolically depicted in Fig. 6.11.

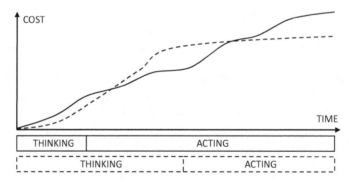

Fig. 6.11 Benefits from thinking before acting

---

[6]As Soon As Possible.

The curves symbolically present the cost of performing the same activity (for example, solving some testing problem) in two settings. The cost includes personnel costs, effort, amount of work done *vs.* planned to do and so on. The first curve, denoted with the solid line, represents the situation in which we don't think too much and immediately start acting. The second one, denoted with the dashed line, refers to the situation where we spend more time on thinking and analyzing and move to acting later. In general, when we think thoroughly about the problem, we may come up with a much better and effective solution, so we may perform the task in a shorter time and with lower cost.

Example

Suppose we decide to implement the automation project across the company, in all projects. We implement the necessary environment and start transforming manual regression test cases into automated test scripts. In project X the transformation took us 80 h in total, including time for solving a lot of technical problems. But when we finally did this, it turned out that we will only have two releases of the product, so the regression will be executed only twice. Regression done manually takes 15 h in total. This means that by automating the regression we saved 30 h.

However, if we thought prior to deciding hastily that we automate everything, we would come up to the conclusion, that there will be only two regression test suite executions. Hence, this will take us 30 h. Comparing it with the 80-h automation project it means that we would be able to spend the remaining 50 h on additional test/QA activities! Even if we assume that the thinking process took 10 additional hours, we still have 40 h for other valuable testing activities in the project.

Of course, we should always try to find a sweet spot in a trade-off analysis between the time spent on thinking vs. acting. The benefit from thinking will not monotonically increase with the increase of time spent on planning and analyzing. At the end of the day, we have to *do* the job. Hence, thinking is important, but we should spend on it as much time as it requires—and no more.

6.9   Using the Tools: You're Doing It Wrong!

We live in the era of automation. When we investigate the software testing conference agendas, we immediately notice that the most interesting thing the testers want to talk about, is automation and tools. As automation has became de facto a standard approach to testing, the more we should be aware of the risks involved with tools.

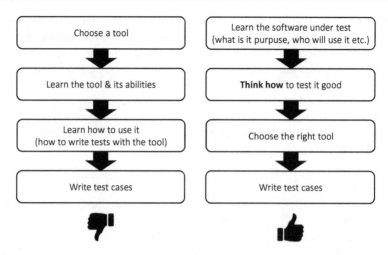

Fig. 6.12 Using the tools: bad strategy and good strategy

There is a famous quote about tools, often attributed to Marshall McLuhan: 'We are what we behold. We shape our tools and then our tools shape us'.[7] In the context of using tools in testing this is a pessimistic observation: a *tester should never allow herself to be guided by a tool*. It is a tester who needs to be in control. It is a tester who rationally and consciously uses the tool to increase her effectiveness—not the opposite.

This phenomenon of a tool being the guide for testing occurs often in companies that are, for some reason, accustomed to using a certain automation framework, or attached to a certain tool type. This may result in a dangerous bias in testing, because by relying solely on a given type of a tool, the testers are able to perform only certain types of testing. Their thinking about defects, risks and possible test approaches are biased toward the techniques offered by this tool.

A good example may be the capture and reply tools, like Selenium or Robot Framework. If there is a company culture in which the only way of testing is via this type of tool, the testers will (unconsciously) perform only the GUI testing or GUI-related testing. This is dangerous, because many types of defects may remain undetected.

Figure 6.12 presents two approaches to tools. The left one can be observed much more frequently, but it is a wrong approach. It leads to the bias in testing. In this

---

[7]This quote is frequently attributed to Marshall McLuhan and is said to be found in his book 'Understanding Media', but it does not appear there at all. Primarily it was coined by John Culkin SJ, a professor of communication at Fordham University ('We shape our tools, and thereafter our tools shape us'). He was a friend of McLuhan and explored the idea in 'A schoolman's guide to Marshall McLuhan' (The Saturday Review, 18 March 1967). The sentence is, in turn, a paraphrase of Winston Churchill words 'We shape our buildings and afterward our buildings shape us', which he said addressing UK Parliament on the subject of plans for rebuilding the bombed-out House of Commons.

Fig. 6.13 A multifunctional knife

approach the tool commands the tester. The approach on the right is a rational one. The starting point is the quality-related analysis of the software. Only then we select the tool—the one that will be useful in performing the test activities analyzed and planned *prior* to tool purchase and use. In this approach the tester commands the tool.

The implications of these two approaches are quite obvious. The first one results in weak tests, biased toward the tool abilities. The second one results in strong, thought-out and hence effective tests, designed upon the rational analysis of the software, business expectations and so on. In the second approach two keywords are bolded: **think how** to test. It means that the analysis itself should be creative and independent of any tool: during the analysis we must not have any particular tool in mind, because otherwise our analysis would be biased. We should also not rely on any technical way of performing the tests—this step will be done after the analysis, when we finally need to choose the tool. Its abilities will impact all the technicalities.

Another, opposite problem with the tools is their multiplicity. Of course it is good to have many different tools, but we should not use them at the same time. Think about the multifunctional knife (Fig. 6.13)—it is a perfect and very handy thing, but when you open at the same time all the knives and other tools it offers, you will probably cut yourself. When solving any testing problem, focus only on the tool that really solves this problem. Do not try to build the 'all-purpose testing environment' for performing every kind of testing. It never works.

Finally, every tester should remember the important saying about the tools: 'a fool with a tool is still a fool'. Notice that foolishness is the opposite of thinking. Tools will be effectively used only if you command the tool, not the other way round.

Kata and Exercises for Testers

7

7.1   Introduction

In this chapter we present a set of exercises that allow the tester to develop her intellectual skills needed in the everyday work. After describing two types of the exercises (Sect. 7.2), and some tips on how to solve the exercises (Sect. 7.3), in the consecutive sections we present the exercises. We grouped them according to the type of skills they refer to. These are:

- logical thinking and reasoning (Sect. 7.4),
- creativity and out-of-the-box thinking (Sect. 7.5),
- counting and estimating (Sect. 7.6),
- analytical thinking (Sect. 7.7).

For each area we provide two types of exercises, so-called kata and 'concrete' exercises. In the following two sections we discuss in detail the differences between them and the ways to approach them. In Sect. 7.8 we provide solutions to exercises. We also explain what types of analytical skills are checked in each exercise and we discuss the lessons that can be learned by testers from these exercises.

7.2   What Is Kata?

The word *kata* literally means 'form' in Japanese (see Fig. 7.1). It refers to different choreographical forms of movements practiced mainly in martial arts like karate or kung-fu. This idea comes from the original kata—a set of exercises being teaching and training methods used to practice combat techniques. Rosenbaum defines its purpose as follows: 'The basic goal of pre-arranged training is to preserve and transmit proven techniques. By practicing kata in a repetitive manner the fighter develops biomechanical responses that enable him or her to execute those techniques and movements in a natural, reflex-like manner. The ultimate goal is to internalize

Fig. 7.1 Kata

the movements and techniques of each pre-arranged sequence (kata) so that they can be executed under almost any circumstances, without thought or hesitation' [107].

For programming, this term was probably first coined by Dave Thomas (codekata.com), a co-author of the book 'The Pragmatic Programmer' [108]. Thomas proposes the Code Kata—a set of programming exercises that allows you to practice the art of the programming. The idea is that systematically practicing the Code Kata makes you a better programmer.

We adopt the notion of kata for similar exercises for testers. The ultimate goal here would be not to internalize physical movements, but intellectual activities. In other words, kata for testers prepare the testers' minds to effectively solve testing problems. They strengthen the good habits related to the way of thinking about the testing problems.

As Kanazawa wrote in a foreword to his book on kata: '(...) Gichin Funakoshi states: 'Perform kata exactly. Actual combat is another matter'. As the master wisely points out, kata are made up of more than merely offensive and defensive techniques. They contain elements that offer opportunities for deep learning about physical education, art, history and, particularly, philosophy' [109].

We can relate this very wise advice to the testing profession. Traversing Funakoshi's words: perform testing kata exactly—real testing is another matter. You cannot expect to face in your job as a tester exactly the kinds of problems described in this book. But—you may ask—if the real problems are totally different than kata—why bother? Well, there is a very good reason for that. It is true that real testing is very complicated. In some situations you will have to be very careful and detailed, in some others the best strategy will be to forget about the 'formal' approach and perform your job in a slack way. In some situations you will create absolutely no plans and immediately get your hands dirty on testing, in some others the planning will be the most important thing. But regardless of the way you choose, if you want to be successful, you will always need to think critically and analytically.

You will not learn this effectively by solving really hard problems. In fact, to be able to solve them you need to possess the above-mentioned analytical skills in advance. The best way to do this is to start with kata. These exercises are a bunch of carefully selected problems that will guide you systematically through many different types of situations and problems that you will recognize later in your real job as a tester. Kata described in this book will also allow you to train your brain and to master your analytic skills. Shortly speaking, they will improve your thinking—the most important tester's skill.

7.3   How to Practice the Tester's Kata and Exercises?

The following sections contain two kinds of exercises, called 'kata' and 'exercises'. Kata are designed for systematic, repetitive practicing. Exercises are the concrete, single problems to solve. To make the learning process as effective as possible, you need to 'perform kata exactly'. You should solve each kata and exercise in a very precise and detailed way. Don't rush. Take your time. If you feel that you are not able to solve a given problem (for example, you cannot generate any additional test ideas), don't look immediately to the solution, even if it is very tempting. Take a break, go for a walk, take care of something else. Maybe even come back to this exercise next day. And then try again to provide some other ways to solve the problem described in a given exercise.

Write down your complete solution before you look to the solution in the book. This process is not an art for art's sake. Practicing this way will improve your skills, such as precision, planning, analytical thinking, reasoning, associating facts. If you don't believe, just try it. You will immediately notice that many new, good ideas will come to your mind just because of writing down your solution.

In karate you should practice the same set of kata through all of your life. Testing exercises are a bit different. When you solve an exercise and look up the solution it makes no sense to repeat the same exercise immediately. Apart from the exercises, each section contains several testing kata. These exercises, in contrast, are generic and do not refer to concrete problems, but to the abstract ways of thinking (or, to the *practice of thinking*). Kata can be executed repetitively for many different, practical test situations, systems under test and so on.

It is a very good habit to think about and practice these kata regularly, for different test problems you encounter in your everyday work and life. Every next use of kata can be enriched with your experience. Have you found some interesting bug lately? Or maybe you have read some interesting book on philosophy, economy or history? *Any* situation may inspire you to think about new approaches to the previously solved kata. You can then extend your solution by adding the new case. You may even be inspired to develop some new approaches to testing—that is, new kata.

For some kata we give some solutions, suggestions or practical examples. They are by no means complete, 'universally true' or exhaustive. They are just examples. In a real life, the testing process is constrained by many factors, including technology, time, budget, acceptable risk level, etc. This often results in a reduced scope of testing. When exercising kata remember that there are no constraints. Provide as many possible good test cases, as you can imagine. Don't be angry, when you see that your solution has only 10 good test cases, while the proposed solution contains or suggests 50 or 100 of them and you missed so many opportunities as a tester. You need to learn the lesson from that kata. When solving the next one or when applying the same kata to another problem your result will be much better. After some time you will find that you are even able to provide effective tests that are not mentioned in this book. Such a thing is a good sign—a black belt in testing is at your fingertips!

7.4   Kata and Exercises on Logical Thinking and Reasoning

7.4.1   Kata #1: Logical Analysis

> Take any document and analyze its logic.

This kata allows you to practice the logical reasoning, following and analyzing the rules and checking their consistency.

The document can be literally anything: a legal act, regulations, regimen, statute, requirements specification, instruction, etc. Does the document contain any rules? Can you reformulate the document in the formal language of logic? Does the document contain any logical fallacies/contradictions (see the example with the Constitutional Court given in Sect. 2.2.4)? Notice that sometimes formal logic and 'everyday' logic may be quite different. Figure 7.2 shows a sign present in every liquor store in Poland. The sign literally says: 'we do not sell alcohol to people who are under the age of 18 and intoxicated.

When we analyze this sentence from the logical point of view, we should come to the following conclusion. The sentence gives a conjunction of two conditions which, if fulfilled, means that the alcohol cannot be sold. It can be reformulated as $Y \wedge U \Rightarrow P$, where Y means 'a person is under the age of 18', U means 'a person is unsober' and P means 'we cannot sell alcohol to this person'. If someone is under the age of 18 and sober, the implication's predecessor is false (because the conjunction of true and false is false). This makes the whole implication true no matter what is the logical value of P. So, P can be false. This means that if someone is too young but sober, or old enough but drunk, he can buy alcohol.

Of course, the intention of this sign is that it gives two independent conditions such that if *any* of them is fulfilled, the alcohol sale is prohibited. Testers need to be very careful when analyzing the logic given in the requirements and should be able to distinguish between 'everyday' and formal logic.

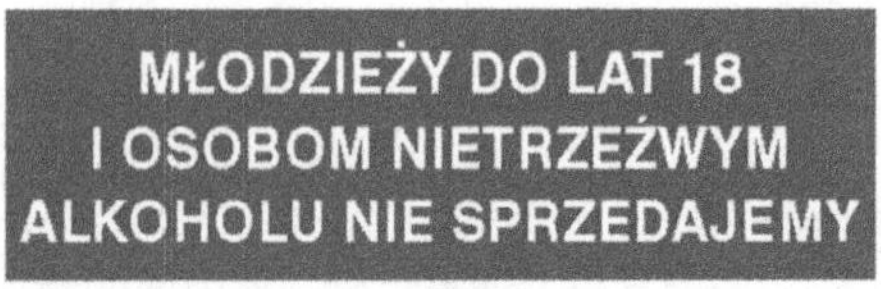

Fig. 7.2 Polish sign with a sentence interesting from the logical point of view

MŁODZIEŻY DO LAT 18
I OSOBOM NIETRZEŹWYM
ALKOHOLU NIE SPRZEDAJEMY

7.4.2 Kata #2: What-If Analysis

> Consider any kind of a process, situation or procedure and think what would happen (what would be the consequences) if something was changed in it. Analyze many different changes within the same process.

This kind of a 'what-if' analysis allows us to realize the importance of some actions, steps or procedures defined within processes.

Consider the following example: in Poland every citizen has a so-called PESEL number (Personal Identification Number). Its first six digits encode the date of birth (for example, if you were born May 6th 1975, your PESEL starts with 750506). In many official procedures, when a citizen has to fill in some form, she has to write in both PESEL *and* date of birth. But if the PESEL number contains this date, why enter a redundant information?

What would happen if the form didn't ask about the birth date, but only for a PESEL? We should immediately notice that the redundant information gives us a 'double-check' procedure for data correctness. If we have to enter only a PESEL number and made a mistake in it, it might not be detected. When a system has also the information about the birth date, it may compare the first six PESEL digits with this date and therefore verify the correctness of this data.[1]

7.4.3 Exercise: Logical Thinking

This exercise comes from https://www.theguardian.com/science/2016/mar/28/can-you-solve-it-the-logic-question-almost-everyone-gets-wrong. It requires a bit of logical thinking. The puzzle is as follows:

> *Jack is looking at Anne, but Anne is looking at George. Jack is married, but George is not. Is a married person looking at an unmarried person?*
>
> *A. Yes*
> *B. No*
> *C. Cannot be determined*

7.4.4 Exercise: Who Lies?

Mr A says that Mr B lies. Mr B says that Mr C lies. Mr C says that both Mr A and Mr B lie. Who tells the truth and who lies?

---

[1]In fact, in case of the PESEL number the situation is even simpler, as one of the PESEL digits is a so-called check digit, which is a redundancy check for error detection in the PESEL number.

7.4.5 Exercise: Bob's Daughters

Andy and Bob—two school mates meet after a long time at the alumni reunion. Here is their conversation:

Andy: How are you? I heard that you have three daughters.
Bob: Yes. Imagine that all three of them celebrate their birthdays on the same day!
A: Can I ask what are their ages?
B: Guess. I'll give you a hint: the product of their ages is 36.
A: Well, it's rather too little information. . .
B: OK. I'll give you another one. The sum of their ages equals the number of the windows in the opposite building.
(Andy looks at the building and counts its windows)
A: Hmm. . . Unfortunately, I need another clue.
B: Alright. I can tell you that the oldest one has red hair, and the younger ones are blond.
A: Ah, so now everything is clear!

What are the ages of Bob's daughters? Reconstruct the way of Andy's reasoning. How did he come up to the right answer and why he needed all three clues (some of which being rather weird. . .)?

7.4.6 Exercise: Mismatched Figure

This puzzle is due to the Russian mathematician, Tatiana Chovanova. Figure 7.3 shows five figures. One of them does not match the rest. Which one is the mismatched one?

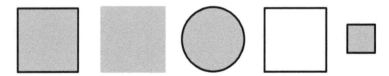

Fig. 7.3 Tatiana Chovanova's puzzle

7.5   Kata and Exercises on Creativity and Out-of-the-Box Thinking

7.5.1   Kata #3: Generation of Ideas

> Apply the TQED analysis to an arbitrary problem, object or process. Generate as many characteristics and test ideas as you can.

This kata allows you to practice the creativity boosting with the help of the TQED model, that is, to generate valuable, interesting and practical test ideas.

It is recommended to apply it not only to the objects 'typical' from the tester's point of view (system, requirements, etc.), but also to everyday activities as well as atypical, weird or uncommon things, situations and actions. Table 7.1 gives you some examples.

7.5.2   Kata #4: Bypasses and Detours

> Think about how to bypass something. It may be a very practical situation as well as an abstract or fantastic one. Generate as many ideas as you can.

This kata trains you in the dirty testing. It may be helpful in situations which require you to provide the negative, malicious test data, user actions and so on (for example, in API testing, security testing, etc.).

To develop your creativity more effectively, do not restrict yourself only to the IT examples. You may think about very abstract or fantastic examples, for example:

- how to enter a party without the invitation?
- how to get into the tube without a valid ticket and not get caught?
- how to bypass the security control at the airport?
- how to sneak into conclave?
- how to assassinate the president and not get caught?

Table 7.1 Example entities for the TQED analysis

Entity	Examples
Static object	Bike, mouse trap, road sign, dog, solar system
Problem	Finding the shortest path, taking the child to school, playing the piano
Process	Granting a loan, grading the exam, baking the pizza

7.5.3   Exercise: The Right Question

You are imprisoned in a cell with two doors. One of them is the exit and behind the second one there is a poisonous gas that will kill you instantly if you open it. You are allowed to open one door. If you select the exit, you may leave the prison. Unfortunately, you don't know which one is that. The doors are guarded by two prison guards. One of them (you don't know which one) always tells the truth and the second one always lies. You can ask only one question to only one guard. What question would you ask, so that the answer allows you to get the freedom back?

7.5.4   Exercise: Connecting the Dots

Can you connect the nine dots shown in Fig. 7.4 using at most four straight lines, without lifting the pen and without tracing the same line more than once?

7.5.5   Exercise: Find the Rule

Consider the following relations between numbers:

$$f(8809)=6 \quad f(7111)=0 \quad f(2172)=0 \quad f(6666)=4 \quad f(1111)=0$$
$$f(3213)=0 \quad f(7662)=2 \quad f(9313)=1 \quad f(0000)=4 \quad f(2222)=0$$
$$f(3333)=0 \quad f(5555)=0 \quad f(8913)=3 \quad f(8096)=5 \quad f(7777)=0$$
$$f(9999)=4 \quad f(7756)=1 \quad f(6855)=3 \quad f(9881)=5 \quad f(5531)=0$$

Find out the rule for f and compute $f(2581)$.

Fig. 7.4 Nine dots puzzle

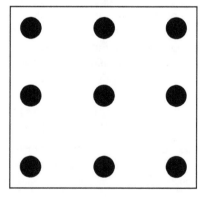

7.5.6   Exercise: Four Triangles

Build four equilateral triangles from six segments of the same length.

7.6   Kata and Exercises on Counting and Estimating

7.6.1   Kata #5: Estimations for Counting

> Estimate the number of objects for which there is no simple formula to calculate it.

The goal of this kata is to practice both the creative approach and estimation skills. The most important thing here is not to provide the exact answer, but to design a reasoning that might bring us to the reasonable estimation.

Here are some example things to estimate:

• what is the number of trees in the United States?
• what is the average number of airplanes flying in a given moment of time?
• how many ping-pong balls fit in the bus?
• how many people use public transportation every day in your city?

And here is a more concrete example. Suppose you want to count the total number of windows in all the buildings in New York. You may start with estimating the number of people living in New York, average number of windows in one flat, and average number of family members. Then do the same for the office buildings—here you may, for example, estimate first the number of New York inhabitants that work in the office, estimate the average number of employees in one office and divide these two numbers, obtaining the estimation of the number of office buildings. This would give you some estimate.

You may use a different approach: estimate the area A of New York, the average building density per area unit (B), the average number F of floors in a building and the average number of windows W on a single floor. Then the final estimation would be $A \cdot B \cdot F \cdot W$.

It is very instructive if the exercise is solved by a group of people. Each person estimates the result on her own and then everyone compares the results and discusses the methods they use to come up with the final solution.

7.6.2 Kata #6: Time Estimations

> Estimate the time of a future activity and after completing it compare your estimation with the actual time.

This kata is similar to the former one, but is related to time estimation, which is also a crucial thing in test planning.

In this kata you are able to compare your guess with the real result, because you can apply your estimation to a real activity that you are going to perform. The example activities for which you can measure the time are:

- how long will it take to drive from home to work?
- how long will it take to read a book/a certain number of book's pages?
- how long will it take to fill in a defect report?

When you do the estimate, you probably make many assumptions. When comparing your prediction with the actual results you know what you've missed or what you've under- or overestimated. If the activity you estimated is a repetitive action, you can repeat the time estimation task for the same activity in the future, considering the 'lessons learned' from the previous estimations. You should notice better and better precision in estimating this activity.

7.6.3 Exercise: Monty Hall Problem

This famous problem comes from the 'Ask Marylin' column in Parade magazine from 1990:

> *Suppose you're on a game show, and you're given the choice of three doors: Behind one door is a car; behind the others, goats. You pick a door, say No. 1, and the host, who knows what's behind the doors, opens another door, say No. 3, which has a goat. He then says to you, 'Do you want to pick door No. 2?' Is it to your advantage to switch your choice?*

This is the exercise from Sect. 2.2.5, where a solution using the 'rescale strategy' is given. Now, try to solve it in a more formal way. *Hint*: this problem can be solved by providing a formal proof using the notion of conditional probability, but you may come up to the solution by performing a very simple analysis of the problem (what is the probability that your first choice is right and will it change after the host opens another door?).

7.6.4 Exercise: Probability

A certain test for checking the presence of a virus gives the correct answer in 95% of cases. This means that a probability of the negative result for a sick patient is 5/100 and so is the probability of the positive result[2] for a patient without the virus. It is known that 1% of the population is a virus carrier. The test was performed for a randomly chosen patient and it gave the positive result. What is the probability that this patient indeed is the virus carrier? Will it be very high? How would you estimate it without performing the exact computations?

Hint. You can calculate this probability directly from Bayes theorem, but you may deduce the probability level without referring to the theory.

7.6.5 Exercise: Simple Counting

Read the text below and count the number of occurrences of the letter F. How many letters F did you count?

FINISHED FILES ARE THE
RESULT OF YEARS OF SCIENTIFIC
STUDY COMBINED WITH THE
EXPERIENCE OF YEARS

7.7 Kata and Exercises on Analytical Thinking

7.7.1 Kata #7: Risk Analysis

Perform a risk identification and analysis for an everyday activity. Identify as many risks as you can. If possible, group them into the categories. Analyze each risk (calculate its likelihood and impact).

This kata develops your analytical thinking via performing a risk analysis. It is very helpful for negative testing and also for identifying the most effective strategy for different parts of the project.

For example, you may think about your travel from home to work. What can go wrong? You may oversleep, there may be a traffic jam, you may forget something and have to go back, there may be a public transportation strike, and so on.

---

[2]Negative result means that the test did not detect the presence of the virus. Positive result means that it did.

7.7.2   Kata #8: Abstract Testing

Think about how would you test a given object. Think not only about the test ideas or test cases, but also what questions you should ask prior to testing, to get enough amount of knowledge about this object, its purpose, test environment, test goals and so on.

Practicing this kata will develop your creativity in testing. It is important to perform this exercise for many different types of objects—not only the real, typical things, but also the abstract ones and even ones that even do not exist, for example:

- typical objects, like: hammer, glass, book, bridge, elevator, etc.
- abstract/nonexistent objects, like: teleport, intergalactic spaceship, test oracle, sorting algorithm, etc.

7.7.3   Exercise: Testing a Chair

You are asked to propose a test approach for testing a chair. What would be your next steps? What other things you think you should know? How would you test the chair if you have enough knowledge about the test object?

7.7.4   Exercise: The Fly and the Trains

Two trains are 200 km apart and travelling towards each other in a straight line at 50 km/h each. From one train a fly takes off and flies straight above the rails to the other train at the speed of 65 km/h. When it reaches the other train, it immediately bounces off and flies back to the first train. This movement is repeated till the trains crash together.

What is the total distance traveled by the fly?

Hint: There is a straightforward and, at the same time, quite complicated solution to this puzzle. However, there also exists a much simpler solution.

7.7.5   Exercise: Code Analysis

This exercise checks the tester's ability to provide counterexamples—a very important skill in testing. In Sect. 5.2.2 we presented the example of an algorithm that verified whether the sorting algorithm indeed returned the correct, sorted sequence:

Example

Suppose that our SUT implements a new, fast sorting algorithm. We would like to test it with millions of random test cases. The system accepts an array of numbers as input and returns the same sequence, but in an ascending order. The pseudo-code shown below implements a simple oracle for verifying if the output is correct (the notation O[i] means the i-th element of the array O):

```
function oracle
input: I (input array of size m), O (output array of size n)
1. if (m≠n) return 'wrong result - test failed';
2. for (i in 1...n-1) do
3.    if O[i+1] < O[i] return 'wrong result - test failed';
4. for (i in 1...m) do
5.    if I[i] is not in O return 'wrong result - test failed';
6.    remove I[i] from O
7. return 'test passed'
```

Assume line 6 is removed from the above code. Will the oracle still work fine? If not, give the counterexample (that is, an input I and O for which the oracle will return the wrong answer).

7.8   Solutions to Exercises

7.8.1   Solution to Exercise 7.4.3

The correct answer is A. According to The Guardian, only 28% of responders chose the right answer. 4% chose B and over 67% said that the answer cannot be determined! It's probably because the question is tricky—it seems that it gives us insufficient information: we don't know whether Anne is married or not. However, this information is irrelevant to the answer: if she is married, we know that a married person is looking at an unmarried person (Anne is looking at George). If she is not married, then—again—a married person is looking at an unmarried person (Jack is looking at Anne). To see it better, we may symbolically represent the situation denoting by "a > b" the fact that a is looking at b:

Jack > Anne > George

We are interested only in the marital status of the persons, so we transform the diagram:

married > ? > unmarried

If Anne is married we have:

married > **married** > **unmarried**

If Anne is unmarried we have:

married > **unmarried** > unmarried

We see that in each case we have the "married > unmarried" situation (bolded in the diagrams above).

The lesson from this exercise is that sometimes we do not need to have every possible information to get the right answer. Some information may be irrelevant.

7.8.2 Solution to Exercise 7.4.4

A and C are liars, B is a truth-teller. We can solve it at least in two ways: by logical reasoning and using formal logic. Let us present both solutions.

The solution using logical reasoning If C is a truth-teller, then it is true that both A and B are liars. But A says B lies, so if A is a liar, B must be a truth-teller. It contradicts the former conclusion that B is a liar. Hence, C cannot be a truth-teller. Suppose now that C lies. It means that at least one of A and B is a truth-teller. Since B says that C lies, B must be a truth-teller. And since A says B lies, A must by a liar.

The solution using formal logic Denote by $P(x)$ the predicate that can be read as 'x tells the truth'. The sentence 'x says y' implies that $P(x) \Leftrightarrow y$: if x tells the truth and x says y, then it is true that y. If x lies, and x says y, then it is not true that y. Using this formalism, we can write the three sentences from the exercise as follows ($\neg$ is a negation and is read as 'it is not true that. . .'):

(1) $P(A) \Leftrightarrow \neg P(B)$ A says B lies
(2) $P(B) \Leftrightarrow \neg P(C)$ B says C lies
(3) $P(C) \Leftrightarrow \neg P(A) \wedge \neg P(B)$ C says that both A and B lie

Let us transform (3) by substituting its right-hand side elements using (1) and (2). Notice that $p \Leftrightarrow q$ is equivalent to $\neg p \Leftrightarrow \neg q$. We have:

$P(C) \Leftrightarrow \neg P(A) \wedge \neg P(B)$
$\Leftrightarrow P(B) \wedge \neg P(B)$ from (2)
$\Leftrightarrow false$ because $p \wedge \neg p$ is false.

Hence, we have $P(C) = false$, which means that C lies. So, from (2) we have that B tells the truth and then, from (1) that A lies.

The lesson from this exercise is that formal logic is a powerful tool. Also, some simpler logic problems can be solved by considering all possible situations (case 1: C tells the truth, case 2: C lies). The second solution seems to be a bit longer and also requires some mathematical knowledge. But notice that if the problem were more complicated (for example, there might be more persons and every person would say something about other persons), the straightforward analysis might have been difficult to carry. In such a case the formal logic would be the best option to use. There are some logic-based programming languages, like Prolog, that enable us to encode such problems into a software code and solve them automatically.

7.8.3   Solution to Exercise 7.4.5

The product of the ages is 36, so the possible combinations (regardless of their ordering) are:

1, 1, 36
1, 3, 12
1, 4, 9
1, 2, 18
1, 6, 6
2, 2, 9
2, 3, 6
3, 3, 4

This information doesn't allow us to choose the right answer. The second clue is about the sum of the daughter's ages. These sums for the above combinations are:

38—for 1, 1, 36
16—for 1, 3, 12
14—for 1, 4, 9
21—for 1, 2, 18
13—for 1, 6, 6
13—for 2, 2, 9
11—for 2, 3, 6
10—for 3, 3, 4

Bob says that the sum of the ages equals the number of windows in the opposite building. We don't know this number, but we know a very important thing, that Andy—knowing this number—is still not able to solve the puzzle. This means that the solution must be still ambiguous. Hence, the only two possible solutions are the ones with 13 as the sum of the ages:

1, 6, 6
2, 2, 9

If the sum was different than 13, the second clue would clearly give us the right answer. The third clue has nothing to do with the ages, so it seems to be not very informative. However, it says that *the oldest* daughter has red hair. This eliminates the solution 1, 6, 6 and we come up to the final solution: the oldest daughter is 9 years old, and two others are 2 years old.

To be honest, an inquisitive tester might have some doubts about this solution. The first one is that ages don't necessarily have to be integer numbers. Although the sum of the ages is integer (as it is the number of the windows), as well as the product, it does not necessarily mean that all three numbers have to be integers (the question is, if it is possible in our case). The second thing is that there may be two non-twin daughters that were born 11 months one after another, so their age, expressed in the integer numbers, is equal, but one of them is older than the other. In this case, 1, 6, 6 would also be the correct solution, and after the third clue the solution would still be ambiguous.

The lesson from this exercise is that sometimes the data bring us more information than it seems at first glance. We just have to connect the dots. Also, notice that in this puzzle we were analyzing and explaining the situation that has happened—we didn't know some information that Andy knew (number of windows), but it wasn't necessary. The crucial information was that he was not able to answer right after the second clue.

7.8.4   Solution to Exercise 7.4.6

The mismatched figure is the first one, because... it matches all the characteristics that describe the figures! Here's how it works:

- the second figure is the only one that does not have the black border,
- the third figure is the only one that is not a square,
- the fourth figure is the only one that is not gray,
- the fifth figure is the only one that is smaller than all the others.

Only the first figure has all these features. It seems at the beginning that it is 'the most matched' figure, because of the border, shape, color and size. However, each of the other figures is mismatched because of just one characteristic. Hence, the first figure is mismatched, because... it is 'too matched'.

The lesson from this exercise is that sometimes the most typical thing, event or data may be the most suspicious. When we solve the puzzle, we automatically pay attention to all but the first figure, which, paradoxically, distinguishes it from all the others. The tester needs to pay attention to all the data she has. Many bugs can be unnoticed because of the dulled vigilance.

7.8.5 Solution to Exercise 7.5.3

As we don't know which guard is a truth-teller and which one always lies, we need to ask the question in a way that would relate the answer with the other guard. One of the possible solution is to ask any of the guards the following question: 'if I asked the other guard to point at the exit door, which one would he point at?'.

If we ask the truth-teller, he would point at the door with the gas behind them, because he knows that the other guard lies. If we ask the one that always lies, he knows that the truth-teller would point at the exit door. So he points at the other one, because he always lies.

Hence, no matter which guard asks the question, he will always point at the non-exit door. We need to open the other one.

The lesson from this exercise is as follows. If you didn't know this puzzle before, it might have been difficult to you. This is because the answer requires a detailed analysis of the whole 'system' together with the relations between its components. In our case the system is composed of two guards with different properties. The solution can be obtained by analyzing the relation between these components. This puzzle is a nice, 'logical' version of the system thinking activity.

7.8.6 Solution to Exercise 7.5.4

The solution is presented in Fig. 7.5a. It requires *literally* to think outside the box, as the lines have to go outside the square that frames the dots.

Figure 7.5c–e shows another, trial-and-error approach. It is easy to connect the lines with one curved line (c). We can imagine that this is a rubber string and stretch it in a way that it fits more and more to the four straight lines. Finally, we correct the almost optimal solution (d) and arrive with the setting (e).

As in the previous exercises, testers may want to clarify some things. For example, if we treat nine dots not as the points, but as the circles having a non-zero area, we can find a solution similar to the one shown in Fig. 7.5b. Probably the dots should be treated as points in space, with no length or width. Similarly, the lines should be treated as geometric lines with a positive length, but with zero width. Another interesting question is about the space in which the dots are drawn. For example, if they were drawn on a different surface—a sphere, they could be connected using only one single line, as shown in Fig. 7.6.

The lesson from this exercise is that a good tester—when designing the tests— cannot allow herself to be limited by any rules, tools or methods. She should take advantage of everything that can make her work more effective. If she can benefit from any unconventional, weird, nonstandard method—she should definitely go for it.

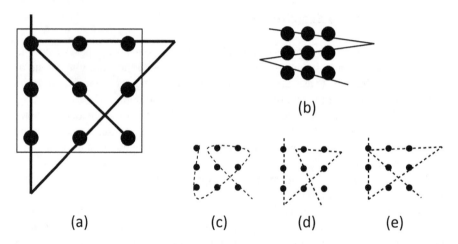

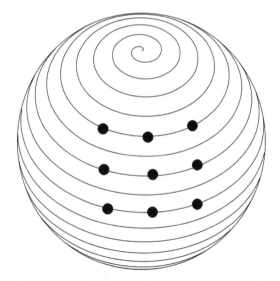

Fig. 7.5   Solution to the nine-dots puzzle

Fig. 7.6   Another solution of the nine-dots puzzle

7.8.7   Solution to Exercise 7.5.5

The correct answer is $f(2581) = 2$. Function f counts the number of closed areas in the graphical representation of digits. For example, digits 0, 6 and 9 have one closed area. Digit 8 has two. All other digits have no closed areas. The difficulty of this puzzle is that when we see digits and functions, we expect that the relation has to be of an arithmetic nature. However, the function f checks the geometric properties of the digits' shapes. The property sought is not visible at first glance. We need to switch from the 'arithmetic' thinking into 'topological' thinking.

It is interesting, though, that f can be represented in a formal, 'arithmetic' way. Here's the function definition (we assume it is defined for all natural numbers):

$$f(1) = f(2) = f(3) = f(5) = f(7) = 0,$$
$$f(0) = f(4) = f(6) = f(9) = 1,$$
$$f(8) = 2,$$
$$f(x) = f([x/10]) + f(x \bmod 10) \text{ for } x > 9,$$

where $[x]$ means the integer part of x, and $x \bmod y$ denotes the rest from dividing x by y. For example:

$$f(2581) = f(258) + f(1)$$
$$= f(25) + f(8) + f(1)$$
$$= f(2) + f(5) + f(8) + f(1)$$
$$= 0 + 0 + 2 + 0$$
$$= 2.$$

The observant tester will notice that in the original puzzle no argument to f contains the digit 4. The possible reason is that 4 can be written in two ways: with one or zero closed areas.

The lesson from this exercise is that we shouldn't go always with the easiest, most visible solution. Sometimes we stumble upon the problems, for which the optimal solution is more difficult to spot.

7.8.8   Solution to Exercise 7.5.6

The solution is shown in Fig. 7.7. It requires a creative trick: transforming the problem into higher dimension. The solution is a tetrahedron, which is a 3D figure. It is impossible to solve the puzzle in two-dimensional space.

The lesson from this exercise is that creativity and the ability to go out from our comfort zone are very powerful tools. We are accustomed to work with two-dimensional space, because it is natural for us. In our everyday work we don't even think about it. Every professional tester should have this ability to think out-of-the-box. This can be practiced by an unceasing analysis of the problems as well as the *tools we use to solve them.*

7.8.9   Solution to Exercise 7.6.3

The answer, from the probabilistic point of view, is clear: we should definitely change our choice. Let us present now two approaches to the problem. The first one is quite concrete, but does not involve any formal mathematics, like Bayes theorem

Fig. 7.7 Solution to the four
triangles puzzle

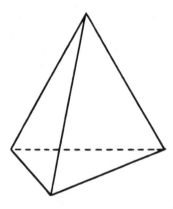

and conditional probabilities. It operates only on the general properties of the probability. The second one is more informal and uses a 'rescale' method that allows us to see the crucial observation needed to solve the puzzle.

Solution 1 It is clear that the probability of choosing the door with a car behind it is 1/3. Notice that this probability does not change when the host opens some other door (it will always be the door without a prize behind it). Hence, the rest 2/3 of the total probability 'goes' to the other closed door, because the probabilities of all possible elementary events need to sum up to 1. Therefore, changing our decision increases the probability of success twice.

Solution 2 Imagine that the number of doors is equal to the number of possible combinations in the EuroMillions lottery (that is, 116,531,800). The probability of choosing the door with a car behind it is equal to 1/116,531,800, which is... almost zero (it is around 0.000000008). Now imagine that the host opens *all* the doors except the one you have chosen and some other. Of course, the host knows where the prize is, so behind all the opened doors there is no car. Now, what is more likely: that the car is behind the door you selected, or that the car is behind the other not opened door? We are almost 100% sure that the car is behind the other door.

The lesson from this exercise is that probability theory is full of paradoxes and unexpected phenomena. A professional tester should know at least some fundamentals of the probability theory, because it is very helpful in estimation and prediction.

7.8.10 Solution to Exercise 7.6.4

The probability that the patient indeed is a virus carrier is unexpectedly low—it is around 16%. Why is it so? Intuitively, we think that if the test gives a wrong answer only in 5 out of 100 cases, the probability we are looking for should be around 95%. However, it isn't.

The reason why it is too low is the enormous disproportion between the sizes of healthy people and virus carriers. Look at Fig. 7.8. The whole population is denoted by two black circles—the big one represents the healthy part, the smaller the virus carriers. Gray filled circles represent the part of the population for which the test gives positive result. It is 95% of the virus carriers' population and 5% of the healthy people. We know that the test gave the positive result, so we know that a patient for which the test was performed, is in one of these two circles. We are looking for the ratio of the smaller one and the sum of both of them. But 5% of the 99% of population is much bigger than 95% of the 5% of population. Hence, the probability is so small.

We can solve the puzzle formally by using the Bayes theorem. Denote by P the event 'test gives the positive result', by V the event 'patient is a virus carrier' and by H the event 'patient is healthy'. We are looking for $Pr(V|P)$. From Bayes theorem we have:

$$Pr(V|P) = \frac{Pr(P|V)Pr(V)}{Pr(P|V)Pr(V) + Pr(P|H)Pr(H)} = \frac{0.95 \cdot 0.01}{0.95 \cdot 0.01 + 0.05 \cdot 0.95} \approx 0.16.$$

The lesson from this exercise is that sometimes the details matter. In this case the most important fact was the disproportion in the groups sizes.

7.8.11 Solution to Exercise 7.6.5

The answer is six. Here's the explanation from http://www.tsfx.com.au/brainboosters:

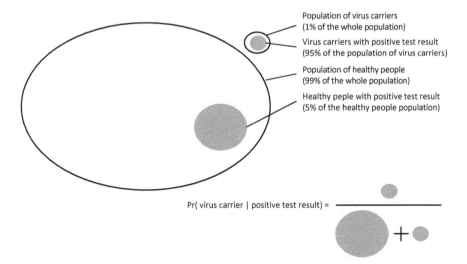

Fig. 7.8 Explanation of the solution to the virus puzzle

Almost everyone guesses three. Why? It seems that the brain cannot correctly process the word 'OF'. The letter F usually makes the 'f' sound, like in 'fox'. However, in the word 'of', it makes a 'v' sound. Somehow, your brain overlooks the word 'of' as it scans for the sound of 'f'.[3]

The lesson from this exercise is that a professional tester needs to be precise and attentive. It is very easy to miss even the most obvious things.

7.8.12 Solution to Exercise 7.7.3

The solution below is just an example—there is no one correct answer.

Before we start testing, we should be sure that we understand the problem and its setting. There are many questions that should be answered to get to this point. For example:

- what type of chair is it?
- for whom is the chair manufactured? who will be the client?
- how long will the chair be used?
- for what purposes the chair will be used?
- how intensively will the chair be used?
- what particular chair functions/characteristics are important for the client?
- how much time have we for tests?
- what is the type of the chair? what kind of material is it made of?
- in what environment will the chair be used?
- what has already been tested and what were the results?
- what should not be tested and why?
- what are the functional requirements?
- what are the non-functional requirements and how can we verify them?
- is the color important?
- what about usability? will the chair be used by a particular person, or it is a 'commercial off-the-shelf' product?
- if we damage or destroy the chair during the tests, will we get a new one?
- is there any technical documentation and assembly instruction from the producer?
- in what form will the chair be delivered to tests? will it be necessary to assemble it by ourselves?
- . . . and so on

Only after getting the answers to all of our questions we are able to perform the rational, effective tests that bring an add-on value to the product. The first question is very important, and the answer to this question may result in some other questions

---

[3]It might be an interesting experiment to check the results of this exercise for the people whose native language is not English. If the explanation is correct, the non-English people should achieve better results than English people.

not mentioned in the list above. For example, if it turns out that this is. . . an electric chair, we should definitely do some tests regarding the current, electricity and so on.

This type of question is quite popular during most job interviews for testers, but it is often misused. Interviewers usually want the tester to provide as many different test cases as possible. However, the tests themselves are not as important as the questions the tester should ask before providing any test suite. The more questions she asks and the more rational and reasonable they are, the more professional the tester is. Asking the questions, drilling down the problem, the requirements, the constraints, etc. has one major goal: a tester needs to know where to start and where to go. In other words: what *exactly* is expected to be tested, what is important, what is irrelevant, what are the evaluation criteria, and so on.

7.8.13 Solution to Exercise 7.7.4

The most straightforward solution is to figure out how long is the first journey, then the return journey, and so on. However, this is very complicated. There is a simple, quick and elegant solution. Notice, that the trains will meet each other in 2 h (the distance between them is 200 km and their total speed is 100 km/h), so the fly will be flying for 2 h at 65 km/h. Hence, it will travel 130 km.

The lesson from this exercise is that some problems are apparently hard and sometimes the solution is very simple, when we look on the problem at a different angle.

7.8.14 Solution to Exercise 7.7.5

If we remove the line 6., the oracle may return an incorrect result in case there are repetitions in the input sequence. For example, if $I = (2, 2, 5)$ and $O = (2, 5, 5)$, the oracle will work as follows:

- condition in line 1. is true, because the size of I (3) equals the size of O,
- loop in lines 2.–3. will not return the wrong result, because O is sorted,
- loop in lines 4.–5. (with line 6. removed) goes through elements 2, 2 and 5; each of these elements is present in O, so there will be no error.

However, when the line 6. is present, during the first loop execution the element 2 will be removed from O. In the second iteration of the loop, another element 2 will be searched in O, but it won't be found. The oracle will detect that O is not the sorted version of I.

The lesson from this exercise is that analytical thinking helps us not only in the technical aspects of the tester's work, but also it allows us to optimize things. If it had turned out that line 6. is irrelevant, we would have erased it and the algorithm would have worked faster.

Appendix A. Glossary of the Most Important Terms

Acceptance Testing Validating that the software or its part fulfills the high-level, business requirements. Usually it takes place at the final part of the development process and refers to the final product. The main goal of the acceptance testing is not finding defects, but making sure that the software really solves the problem it was supposed to solve.

API Testing A type of software testing that involves testing application programming interfaces (APIs) directly and as part of integration testing to determine if they meet expectations for functionality, reliability, performance, and security [110].

Black-Box Testing Testing that does not refer to the internal structure of the object under test. In the case of software, the test basis is usually some requirement document and black-box testing does not refer to the source code. In the case of documentation we do have the access to its internal structure by definition, so documentation testing is always white-box testing.

Boundary Value Analysis A domain-based black-box testing technique that analyzes if software works well for the data lying on the boundaries of previously defined equivalence classes. For example, if we have to verify the correctness of the implementation of the condition $a \leq x \leq b$ for a variable x, we identify the boundaries of the area to be verified, that is—minimal and maximal values for a given equivalence class (in our case this is the class $[a, b]$ with boundaries a and b). For each boundary we perform a test for this boundary and another one for the value closest to the boundary, but outside the boundary. In our example, if the domain is integers, we would have four tests for the class $[a, b]$: $a - 1, a, b, b + 1$. The extended version of the boundary value analysis is the domain analysis, which allows us to test the combinations of boundaries for high-dimensional domains.

© Springer International Publishing AG 2018
A. Roman, *Thinking-Driven Testing*, https://doi.org/10.1007/978-3-319-73195-7

Fig. A.1 A cause-effect
graph

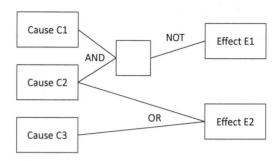

Bug *See defect.*

Cause-Effect Graph Testing A logic-based, black-box testing technique in which
tests are derived from a model called a cause-effect graph that represents the logical
relations between inputs (causes) and outputs (effects) in a system. A cause-effect
graph is the graphical representation of the set of logic functions. Figure A.1 presents
the example cause graph with three causes: C1, C2, C3 and two effects: E1 and E2
connected by logical relations. This graph is a realization of the set of two Boolean
functions: $f_{E1} = \neg (C1 \wedge C2), f_{E2} = C2 \vee C3$. It means that, for example, if C1 holds
and C2, C2 do not hold, E1 will happen (because $\neg(true \wedge false) = \neg false = true$)
and E2 will not happen, because (*false* $\vee$ *false* $=$ *false*). Cause-effect graphs can be
transformed into decision tables and vice versa.

Classification Tree A visual, hierarchical representation of the system in terms of
its characteristics and possible values of these characteristics. This model is often
considered as a combinatorial testing method, but classification tree itself does not
provide any tests. It only shows the system's elements and the relations between
them. To provide the tests that cover, for example, certain combinations of these
elements, one needs a separate algorithm for this, for example an algorithm for
generating the tests achieving pair-wise coverage. Figure A.2 presents a sample
classification tree. The system is represented by three features: A, B and C. Feature A
can take one of the values A1, A2 and A3. Feature B can take one of the two values:
B1 and B2, but B1 is further classified into two possible versions, B1.1 and B1.2.
Feature C can take one of the values C1 and C2. The gray rectangles represent the
possible final values of the three features. There are three possibilities for A (A1, A2,
A3), three for B (B1.1, B1.2, B2) and two for C (C1, C2). Each test may be a
combination of the values of A, B and C. *See also: decision table.*

CMMI Model Capability Maturity Model Integration—a performance improvement model for organizations. It measures and helps to improve the process maturity
within an organization. It classifies the maturity into five levels [111]: initial

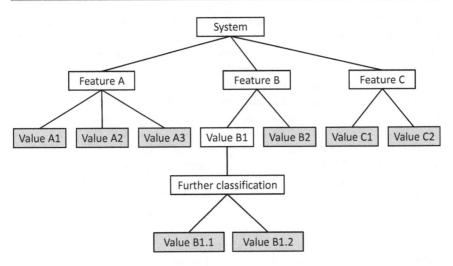

Fig. A.2 Classification tree

(unpredictable, reactive), managed (managed on the project level; projects are planned, performed, measured and controlled), defined (proactive; organization-wide standards provide guidance across projects, programs and project portfolios), quantitatively managed (measured and controlled; organization is data-driven with quantitative performance improvement objectives that are predictable and align to meet the needs of internal and external stakeholders), optimized (stable and flexible; organization is focused on continuous improvement and is built to pivot and respond to opportunity and change; stability provides a platform for agility and innovation). The CMMI model provides a set of practices that, when implemented, should allow the organization to reach higher and higher maturity levels.

Code Review A static technique for systematic examination of a source code. The intention of this practice is at least twofold: (1) to find defects, especially the ones that are difficult to discover during the late SDLC phases (the typical example are design/architectural defects), (2) to understand how the code works. There are several types of code review, varying from very informal to very formal, for example 'over-the-shoulder', pair-programming, desk-checking, inspection. *See also: inspection.*

Code Unit A logically distinguished part of a software code. It may be a formal, structural part of the code (like function, class, module, sub-system, procedure), or an informal one, for example the 'programmer's unit of work'. *See also: unit testing.*

Cohesion The strength of relationship between different functionalities within a given code unit, that is—a measure of how well modules fit together. Usually modules with high cohesion are preferable, because high cohesion is related with better reliability, maintainability and understandability. Cohesion can be measured quantitatively and in fact there are many different definitions. For example, the original Lack of Cohesion metric, introduced by Chidamber and Kemerer [112], is defined as follows: given n methods $m_1, \ldots, m_n$ contained in a class C and let I_i be the set of instance variables used by m_i. Then $LCOM(C) = \max \{0, |P| - |Q|\}$, where $P = \{(I_i, I_j) : I_i \cap I_j = \varnothing\}$ and $Q = \{(I_i, I_j) : I_i \cap I_j \neq \varnothing\}$; if all $I_i = \varnothing$, then $LCOM$ $(C) = 0$. Note that LCOM metric for a class where $|P| = |Q|$ will be 0. But this does not imply the maximal cohesiveness, since within the set of classes with LCOM=0, some may be more cohesive than others [112]. *See also: coupling.*

Combinatorial Testing A form of testing based on the Experimental Design methods. In combinatorial testing the test suite is designed to cover some combinations between different parameters under test. *See also: pair-wise testing, Each Choice testing.*

Concurrency Testing (1) testing performed to identify the defects related to the situation in which multiple users use the application at the same time; (2) testing the correctness of the concurrent computations performed by the SUT.

Condition A logical expression that does not contain any logical operators. For example, the decision x>5 AND y==0 consists of two conditions: x>5 and y==0.

Condition Coverage A code coverage that requires each condition in each decsion to be evaluated at least once to TRUE and at least once to FALSE. For example, for a decision A OR B we have two conditions: A and B. Two tests: (A=TRUE, B=FALSE), (A=FALSE, B=TRUE) achieve the coverage, because both A and B are evaluatet to TRUE and FALSE. The condition coverage do not subsume the decision coverage. In our example, our two tests do not achieve the decision coverage, as in both cases the decision outcome is TRUE.

Condition/Decision Coverage (C/D) A code coverage that requires both condition and decision coverage.

Control Flow Graph A graph representation of all possible paths of executable statements that may be traversed through a program during its execution. A control flow graph is a directed graph $G = (V, E)$ where each vertex from the set V represents

Fig. A.3 A piece of code and its control flow graph

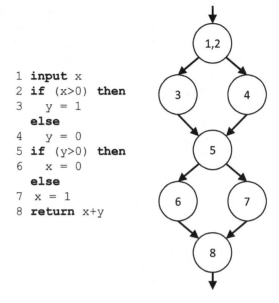

```
1 input x
2 if (x>0) then
3    y = 1
  else
4    y = 0
5 if (y>0) then
6    x = 0
  else
7  x = 1
8 return x+y
```

a basic block[1] and edges from $E \subset V \times V$ represent the possible jumps of the control flow between the basic blocks. Every program execution can be represented as a path in G, but it does not always work the other way round. Namely, there may be some paths in G which are syntactically correct, but are infeasible due to the dependencies between different parts of the code. This is an important thing from the tester's point of view: when the tests are designed according to the control flow graph, a tester must be sure that every generated path has a feasible realization in a SUT. Figure A.3 shows the example of control flow graph containing the infeasible paths. Note that path $1, 2 \rightarrow 3 \rightarrow 5 \rightarrow 7 \rightarrow 8$ is infeasible, because the transition $1, 2 \rightarrow 3$ will result in y=1, but then condition in line 5 will be always true, so the control flow will go through the path $5 \rightarrow 6$.

Coupling Degree of independence between software modules. Coupling is usually related to cohesion: low coupling implies high cohesion and vice versa. Low coupling is preferable, because it supports software maintainability and understandability. There are many operational definitions of coupling. For example, Fenton and Melton [34] proposes the following one: coupling between objects x and y is defined as $c(x, y) = i + n/(n + 1)$, where n is the number of interconnections between x and y, and i is the level of the highest (worst) coupling type found between x and y. The level of coupling type is based on the Myers classification and is assigned a numeric value from 0, 1, 2, 3, 4 or 5. *See also: cohesion.*

---

[1]A basic block is a 'straight-line' piece of code without any jumps into and out of this piece. This means that if one of the instructions within a basic block is executed, then all the instructions in this block will be executed in a linear order.

Coverage The measure to describe the degree to which a given object is exercised by a particular test suite. Note that coverage is always defined for a concrete set of tests. The examples of coverage measures are: statement coverage (fraction of executable instructions executed during the tests), decision coverage (fraction of decision outcomes exercised during the tests) and so on. The most natural coverage measures are the ones for the white-box techniques, but we can also define coverage for black-box models. For example, state machine coverage may be defined as the fraction of transitions executed during the tests; decision table coverage may be defined as the fraction of a table's columns related to the tests executed; and so on.

CRUD Testing Data-oriented testing technique that verifies the correctness of the operations on data: Creating, Reading, Updating and Deleting. There are many different variants of the CRUD testing. The simplest one requires that we should examine each of the C, R, U and D operations for each data. The more complicated ones require us to provide a more complicated scenario, where a given data is first created, then read, then updated and finally deleted (destroyed).

Cyclomatic Complexity Measure of the program's complexity. Defined as the number of decision points in a code + 1. For example, the cyclomatic complexity for a control flow graph from Fig. A.3 is 3, because there are two decision points (in nodes 1, 2 and 5). There is a beautiful theory by McCabe that binds together cyclomatic complexity and the number of so-called linearly independent paths in the code. It says that these two numbers are equal. *See also: control flow graph.*

Data-Driven Testing A test automation technique that separates test scripts and test data. This way, one script can be executed with many different sets of test data. Scripts written in the data-driven approach are easier to maintain than scripts with hard-coded data. If we have to modify a script, we do it only once.

Data Accuracy Testing Testing whether the data values used by the SUT are correct, that is, whether they have the right values, and are represented in a consistent and unambiguous form.

Data Completeness Testing Testing that all data necessary to meet a given business demand are available.

Data Consistency Testing Testing whether the data is written, used or transformed in the way that would violate the database rules regarding data relationships, constraints, redundancy, compatibility, etc.

Data Durability Testing Testing the long-time protection of the stored data, for example, that it will not suffer from degradation or corruption. It may verify the existence of the protection mechanisms like data redundancy or data quality control.

Data Flow Graph Control flow graph enriched with the information on variables' definitions and uses. Data flow graph allows us to identify paths that start with the variable definition and end with definition use. Tests may be designed to cover these paths. There are several variants of this method (all-defs coverage, all-uses coverage, all-du-paths coverage and so on). Data flow graphs may also serve as a basis for the code inspection. Such a review can reveal different anomalies related to data operations (for example, a variable used before being defined). *See also: control flow graph.*

Data Flow Testing Testing the correctness of the data processing, in which data flow graphs are used to design the test cases.

Data Timeliness Testing Testing that refers to the time expectation for the accessibility of data. Timeliness can be measured as the time between when data is expected and when it is readily available for use [113].

Data Validity Testing Testing that data is correct and valid, in terms of both the syntax and semantics.

Debugging A process of analyzing, finding and correcting defects in the code. This is usually done by a developer who is the author of the code.

Decision (1) an expression that can be evaluated to TRUE or FALSE. (2) a point in the code at which the control flow has two or more alternative routes.

Decision Coverage A code coverage criterion that requires each decision in the code to be evaluated at least once to TRUE and at least once to FALSE. For example, for a decision IF $(x > 5)$ THEN DoSomething() we need two tests to achieve this coverage: one in which $x > 5$ (to make it TRUE) and one in which $x \leq 5$ (to make it FALSE). If a code contains at least one decision, the decision coverage subsumes the statement coverage.

Decision Table A graphical model of representing business rules in a software system. They associate conditions with actions to perform, but in a more compact way than other equivalent models, like flow charts or "IF-ELSE" conditional statements. Decision tables are very useful for detecting bugs in the business logic requirements, like missing rules, contradicting rules or rules with undefined actions. Both conditions and actions are usually represented as the Boolean variables (TRUE/ FALSE), but they may be also represented as the categorical variables (for example, action may represent one of the four possible discounts granted; condition may represent one of the five different intervals representing the user's age; and so on). The examples of decision tables are given in Table 1.7 and Fig. 5.6. See also: *cause-effect graph testing*.

Defect A condition in a software product or in another artifact of the SDLC which does not meet—directly or indirectly—a certain requirement or user expectation. Defects in software product cause failures, which are the direct symptoms of requirement fulfillment failure. *See also: error*.

Defect Management A general name for the process of recording, tracking, analysing and reporting the defects found during the software development life cycle. The purpose of defect management may vary. Its role may be: to support the process of solving and retesting defects, to track defect statuses online, to support defect reporting, to support the defect analysis for the process improvement purposes, to gather information about how the defects were resolved to make the process more effective in the future, and so on.

Dirty Testing *see negative testing*.

Domain Analysis General name for a group of data-based, black-box testing techniques that analyze the input/output domain for choosing systematically or randomly a small set of test data for test cases. There are many domain analysis techniques: equivalence partitioning, boundary value analysis, category-partition, high-dimensional domain testing and so on. The essence of these techniques is to partition a domain into a finite number of subdomains and select representatives of each subdomain for tests. Each technique has different criteria for representative selection.

Du-Path A data flow path in a program going from a place where a given variable is defined (defining node), to a place where it is used. The initial node of a du-path must be the only defining node in this path.

Each Choice Testing The simplest form of the combinatorial testing, in which it is required that each single value of each parameter should be tested. For example, if a test case is a pair (x, y) of values, where x can take one of the values from the set {1, 2, 3} and y from the set {a, b}, we require that each of the values: 1, 2, 3, a, b is covered by at least one test. The example of a test suite that reaches this coverge is:

- test 1: $(x = 1, y = a)$
- test 2: $(x = 2, y = b)$
- test 3: $(x = 3, y = a)$

Equivalence Partition A subdomain of input or output values, for which it is assumed that the system under test behaves in the same way. In particular, it is assumed that if for a given x from the equivalence class X the system fails (resp. works OK), then it also fails (resp. works OK) for any other $y \in X$. Equivalence partitioning is a fundamental test technique, because it allows us to reduce the potentially infinite domain into a finite number of equivalence classes. The concept of equivalence partitioning comes from the fundamental notion of the equivalence relation in mathematics.

Error May have different meanings: (1) a human mistake (human error), (2) a synonym for defect, (3) a synonym for failure, (4) an incorrect internal state of the software. *See also: defect, failure.*

Error Guessing A testing technique that makes use of a tester's skills, intuition, experience and business domain knowledge to identify defects that may be not easily captured by the more formal techniques.

Exploratory Testing A testing technique in which a tester does not design test cases in advance, but designs, implements and executes the tests concurrently, regarding the actual behavior of the SUT.

Failure External, visible symptom of the incorrect software operation, for example: returning the wrong result, working too slow, system crash, etc. *See also: error.*

Finite State Machine An abstract, dynamic model of a system's behavior in time, where the succeeding system state depends only on the previous state s and the event e that has occurred when the system was in state s. The example of a finite state machine is given in Fig. 2.11. Formally, a finite state machine is a tuple $(Q, \Sigma, f, \sigma_0,$

T), where Q is a finite set of states, Σ is a finite set of events, $f : Q \times \Sigma \rightarrow Q$ is a transition function, $\sigma_0 \in \Sigma$ is the initial state and $T \subset Q$ is the set of terminal states. There are many models that extend this simple definition, for example Mealy or Moore automata with output, time automata, tree automata and so on. One of the UML diagrams is a state machine diagram, which furthermore allows us to model concurrency, hierarchical structure of states and so on. There exist many different types of coverage for finite state machine testing, for example: covering each state, covering each transition, covering all incorrect transitions, covering each pair of consecutive transitions. The generalized version of the last one is called N-switch coverage (covering all sequences of transitions of length $N - 1$).

Full Path Testing A white-box technique in which the test cases are designed to cover all possible control flow paths. This is possible only when there are no loops in the code. If the loops exist, full path coverage may be weaken by allowing the loops to be treated separately (for example in terms of the loop coverage). For example, to achieve the full path coverage of the graph from Fig. A.3, we need to provide four test cases, as there are four paths that should be exercised:

1. $1, 2 \rightarrow 3 \rightarrow 5 \rightarrow 6 \rightarrow 8$.
2. $1, 2 \rightarrow 3 \rightarrow 5 \rightarrow 7 \rightarrow 8$.
3. $1, 2 \rightarrow 4 \rightarrow 5 \rightarrow 6 \rightarrow 8$.
4. $1, 2 \rightarrow 4 \rightarrow 5 \rightarrow 7 \rightarrow 8$.

Full path coverage, if possible to be achieved, subsumes the MC/DC coverage.

Function Point A unit of measurement to express the amount of business functionality a software provides to a user. Function points are used to compute a functional size measurement of a system. There are several recognized standards defining function points and function point measurement process, for example "ISO/IEC 19761:2011 Software engineering. A functional size measurement method" or "ISO/IEC 20926:2009 Software and systems engineering—Software measurement—IFPUG functional size measurement method".

Happy Path Testing A testing technique that verifies 'positive'scenarios, that is, the scenarios in which everything should go well, with correct data provided, expected user behavior and without any exceptions. Usually it is related to the use case testing, where the main scenario (happy path) of the use case is tested.

Inspection A peer-review of any work product. One of the most formal inspection types is a so-called Fagan inspection, introduced first by Fagan in IBM in 1976 [114]. Inspections are expensive and time-consuming, but when conducted properly with the right people involved, they may be one of the most effective testing techniques within the whole testing process. *See also:* code review.

Integration Testing Any kind of testing that verifies the communication, integration or interfaces between two or more entities. Integration testing can be performed on different levels—it may take the form of unit integration testing, system integration testing, protocol testing, and so on. In general, integration testing between two entities A and B checks if any type of a message from A to B is properly received and interpreted.

Keyword-Driven Testing An approach to test automation in which a tester builds test scenarios using so-called keywords that represent different business actions. Each keyword should have a clear sound and intelligible name (describing the business action it is responsible for) and may be parameterized. For example a keyword LogIntoTheSystem may have two parameters: login and password. Each keyword has an underlying script which physically realizes the business procedure described by this keyword. The main benefit from the keyword-driven approach is the low maintainability cost (test scenarios built from the keywords are separated from the scripts and may be even separated from the test data *see data-driven testing*). Also there's an opportunity to automate the tests by testers who don't know any programming or script language.

Linearly Independent Paths A set of paths in the control flow graph such that no one of them can be expressed as a combination of the others. The combination of paths is understood as the combination of their corresponding vectors $(x_1, x_2, \ldots, x_N)$, where x_i is the number of times the path traversed the node i. The maximal number of the linearly independent paths equals the cyclomatic complexity of the graph. For example, the control flow graph in Fig. A.4 has four linearly independent paths, for example:

Path 1. $1 \rightarrow 2 \rightarrow 4 \rightarrow 5 \rightarrow 6$; Corresponding vector: $(1, 1, 0, 1, 1, 1)$.
Path 2. $1 \rightarrow 3 \rightarrow 4 \rightarrow 5 \rightarrow 6$; Corresponding vector: $(1, 0, 1, 1, 1, 1)$.
Path 3. $1 \rightarrow 3 \rightarrow 1 \rightarrow 3 \rightarrow 4 \rightarrow 5 \rightarrow 6$; Corresponding vector: $(2, 0, 2, 1, 1, 1)$.
Path 4. $1 \rightarrow 3 \rightarrow 4 \rightarrow 5 \rightarrow 4 \rightarrow 5 \rightarrow 6$; Corrsponding vector: $(1, 0, 1, 2, 2, 1)$.

Any other path can be expressed as the combination of these paths. For example, the path $1 \rightarrow 2 \rightarrow 4 \rightarrow 5 \rightarrow 4 \rightarrow 5 \rightarrow 6$ can be expressed as the combination Path 4 + Path 1 − Path 2, because $(1, 1, 0, 2, 2, 1) = (1, 0, 1, 2, 2, 1) + (1, 1, 0, 1, 1, 1) − (1, 0, 1, 1, 1, 1)$.

Load Testing Testing that checks how the system under test operates under the expected load (for example, the expected number of concurrent users, expected number of requests in a given period of time, etc.).

Fig. A.4 A control flow
graph with four linearly
independent paths

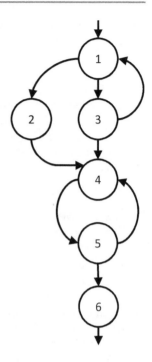

Loop Coverage A code coverage that requires a certain type of coverage of the
loop structures. There are many different approaches to this issue. The most popular
one requires that each loop should be executed: 0 times (the loop condition should be
false when checked the first time), one time, more than one time. In the case of the
inner loops (a loop inside the other loop) the coverage may require some
combinations of this coverage, for example: execute the outer loop one time,
and—within this execution—the inner loop should be executed 0 times, one time
and more than one time.

Maintainability Testing Testing that determines to what extent the SUT meets the
specified maintainability requirements. Maintainability is strictly connected with the
change—whether in the system itself, or in the environment in which the system
operates. Maintainability testing of a system checks how easy is to correct, modify or
update the software. Maintainability can be also considered on the low, code level.
The typical good practices for keeping the high code maintainability are for example:
keeping the variable scope as small as possible, avoiding classes with no methods
(in object-oriented programming), using design patterns, using encapsulation and so
on. This type of testing is very important, because much of the software costs come
from the maintainability after the release.

MC/DC Coverage A code coverage criterion that requires that each condition in a decision is shown to independently affect the outcome of the decision. For example, when testing the decision (A AND B) we need three tests to achieve MC/DC coverage: (1) A=TRUE, B=TRUE, (2) A=FALSE, B=TRUE, (3) A=TRUE, B=FALSE. Test cases (1) and (2) show that A independently affects the outcome of the decision: while B does not change, the change of A modifies the decision outcome: (1) is TRUE, (2) is FALSE. Similarly, (1) and (3) show the same thing for B: while A does not change, the change of B modifies the decision outcome: (1) is TRUE, (3) is FALSE. MC/DC subsumes the decision coverage by definition.

Metric Measurement of a particular characteristic of a software system or any other work product. Every well-defined metric has an operational definition which gives the exact instructions on how to perform the measurement. This is important for the measurements to be consistent and therefore comparable. For example, when we define the Lines of Code metric, we need to know exactly what is understood by a one, single line of code (is it the executable statement? or a physical line of text? do the comments count? and so on).

Module Physically distinguished software component responsible for providing a well-defined functionality (for example, a class, function, procedure, etc.).

Negative Testing Testing by using the inputs, actions or events which are unwanted, malicious, atypical or not expected by a system under test.

Operational Profile Statistical description of a typical or expected software use. Operational profiles may be represented by many different models, for example the probability distributions for the system's load, Markov chains for modeling the sequences of user's actions, etc. Knowing the software's operational profile a tester is able to simulate the typical way the software is or will be used. She can also simulate different anomalies by modifying the operational profile parameters, for example an unexpected heavy load, very large number of concurrent users, atypical software use, etc.

Orthogonal Table (Orthogonal Array) A matrix whose entries are arranged in a way that for every selection of its t columns all ordered t-tuples of the values from the row entries restricted to these columns appear the same number of times. The notion of an orthogonal table comes from the mathematics subdiscipline called experimental design (or combinatorial design). Orthogonal tables can be used in combinatorial testing, for example in pair-wise testing. *See also: pair-wise testing.*

Pair Programming A form of code development combined with an on-line code inspection. In this technique two programmers work together at one workstation. One of them writes the code, while the other one (called observer) observes the coding and reviews it line by line. This is a costly, but effective technique that prevents defect insertion. Another variant of this technique is the one in which the observer is a tester, not developer.

Pair-Wise Testing A form of the combinatorial testing, used when the test is composed by a set of parameters' values. It requires that any pair of values of any two parameters need to occur together in at least one test. Pair-wise technique greatly reduces the number of all possible combinations of all parameters' values, while keeping the ablity to detect the majority of defects. *See also: orthogonal table.*

Pareto Distribution A power law probability distribution, whose probability density function is given by $f(x) = \begin{cases} \alpha\beta^{\alpha}, x \geq \beta \\ 0, x < \beta \end{cases}$. This distribution was first observed by the Italian economist Vilfredo Pareto. It is used in description of many observable phenomena. The practical implication of the Pareto distribution is a so-called Pareto rule, which says that 80% of effects is caused by 20% of causes. For example, ca. 20% of modules contain ca. 80% of all defects. Pareto rule is a good optimization tool, which allows us to prioritize our work so that we do the most profitable things first.

Performance Testing Testing the system performance under a particular workload. Performance testing also verifies the effectiveness of the resource usage (memory, CPU time, disk space and so on). It should be remembered that a single performance test is burdened with error, because the actual performance will depend on many factors, some of which are completely out of our control. Hence, performance testing results should be always treated as random variables. It implies that every performance test should be repeated several number of times and the results should be subject to the statistical analysis.

Quality Control A process that measures the actual quality level of a work product. Testing is a classical tool for quality control. The result of this measurement may be given in terms of the number of defects found, frequency of defects, number of residual risks, number of requirements yet uncovered by tests, number of tests that failed and so on. Quality control is a part of the quality assurance process. *See also: quality assurance.*

Quality Assurance A part of the quality management process focused on providing confidence that quality requirements will be fulfilled. From the tester's point of view, quality assurance includes—apart from the quality control activities—all the activities that prevent introduction of defects into the product.

Race Condition Testing Testing that involves forcing the race conditions to appear in the SUT. A race condition is the system's behavior, where the output is dependent on the sequence or timing of other uncontrollable events.

Rayleigh Distribution A probability distribution parametrized by a scale parameter σ, with a probability density function given by $f(x) = \frac{x}{\sigma^2} e^{-\frac{x^2}{2\sigma^2}}$ for $x \geq 0$. Rayleigh distribution is often observed when the overall magnitude of a vector is related to its directional components. In software quality assurance this distribution models the distribution of defects in function of time. Therefore, Rayleigh distribution may serve as a defect prediction model. Rayleigh distribution is a special case of a Weibull distribution.

Regular Expression A pattern that describes a set of strings (called a regular language). Given a finite alphabet Σ, the family of regular expressions is defined in the inductive way:

- empty set $\varnothing$ is a regular expression,
- empty string ε (representing a word over Σ of length 0) is a regular expression,
- for every $\sigma \in \Sigma$ a single character σ is a regular expression,
- if R and S are regular expressions, then so are SR (concatenation), $R + S$ (alternation) and R^* (Kleene star), where R^* is the smallest set containing ε, R and closed under concatenation.

For example, the regular expression $(a + b)c^*(aa + bb)$ denotes the set of all strings that start with a or b, followed by 0 or more characters c and end with aa or bb. The word $accbb$ matches this pattern, but the word $accba$ does not. Regular expressions are very useful in many text processing tasks, like data validation, parsing or text search algorithms. In the context of software testing they are useful for data generation. They may also serve as the data model which can be verified by a test suite (see Sect. 1.9 for an example).

Reliability Testing Testing the software ability to operate correctly for a particular amount of time. Reliability is usually expressed in terms of mean time between failures (MTBF). The greater this value is, the more stable, mature and reliable the software is.

Review Checking of any work product. *See code review, inspection.*

Requirement Any reasonable expectation of the system defined by a stakeholder (client, developer, tester, etc.). This expectation can be given explicitly (the typical example is the functional requirements specification), but also implicitly (for example, a user wants the software to work fast and reliably, but does not express this directly as his requirement).

Residual Defect A defect remaining in the system after the release. Residual defects found by users after the release are called field defects.

Residual Risk A risk related to the residual defects.

Risk An unexpected event that results in a negative outcome. Risks are characterized by their uncertainty (we do not know if and when they occur)—defined as a probability and impact (the size of loss)—usually defined in monetary terms.

Security Testing A process intended to reveal flaws in the security mechanisms of a system. Security testing can be divided into two main types: business and technical security testing. The first one is related to the verification of security mechanisms provided by the software itself, like the users access rights management, use of passwords and so on. The second group is more about 'hacking' things, like cryptography and different kinds of security attacks (SQL injection, cross site scripting and so on).

Smoke Test A preliminary testing covering the basic software functionality, to check whether the software runs and provides the most important or critical functions.

Soak Testing A type of performance test that verifies the stability of the system's performance characteristics over an extended period of time, where the SUT is subject to a standard load.

Software Maturity A measure of the progress the software products are making towards satisfying the final objectives (usually user requirements). Maturity level is an indicator of the software readiness for the release. The concept of maturity may be also referred to as the process—*see CMMI model.*

Spike Testing A type of performance testing, in which the test object is subject to sudden increase in the magnitude of load. The most interesting part of this testing is checking the system's behavior *between* the consecutive spikes.

SQL Injection Attack A type of the security attack in which the attacker adds a piece of an SQL code to a form field with the intention that this piece of code will be executed on the server side, allowing the attacker to gain access to some resources stored in a database.

Stakeholder Any individual, group or organization who may affect, be affected by, or perceive itself to be affected by a decision, activity or outcome of a project.

Statement Coverage A code coverage that requires each executable line of code to be executed. For example, for the following code:

```
1 INPUT x
2 IF (x==0) THEN
3    DoSomething()
  END IF
4 DoSomethingElse()
```

it is enough to provide one test case with the input value $x=0$ to achieve the statement coverage, as the control flow will go through the executable lines 1, 2, 3, 4.

Strategy According to Merriam-Webster dictionary, a strategy is a careful plan or method for achieving a particular goal usually over a long period of time. In terms of testing, we talk about test strategy, which is the general, planned approach to the test project. Good test strategy defines what should be tested and how and why, keeping in mind the long-term, business-related goals.

Stress Testing A form of the performance testing, where a system is subjected to increasing load going beyond normal operational capacity, in order to determine the breaking points or safe usage limits. In stress testing it is important to increase the load systematically in order to detect the accurate position of a breaking point.

Subsumption A relation between the coverage types. The coverage cirterion C1 subsumes the coverage criterion C2, if *every* test suite that achieves C1 coverage, achieves C2 as well. For example, MC/DC subsumes decision testing.

Syntax Testing A black-box technique that checks the conformance of the input, internal or output data to the syntax of this data. For example, we may check whether a form field accepts only valid e-mail addresses.

System Testing Testing performed on a fully integrated system or its part. This is usually the typical form of testing done by a professional tester. Full integration allows us to perform end-to-end tests referring to certain business scenarios. System testing is therefore more user- than product- or process-oriented.

Test Basis Any source of knowledge about the SUT, its architecture, behavior, etc. Test basis is helpful in providing test cases or designing a test strategy.

Test Condition Any property, characteristic or function that can be tested.

Test Coverage *See coverage.*

Test Idea Any approach for testing a test condition.

Test Management The process of managing the software testing process. Test management activity is necessary, because test process is often complex and subject to restrictions, hence requires a careful planning, organizing the test process and maintaining an effective communication within the test team as well as with the other teams involved in the project. Test management activity also includes defining the test strategy and the ultimate testing goals.

Test Problem Any task to be solved by a tester.

Test Process Totality of activities related to software testing, organized into a logical and rational network of dependent actions. Formal test process definitions usually distinguish between several classical test phases, like: monitoring, control, test analysis, test design, test implementation, test execution, reporting, closure activities.

Test Strategy *See strategy.*

UML Unified Modeling Language, a general-purpose modeling language for visualizing the design of the information systems. Since 1997 UML is maintained and developed by the Object Management Group. Formally, UML consists of different type of diagrams that can be split into structure (static) and behavior (dynamic) diagrams.

Unit *See code unit.*

Unit Testing Testing the software unit in isolation from other units. Typically, performed by the developers who test their own code (modules, classes, functions and so on).

Usability Testing Validating the product from the pure user perspective. Usability testing determines the ease of system's functions understanding, the learning effort for different types of users and the ease of software use in a given environmet.

Use Case Testing A black-box test design technique in which the test scenarios are designed based on the use cases. The use case testing is usually effective in defining the scope of acceptance tests.

UX (User Experience) The totality of the end user's interaction with the company, its services, and its products. UX should be distinguished from the UI (User Interface) and usability, which is a quality attribute related to the UI.

White-Box Testing Testing that uses the information about the internal structure of the tested object. In the case of SUT this is usually the source code, call graph or the low-level design. For the high-level tests the example of an internal structure may be the business process model.

Appendix B. Testing in a Nutshell

In this Appendix we present the fundamental and classical concepts on software testing. We describe the typical testing process phases and the activities of the typical roles involved in the testing. Much of the material in this Appendix is based on the TMap approach [18] and ISO/IEEE/IEC 29119 standard [4].

Definition of Testing According to ISO/IEEE/IEC 29119-1 standard, software testing is defined as a "set of activities concluded to facilitate discovery and/or evaluation of properties of one or more test items".

Why Test? Testing is a form of the software quality evaluation. It prevents reworking costs and damage in production. It allows us to gain faith in the product, when the defects found by testing are fixed and when the testing cannot find any more defects.

Ways of Testing We can define three general ways of testing:

- **Dynamic explicit testing**—where the test cases are explicitly designed to obtain information on the specific quality characteristic. Dynamic explicit testing is scripted, that is, it is planned in advance. Actual results are compared against the expected ones in order to determine, whether the system behaves according to requirements. TMap claims that this is the most usual way of testing [18].
- **Dynamic implicit testing**—where the information about the software is obtained without the explicit use of test cases. The software is evaluated by just using it with no particular test cases in mind. The examples may be exploratory testing, some forms of the usability testing, etc. Dynamic implicit testing can be planned, but it is not necessary.
- **Static testing**—where the end products are assessed without software being run. Static testing is usually done against the source code, but it can be done as well for other software artifacts, like software requirements specification, architectural design, and so on.

© Springer International Publishing AG 2018
A. Roman, *Thinking-Driven Testing*, https://doi.org/10.1007/978-3-319-73195-7

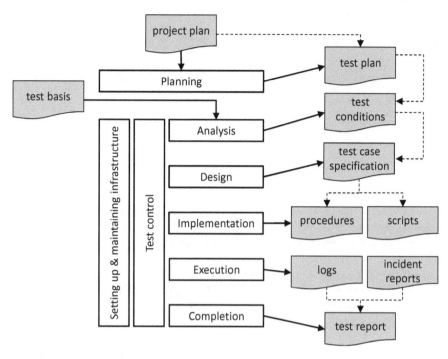

Fig. B.1 A typical software testing process and its artifacts

Testing Process and Its Artifacts A typical testing process is presented in Fig. B.1.
It is important to remember that, although it seems to be a sequential process, in fact
it is not. The phases can occur in parallel, the process may return from one phase to
another, execute them in iterations and so on.

We can distinguish between the following, typical testing phases:

- **Planning.** In this phase the objectives of testing and the specification of test
  activities are defined and included in the test plan. The planning activity is
  important, because it is impossible to test the system completely. Hence, the
  test strategy needs to be defined, where the estimates and planning are determined
  according to a risk analysis process. It is then determined which test techniques
  should be used and to what extent. The objective is to achieve the best possible
  coverage.
- **Control.** The execution of the test plan needs to be continuously monitored. The
  aim of the control activities is to control and report on the test process in an
  optimal manner. It allows the managers (and clients) to react quickly, when the
  process deviates from the planned route.
- **Setting up and maintaining infrastructure.** This phase aims to care of the
  required test infrastructure and resources, such as test tools, test frameworks,

test environments, workplaces. A properly defined test environment is crucial, because no test can be executed without an infrastructure.

- **Analysis.** In the analysis phase the test basis is reviewed to identify the test conditions and their testability. A test basis consists of all documents from which the requirements of a system under test can be inferred. Test cases are based on these documents. A test condition is any property, characteristic or function that can be tested.
- **Design.** In the design phase a tester determines the test case design techniques that provide the necessary test coverage for the test items identified during the analysis phase. Next, the test cases are designed in a way to exercise the identified test conditions.
- **Implementation.** Once the test cases are designed, they are implemented. If the test cases are executed manually, they are "implemented" in a form of the test procedures. If they are to be automated, they are implemented in a form of the test scripts.
- **Execution.** During the execution phase the test cases are executed, and the actual results are compared against the expected ones. The discrepancies are reported as the incidents. The activities related to the test execution are recorded in the logs. This information may be helpful when counting the coverage, assessing the test progress or analyzing the defects during the debugging.
- **Completion.** In the completion phase the tester checks whether the exit criteria are met. These criteria are usually defined in terms of some measure of diligence (for example, the amount of a certain type of coverage). If they are not fulfilled, some additional testing may be performed, if there is enough time, budget and resources. When the exit criteria are met, the testing process (or its phase) is finished. The test closure activities include:
  - writing the test report,
  - delivering the work products to proper team members (for example, passing the reports about the known and not fixed defects to the maintenance/tech support team),
  - archiving the test documentation and other test artifacts like test cases, test environments and so on,
  - participating in the "lessons learned" retrospective meetings in order to improve the test process in the future.

Test Techniques A test technique is a combination of actions to produce a test product in a universal manner. Within the test process many different test techniques can be used (see Fig. B.2):

- **Product risk analysis**—analyzes the product under test with the aim of achieving a shared view, among the test manager and other stakeholders, of the more or less risky characteristics and components of the product to be tested so that the thoroughness of testing can be agreed upon [18].

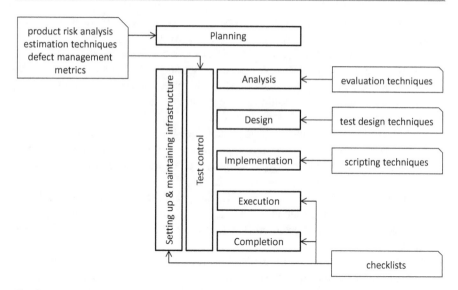

Fig. B.2 Test process and related test techniques

- **Estimation techniques**—a set of techniques to estimate the test effort; estimations can be made on various levels (test level, test phase, test activity) and use different approaches, like: ratio figures, test object size, Work Breakdown Structure (WBS), proportionate estimation, Test Point Analysis, Wideband Delphi technique and many others.
- **Defect management**—a process of managing the defect life cycle and providing various overviews. The overviews, in particular, may be used to make well-founded quality statements.
- **Metrics**—they allow us to express different process and product characteristics in a quantitative way. Due to the uniform measurement process we are able to compare the same aspects of different objects or one aspect of the same object in different moments of time.
- **Evaluation techniques**—allow us to evaluate different types of products. The typical evaluation techniques are:
  - inspection (focuses primarily on achieving consensus on the quality of a work product),
  - review (focuses primarily on finding courses for a solution on the basis of the knowledge, experience and competencies of the reviewers, and on finding and correcting defects),
  - walkthrough (a method by which the author explains the contents of a work product during a meeting).
- **Test design techniques**—the standardized methods to derive, from a specific test basis, test cases that realize a specific coverage. See for example Table 4.3 to recall many classical test design techniques.

- **Scripting techniques**—the techniques used by the developers to write a good quality code. The examples of such techniques are design patterns (for example Page Object Pattern—a very popular technique among software testers), coding standards (commenting, naming conventions, etc.), good practices for code deployment and so on. Using these techniques results in lowering the scripts maintainability costs.
- **Checklists**—used to reduce failure by compensating for potential limits of human memory and attention. They support testers in their everyday work, for example during the risk assessment, establishing the test strategy, evaluating the test process, performing reviews and so on.

Software Testing Roles and Responsibilities We can distinguish between two main roles in software testing: test manager and test engineer. The naming may be different in different organizations. A test manager may be called 'test director' or 'test lead'. Test engineer is sometimes referred to as: tester, QA engineer, QC engineer, software quality engineer, etc.

Test manager is responsible for the managerial part of the testing process which includes: test planning, tasks assignment, monitoring the progress, reporting to the management, etc. Test engineer is responsible for the 'technical' activities: analyzing the test basis, designing, implementing and executing test cases, reporting the incidents, etc.

Test Levels A test level is a group of test activities that are managed and executed collectively. The typical test levels are:

- **Unit testing**—testing an isolated unit of the developer's work (usually a module, class, function, procedure and so on) to demonstrate that this unit meets the requirements defined in the technical specification.
- **Integration testing**—testing an interaction between two or more units or systems. In this type of testing a tester is interested only in the communication between the tested objects, not in testing the objects themselves.
- **System testing**—testing the functional and non-functional characteristics of a fully integrated system. During the system testing we are able to test the end-to-end business processes.
- **Acceptance testing**—testing the fully integrated system in order to verify that the business requirements are met. Often done by the end users.

Test Types A test type is a group of test activities with the intention of checking the information system in respect of a number of correlated quality characteristics. The typical test types are:

- **Functional tests**—they check *what* the system does by verifying that data processing is correct and complete, in accordance with the description in the functional specification. These are usually the 'black-box' tests, as they ignore the internal structure of a system, taking into account only the specification.
- **Non-functional tests**—they check *how* the system works and are related to the so-called quality characteristics, like reliability, security, performance, usability, maintainability, etc. As in the case of the functional tests, they are also usually the 'black-box' tests.
- **Structural tests**—tests that are designed in a way to cover a certain type of the internal structure of the SUT. They require the knowledge about this internal structure. They are often called 'white-box' or 'glass-box' testing.

Incident Life Cycle Once a discrepancy between the actual and expected results occurs, or when the tester just feels that something is wrong, we say that the incident happened. The incident does not necessarily mean that we discovered a defect or a failure. It means that we need to investigate and resolve it. An incident may indeed be a defect or a failure. In this case, the incident report is passed to the developer or other person that corrects a given object under test. After the correction a retest should be done. A retest means executing the test that detected the problem, in order to make sure that the problem has been fixed. An incident may turn out to be a perfectly correct situation, for example, due to the recent requirements change or just because the tester was wrong in his judgement.

Universal Rules of Testing Regardless of the SDLC, type of the SUT, test strategy and other factors, there are some universal rules that hold in all testing projects:

- **Testing shows presence of defects, but it cannot prove that the code is defect-free.** Testing reduces the number of undiscovered defects, but cannot guarantee that we removed all of them. Therefore, the designed test cases should be strong, that is, they should be able to detect as many defects as possible.
- **Exhaustive testing is impossible.** It is impossible to check the software behavior for each possible input. Usually the input domain is infinite. Also, the existence of a loop in a code means that there is an infinite number of paths to be covered. This rule can be even formalized as a math theorem, by reducing the testing problem to the so-called *halting problem*,[2] which is known to be undecidable.

---

[2]In computability theory, the halting problem is the problem of determining, from the description of an arbitrary algorithm and its input, whether the algorithm will finish running or continue to run forever for this input data. In 1936 Alan Turing proved that a general algorithm to solve the halting problem cannot exist.

- **The earlier the tests are performed, the better.** Early testing results in detecting many faults that are hard to detect in the later phases (for example, desing defects or defects in the requirements). Early defect detection means also the low fixing costs.
- **Defect distribution is not uniform.** Defects like to occur in 'clusters'. For example, the defect distribution across the system modules is usually a Pareto-like or exponential-like distribution. Hence, if we detect a lot of defects in some part of the code, we should probably investigate this part even more, because this area is probably error-prone and it is likely that there are even more defects.

Bibliography

1. Spillner, A., Rossner, T., Winter, M., Linz, T.: Software Testing Practice: Test Management, rocky nook (2007)
2. Pinkster, I., van de Burgt, B., Janssen, D., van Veenendaal, E.: Successful Test Management. An Integral Approach. Springer, Berlin (2006)
3. Farrell-Vinay, P.: Manage Software Testing. Auerbach Publications, Boca Raton (2008)
4. ISO/IEC/IEEE 29119 – Software Testing Standard. International Organization for Standardization, 2013-2016
5. Koomen, T., Pol, M.: Test Process Improvement: A Practical Step-by-Step Guide to Structured Testing. Addison-Wesley, Reading (1999)
6. Bath, G., van Veenendaal, E.: Improving the Test Process: Implementing Improvement and Change, rocky nook (2014)
7. Graham, D., Fewster, M.: Experiences of Test Automation. Addison-Wesley, Upper Saddle River (2012)
8. Beyer, B.: Critical Thinking. Phi Delta Kappa Educational Foundation, Bloomington, Indiana (1995)
9. Cross, N.: Design Thinking: Understanding How Designers Think and Work. Bloomsbury Academic, London (2011)
10. Jorgensen, P.: Software Testing. A Craftsman's Approach. CRC Press, London (2014)
11. Pressman, R., Maxim, B.: Software Engineering. A Practitioner's Approach. Mc Graw Hill, Boston (2015)
12. Biggs, N.: Discrete Mathematics. Oxford University Press, Oxford (2002)
13. Senge, P.: The Fifth Discipline: The Art and Practice of the Learning Organization. Random House, New York (2010)
14. Whittaker, A.: Exploratory Software Testing. Tips, Tricks, Tours and Techniques to Guide Test Design. Addison-Wesley, Upper Saddle River, NJ (2010)
15. Thomas, T., Badgett, T., Sandler, C., Myers, G.: The Art of Software Testing. Wiley (2011)
16. Patton, R.: Software Testing. Sams Publishing, Indianapolis, IN (2006)
17. Beizer, B.: Software Testing Techniques. Dreamtech Press (2002)
18. Koomen, T., van der Aalst, L., Broekman, B., Vroon, M.: TMap Next for Result-Driven Testing. UTN Publishers (2006)
19. I.M. Testy (2006) https://blogs.msdn.microsoft.com/imtesty/2006/07/13/the-purpose-of-soft ware-testing/. Accessed 07 08 2016
20. Alanpa (2006) https://blogs.msdn.microsoft.com/alanpa/2006/07/10/testing-bug-finding/. Accessed 07 08 2016
21. Eversystems http://eversystems.eu/Document/18/The_Five_Goals_of_Software_Testing. Accessed 07 08 2016
22. Garvin, D.: What does product quality really mean? MIT Sloan Manage. Rev. **26**(1), 25–45 (1984)
23. Jawadekar, W.: Software Engineering. McGraw-Hill, New Delhi (2004)

© Springer International Publishing AG 2018
A. Roman, *Thinking-Driven Testing*, https://doi.org/10.1007/978-3-319-73195-7

24. Agarwal, B., Tayal, S.: Software Engineering, 2nd edn, Firewall Media (2009)
25. Kan, S.: Metrics and Models in Software Quality Engineering. Addison-Wesley, Boston, MA (2003)
26. Hoffman, D.: The Darker Side of Metrics. Software Quality Methods, LLC (2000)
27. Kaner, C.: The ongoing revolution in software testing. In Software Test and Performance Conference 2004 (2004)
28. Jones, C., Bonsignour, O.: The Economics of Software Quality. Pearson, Boston (2012)
29. Cohen, D., Dalal, S., Kajla, A., Patton, G.: The automatic efficient test generator (AETG) system. In: Proceedings of the 5th International Symposium on Software Reliability Engineering (1994)
30. Kuhn, D., Reilly, M.: An investigation of the applicability of design of experiments to software testing. In: Proceedings of the 27th Annual NASA Goddard Software Engineering Workshop, Washington (2002)
31. Kuhn, D., Kacker, R., Lei, Y.: Introduction to Combinatorial Testing. Taylor & Francis, London (2013)
32. Compton, T., Withrow, C.: Prediction and control of ADA software defects. J. Syst. Softw. **12**, 199–207 (1990)
33. Lind, R., Vairavan, K.: An experimental investigation of software metrics and their relationship to software development effort. IEEE Trans. Softw. Eng. **15**(5), 649–653 (1989)
34. Fenton, N., Neil, M.: A critique of software defect prediction models. IEEE Trans. Softw. Eng. **25**(5), 675–688 (1999)
35. Bach, J., Bolton, M.: Exploratory Testing 3.0 (2015) http://www.satisfice.com/blog/archives/1509. Accessed 2016
36. Itkonen, J., Mäntylä, M.: Are test cases needed? Replicated comparison between exploratory and test-case-based software testing. Empir. Softw. Eng. **19**, 303–342 (2014)
37. GAO: Patriot Missle Defense. Software Problem Led to System Failure at Dhahran, Saudi Arabia. United States General Accounting Office (1992)
38. EuroStar 2012 Conference. What is the most important skill a software tester should have? 12 09 2012. https://www.youtube.com/watch?v=OLxaG0TNgMM. Accessed 2016
39. von Thun, F.S.: Miteinander reden: Störungen und Klärungen. Psychologie der zwischenmenschlichen Kommunikation. Rowohlt, Reinbek (1981)
40. Kramer, A., Legeard, B.: Model-Based Testing Essentials. Wiley (2016)
41. van Veenendaal, E.: Practical Risk-Based Testing. The PRISMA Approach. UTN Publishers (2012)
42. Goues, L.C., Yoo, S.: Search-based software engineering. In: 6th International Symposium, SSBSE 2014, Fortaleza, Brazil (2014)
43. McMinn, P.: Search-based software test data generation: A survey. Softw. Test. Verif. Reliab. **14**(2), 105–156 (2004)
44. Cadar, C., Dunbar, D., Engler, D.: KLEE: Unassisted and automatic generation of high-coverage tests for complex systems programs. In: USENIX Symposium on Operating Systems Design and Implementation (2008)
45. Thomas, D.: Agile is Dead (2015) https://www.youtube.com/watch?v=a-BOSpxYJ9M. Accessed 2016
46. Haselton, M., Nettle, D., Andrews, P.: The evolution of cognitive bias. In: Buss, D.M. (ed.) The Handbook of Evolutionary Psychology, pp. 724–746. Wiley, Hoboken, NJ (2005)
47. Confirmation bias. https://explorable.com/confirmation-bias. Accessed 2016
48. Wason, P.: On the failure to eliminate hypotheses in a conceptual task. Q. J. Exp. Psychol. **12**(3), 129–140 (1960)
49. Festinger, L.: A Theory of Cognitive Dissonance. Stanford University Press, Stanford, CA (1957)
50. Conway, M.: How do committees invent? *Datamation*. **14**(5), 28–31 (1968)
51. Csíkszentmihályi, M.: Flow: The Psychology of Optimal Experience. Harper and Row (1990)

52. Zeller, A.: Why Programs Fail: A Guide to Systematic Debugging. Morgan Kaufman, San Francisco (1999)
53. Parkinson, C.: Parkinson's Law. The Economist, November 19 (1955)
54. Visser, J.: Building Maintainable Software. O'Reilly (2016)
55. Martin, R.: Clean Code. A Handbook of Agile Software Craftsmanship. Prentice Hall (2009)
56. Popper, K.: Conjectures and Refutations: The Growth of Scientific Knowledge. Routlege & Kegan Paul, London (1963)
57. Cohn, M.: Succeeding with Agile: Software Development Using Scrum. Addison-Wesley (2010)
58. Fowler, M.: Test Pyramid. 1 5 2012. http://martinfowler.com/bliki/TestPyramid.html. Accessed 2016
59. Whittaker, J.A.: How to Break Software. A Practical Guide to Testing. Pearson Education, Boston, MA (2003)
60. Whittaker, J., Thompson, H.: How to Break Software Security. Effective Techniques for Security Testing. Addison-Wesley (2004)
61. Andrews, M., Whittaker, J.: How to Break Web Software. Functional and Security Testing of Web Applications and Web Services. Addison-Wesley (2006)
62. Kaner, C., Falk, J., Nguyen, H.: Testing Computer Software. Wiley, New York (1999)
63. Binder, R.: Testing Object Oriented Systems. Models, Patterns, and Tools. Addison-Wesley (1999)
64. Robinson, H.: In: Workshop on Model-Based Testing, Melbourne, Florida (2001)
65. Meijer, E.: One Hacker Way (Reaktor Dev Day 2014) (2014) https://vimeo.com/110554082. Accessed 2016
66. Adzic, G.: Specification by Example: How Successful Teams Deliver the Right Software. Manning Publications, Westampton (2011)
67. Anderson, D., Dumitriu, D.: From Worst to Best in 9 Months: Implementing a Drum-Buffer-Rope Solution in Microsoft's IT Department. Microsoft Corporation (2005)
68. Kuhn, M., Johnson, K.: Applied Predictive Modeling. Springer (2016)
69. McInerny, D.: Being Logical. A Guide to Good Thinking. Random House (2005)
70. Belden, T., Belden, M.: The Lengthening Shadow: The Life of Thomas J. Watson, Little, Brown and Company (1962)
71. Pyzdek, T., Keller, P.: The Six Sigma Handbook. McGraw-Hill (2014)
72. Facione, P.: Critical Thinking: A Statement of Expert Consensus for Purposes of Educational Assessment and Instruction (1990)
73. Smith, R.: Systems thinking tester. In: Pacific Northwest Software Quality Conference Proceedings, Portland (2015)
74. Fell, J.: Enterpreneur (2011) https://www.entrepreneur.com/article/220604. Accessed 2017
75. Agile Manifesto (2001) http://agilemanifesto.org/
76. Carroll, L.: Alice's Adventures in Wonderland (1865)
77. Tague, N.: The Qualty Toolbox. ASQ Quality Press (2005)
78. Ritchey, T.: Analysis and synthesis: on scientific method – based on a study by Bernhard Riemann. Syst. Res. **8**(4), 21–41 (1991)
79. Witztum, A.: Introduction to Economics, LSE Kick Day Off 2011 (2011) https://www.youtube.com/watch?v=Lq4HXW_JYd4.
80. Chaos Report. Standish Group (2015)
81. Offutt, J., Ammann, P.: Introduction to Software Testing, 2nd edn. Cambridge University Press (2016)
82. Hall, T., Beecham, S., Bowes, D., Gray, D., Counsell, S.: A systematic literature review on fault prediction performance in software engineering. IEEE Trans. Softw. Eng. **38**(6), 1276–1304 (2012)
83. Boehm, B.: A spiral model for software development and enhancement. ACM SIGSOFT Softw. Eng. Notes. **11**(4), 14–24 (1986)

84. Boehm, B.: Spiral Development: Experience, Principles, and Refinements. Software Engineering Institute, Special Report CMU/SEI-2000-SR-008 (2000)

85. Copeland, L.: A Practitioner's Guide to Software Test Design. Artech House Publishers (2003)

86. Kaner, C., Padmanabhan, S., Hoffman, D.: The Domain Testing Workbook. Context Driven Press (2013)

87. Krug, S.: Don't Let Me Think, Revisited: A Common Sense Approach to Web Usability, 3rd edn. Pearson Education (2014)

88. Molyneaux, I.: The Art of Application Performance Testing. O'Reilly (2015)

89. Kim, P.: The Hacker Playbook: Practical Guide to Penetration Testing. Secure Planet LLC (2014)

90. U.S.B. Congress. USBC rulebook (2017) http://usbcongress.http.internapcdn.net/usbcongress/bowl/rulebook/2016-2017Rulebook.pdf. Accessed 2017

91. FIFA document "How are points calculated in the FIFA World Ranking?". http://www.fifa.com/mm/document/fifafacts/rawrank/ip-590_10e_wrpointcalculation_8771.pdf

92. Linux source code repository. https://github.com/torvalds/linux/blob/master/kernel/pid.c. Accessed 2017

93. McCall, J., Richards, P., Walters, G.: Factors in Software Quality. Rome Air Development Center, Air Force Systems Commandm Griffiss Air Force Base, New York (1977)

94. Boehm, B., Brown, J., Kaspar, H., Lipow, M., McLeod, G., Merritt, M.: Characteristics of Software Quality. North Holland (1978)

95. Kitchenham, B., Pfleeger, S.: Software quality: the elusive target. IEEE Softw. **13**(1), 12–21 (1996)

96. Wagner, S.: Software Product Quality Control. Springer (2013)

97. Yourdon, E.: When good enough software is best. IEEE Softw. **12**(3), 79–81 (1995)

98. Chillarege, R., Bhandari, I., Chaar, J., Halliday, M., Moebus, D., Ray, B., Wong, M.-Y.: Orthogonal defect classification – a concept for in-process measurements. IEEE Trans. Softw. Eng. **18**(11), 943–956 (1992)

99. Schroeder, P., Bolaki, P., Gopu, V.: Comparing the fault detection effectiveness of n-way and random test suites. IEEE International Symposium on Empirical Software Engineering, pp. 49–59 (2004)

100. Bryce, R., Rajan, A., Heimdahl, M.: Interaction testing in model based development: effect on model coverage. IEEE 13th Asia Pacific Software Engineering Conference, pp. 259–268 (2006)

101. Basili, V., Weiss, D.: A methodology for collecting valid software engineering data. IEEE Trans. Softw. Eng. **10**(6), 728–738 (1984)

102. Tufte, E.: The Visual Display of Quantitative Information. Graphics Press (2001)

103. van Veenendaal, E., Wells, B.: Test Maturity Model Integration. UTN Publishers (2012)

104. Ewijk, A., Linker, B., van Oosterwijk, M., Visser, B., de Vries, G., Wilhelmus, L., Marselis, R.: TPI Next – Business Driven Test Process Improvement. UTN Publishers (2009)

105. Crispin, L.: Using the Agile Testing Quadrants. 8 11 2011. http://lisacrispin.com/2011/11/08/using-the-agile-testing-quadrants/. Accessed 2017

106. Box, G.: Robustness in the strategy of scientific model building. In: Launer, R.L., Wilkinson, G.N. (eds.) Robustness in Statistics. Academic (1979)

107. Rosenbaum, M.: Kata and the Transmission of Knowledge. YMAA Publication Center (2004)

108. Hunt, A., Dave, T.: The Pragmatic Programmer. Addison Wesley (1999)

109. Kanazawa, H.: Karate: The Complete Kata. Kodansha International (2009)

110. Reichert, A.: Testing APIs protects applications and reputations (2015) http://searchsoftwarequality.techtarget.com/tip/Testing-APIs-protects-applications-and-reputations. Accessed 2017

111. CMMI. CMMI model. http://cmmiinstitute.com/capability-maturity-model-integration. Accessed 2017

112. Chidamber, S., Kemerer, C.: A metrics suite for object oriented design. IEEE Trans. Softw. Eng. **20**(6), 476–493 (1994)

113. Loshin, D.: The Practitioner's Guide to Data Quality Improvement. Elsevier (2011)
114. Fagan, M.: Design and code inspections to reduce errors in program development. IBM Syst. J. **15**(3), 182–211 (1976)
115. Ghaith, S., Wang, M., Perry, P., Jiang, Z.M., O'Sullivan, P., Murphy, J.: Anomaly detection in performance regression testing by transaction profile estimation. Softw. Test. Verif. Reliab. **26**, 4–39 (2016)
116. Kaner, C.: What is a good test? In: STAR East Conference (2003)
117. Arnold, D.: The Patriot Missle Failure (2000). http://www.math.umn.edu/~arnold/disasters/patriot.html. Accessed 2016.
118. Wason, P.: Reasoning about a rule. J. Exp. Psychol. **20**(3), 273–281 (1968)
119. Fenton, N., Melton, A.: Deriving structurally based software measures. J. Syst. Softw. **12**, 177–187 (1990)

CPSIA information can be obtained
at www.ICGtesting.com
Printed in the USA
LVHW060426131118
596929LV00008B/524/P